JOHN RANDOLPH,

OF ROANOKE,

AND OTHER

SKETCHES OF CHARACTER,

INCLUDING

WILLIAM WIRT.

TOGETHER WITH

TALES OF REAL LIFE.

BY F. W. THOMAS,

AUTHOR OF "CLINTON BRADSHAW," ETC.

PHILADELPHIA:
A. HART, LATE CAREY AND HART.
1853.

PHILADELPHIA:

T. K. AND P. G. COLLINS, PRINTERS.

Inscribed

TO THE

HONORABLE EDWARD EVERETT,

OF

MASSACHUSETTS,

IN RESPECT FOR HIS LOVE OF LITERATURE;

HIS ENLARGED STATESMANSHIP;

HIS ARDENT PATRIOTISM, AND HIS STAINLESS CHARACTER.

PREFACE.

THESE sketches of character, tales, &c., were written as the occasions presented themselves.

In some instances they were published at the time, and in others they were retained in MS., with the view to a publication like this. Part of the article on the "Development of Mind and Character," is taken from an address delivered before the Miami University, of Ohio.

The differences made by dates, and particularly by deaths, the reader will detect in more than one instance. They are occurring as the proof-sheets pass through the press. For instance, Judge Burnet, of Cincinnati, who, in the sketch of John Randolph, is mentioned as among the living, is numbered, as I write this preface, with the dead. He reached an advanced age, full of honors, and he possessed one of the brightest intellects in the whole West. The second bust, I believe, that Powers ever moulded, was of this gentleman, and it is as life-like a presentment as I have ever seen. But the author merely meant to say that these papers are presented to the reader as they were written, when his mind impelled him to the task; and he would express the hope that they may interest innocently whatever time may be bestowed upon their perusal.

CONTENTS.

JOHN RANDOLPH, OF ROANOKE.

"GREAT WITS TO MADNESS NEARLY ARE ALLIED."

I REMEMBER some years since to have seen John Randolph in Baltimore. I had frequently read and heard descriptions of him; and one day, as I was standing in Market, now Baltimore Street, I remarked a tall, thin, unique-looking being hurrying towards me with a quick impatient step, evidently much annoyed by a crowd of boys who were following close at his heels; not in the obstreperous mirth with which they would have followed a crazy or a drunken man, or an organ-grinder and his monkey, but in the silent, curious wonder with which they would have haunted a Chinese, bedecked in full costume. I instantly knew the individual to be Randolph, from the descriptions. I therefore advanced towards him, that I might take a full observation of his person without violating the rules of courtesy in stopping to gaze at him. As he approached, he occasionally turned towards the boys with an angry glance, but without saying anything, and then hurried on as if to outstrip them; but it would not do. They followed close behind the orator, each one observing him so intently that he said nothing to his companions. Just before I met him, he stopped a Mr. C——, a cashier of one of the banks, said to be as odd a fish as John himself. I loitered into a store close by, and, unnoticed, remarked the Roanoke orator for a considerable time; and really, he was the strangest-looking being I ever beheld.

His long thin legs, about as thick as a stout walking-cane, and of much such a shape, were encased in a pair of tight smallclothes, so tight that they seemed part and parcel of the limbs of the wearer. Handsome white stockings were fastened with great tidiness at the knees, by a small gold buckle, and over them, coming about half-way up the calf, were a pair of what I believe are called hose, coarse and country knit. He wore shoes. They were old-fashioned, and fastened also with buckles—huge ones. He trod like an Indian, without turning his toes out, but planking them down straight ahead. It was the fashion in those days to wear a fan-tailed coat with a small collar, and buttons far apart behind, and few on the breast. Mr. Randolph's were the reverse of all this, and, instead of his coat being fan-tailed, it was what we believe the knights of the needle call swallow-tailed; the collar was immensely large, the buttons behind were in kissing proximity, and they sat together as close on the breast of the garment as the feasters at a crowded public festival.

His waist was remarkably slender, so slender that, as he stood with his arms akimbo, he could easily, as I thought, with his long bony fingers, have spanned it. Around him his coat, which was very tight, was held together by one button, and in consequence an inch or more of tape, to which it was attached, was perceptible where it was pulled through the cloth. About his neck he wore a large white cravat, in which his chin was occasionally buried as he moved his head in conversation; no shirt collar was perceptible; every other person seemed to pride himself upon the size of his, as they were then worn large. Mr. Randolph's complexion was precisely that of a mummy; withered, saffron, dry, and bloodless; you could not have placed a pin's point on his face where you would not have touched a wrinkle. His lips were thin, compressed, and colorless; the chin, beardless as a boy's, was broad for the size of his face, which was small; his nose was straight, with nothing remarkable in it, except, perhaps, it was too short. He wore a fur cap, which he took off, standing a few moments uncovered. I observed that his head was quite small, a characteristic which is said to have marked many men of talent—Byron and Chief-

Justice Marshall, for instance. Judge Burnet, of Cincinnati, who has been alike distinguished at the bar, on the bench, and in the United States Senate, and whom I have heard no less a judge and possessor of talent than Mr. Hammond, of the Gazette, say, was the clearest and most impressive speaker he ever heard, has also a very small head. Mr. Randolph's hair was remarkably fine; fine as an infant's, and thin. It was very long, and was parted with great care on the top of his head, and was tied behind with a bit of black ribbon, about three inches from his neck; the whole of it formed a queue not thicker than the little finger of a delicate girl.

His forehead was low, with no bumpology about it; but his eye, though sunken, was most brilliant and startling in its glance. It was not an eye of profound, but of impulsive and passionate thought, with an expression at times such as physicians describe to be that of insanity; but an insanity which seemed to quicken, not destroy intellectual acuteness. I never beheld an eye that struck me more. It possessed a species of fascination, such as would make you wonder over the character of its possessor, without finding any clue in your wonderment to discover it, except that he was passionate, wayward, and fearless. He lifted his long bony finger impressively as he conversed, and gesticulated with it in a peculiar manner. His whole appearance struck me, and I could easily imagine how, with his great command of language, so appropriate and full, so brilliant and classical, joined to the vast information that his discursive oratory enabled him to exhibit in its fullest extent, from the storehouse of which the vividness of his imagination was always pointing out a happy analogy or bitter sarcasm that startled the more from the fact that his hearers did not perceive it until the look, tone, and finger brought it down with the suddenness of lightning, and with its effects, upon the head of his adversary; taking all this into consideration, I could easily imagine how, when almost a boy, he won so much fame, and preserved it so long, and with so vast an influence, notwithstanding the eccentricity and inconsistency of his life, public and private.

By the by, the sudden, unexpected, and aphoristical way in which Randolph often expressed his sentiments had much to do with his oratorical success. He would, like Dean Swift, make a remark, seemingly a compliment, and explain it into a sarcasm, or he would utter an apparent sarcasm and turn it into a compliment. Many speakers, when they have said a thing, hurry on to a full explanation, fearful that the hearer may not understand them; but when Randolph expressed one of these startling thoughts, he left the hearer for some time puzzling in doubt as to what he meant; and when it pleased him, in the coolest manner in the world he explained his meaning, not a little delighted if he discovered that his audience were wondering the while upon whom the blow would descend, or what principle the remark would be brought to illustrate. A little anecdote, which I heard a member of Congress from Kentucky tell of him, shows this characteristic. The Congressman, on his first visit to Washington (he had just been elected), was of course desirous of seeing the lions. Randolph, though not a member of either house, was there, and had himself daily borne into the Senate or House by his faithful Juba, to listen to the debates. Everybody, noted or unnoted, was calling on the eccentric orator, and the member from Kentucky determined to do likewise and gratify his curiosity. A friend, General ——, promised to present him, saying, though: "You must be prepared for an odd reception, for, if Randolph is in a bad humor, he will do and say anything; if he is in a good humor, you will see a most finished gentleman." They called; Mr. Randolph was stretched out on a sofa. "He seemed," said the member, "a skeleton, endowed with those flashing eyes which ghost-stories give to the reanimated body when sent upon some earthly mission."

The Congressman was presented by his friend, the general, as a member of Congress from Kentucky. "Ah, from Kentucky, sir," exclaimed Randolph, in his shrill voice, as he rose to receive him, "from Kentucky, sir; well, sir, I consider your State the Botany Bay of Virginia."

The Kentuckian thought that the next remark would be a quotation from Barrington's Botany Bay epilogue, applied by Randolph to the Virginia settlers of Kentucky:—

> "True patriots we, for, be it understood,
> We left our country for our country's good."

But Randolph, after a pause, continued: "I do not make this remark, sir, in application to the morals or mode of settlement of Kentucky. No, sir; I mean to say that it is my opinion, sir, that the time approaches when Botany Bay will in all respects surpass England, and, I fear, it will soon be so with regard to your State and mine."

I cite this little anecdote, not for any peculiar pith that it possesses, but in illustration of his character, and in proof of the remark above made.

If Mr. Randolph had lived in ancient times, Plutarch, with all his powers in tracing the analogies of character, would have looked in vain for his parallel. And a modern biographer, with all ancient and all modern times before him, will find the effort fruitless that seeks his fellow. At first the reader might think of Diogenes as furnishing some resemblance to him, and that all that Randolph wanted was a tub; but not so if another

Alexander had asked him what he would have that imperial power could bestow—the answer never would have been a request to stand out of his sunlight. No; Randolph, if he could have got no higher emolument and honor, would immediately have requested to be sent on a foreign mission; that over, if Alexander had nothing more to give, and was so situated as not to be feared, who does not believe that the ex-minister would turn tail on him?

The fact is that Randolph was excessively ambitious, a cormorant alike for praise and plunder; and though his patriotism could point out the disinterested course to others, his love of money would not let him keep the track himself—at least in his later years, when mammon, the old man's God, beset him, and he turned an idolater to that for which he had so often expressed his detestation, that his countrymen believed him. His mission to Russia broke the charm that the prevailing opinion of his disinterestedness cast about him, and his influence in his native State was falling fast beneath the appointment and outfit and salary that had disenchanted it when he died; and now old Virginia will forget and forgive these inconsistencies of one of her greatest sons to do reverence to his memory.

Randolph's republicanism was never heartfelt; he was at heart an aristocrat. He should have been born in England, a noble—there he would stubbornly have resisted the encroachments of all below him upon his own prerogatives, station, dignity, and quality; and he would have done his best to bring the prerogatives, station, dignity, and quality of all above him a little below his level, or at least upon an equality with his. Randolph would have lifted Wilkes up to be a thorn in the side of a king whom he did not like, and to overthrow his minister; had he been himself a minister, his loyalty would have pronounced Wilkes an unprincipled demagogue. Wilkes, we know, when he got an office, said he could prove to his majesty that he himself had never been a Wilkeite. Randolph was intensely selfish, and his early success as a politician and orator impressed him with an exaggerated opinion of his own importance, at an age when such opinions are easily made and not easily eradicated. In the case of Randolph, this overweening self-estimation grew monstrous. "Big man me, John," and the bigness or littleness of others' services was valued and proclaimed just in proportion as it elevated or depressed the interests and personal dignity of the orator of Roanoke. And often, when his interest had nothing to do with the question presented to him, his caprice would sway his judgment, for his personal resentments led him far away from every consideration save that of how he could best wound his adversary.

His blow wanted neither vigor nor venom; his weapons were poisoned with such consummate skill, and he so well knew the vulnerable point of every character, that often when the wound, by an observer, who knew nothing of his opponent, was deemed slight, it was rankling in the heart. Randolph was well acquainted with the private history of the eminent men of his time, the peccadillos, frailties, indiscretions, weaknesses, vanities, and vices of them all. He used his tongue as a jockey would his whip; he hit the sore place till the blood came, and there was no crack, or flourish, or noise, or bluster in doing it. It was done with a celerity and dexterity which showed the practised hand, and its unexpectedness as well as its severity often dumbfounded the victim so completely that he had not one word to say, but writhed in silence. I remember hearing two anecdotes of Randolph, which strikingly type his character. One exhibits his cynical rudeness and disregard for the feelings of others—in fact, a wish to wound their feelings; and the other his wit. I do not vouch for their accuracy, but I give them as I have frequently heard them, as perhaps has the reader. Once, when Randolph was in the city of B——, he was in the daily habit of frequenting the bookstore of one of the largest booksellers in the place. He made some purchases from him, and was very curious in looking over his books, &c. In the course of Randolph's visits, he became very familiar with Mr. ——, the bookseller, and they held long chats together; the orator of Roanoke showing off with great courtesy. Mr. —— was quite a pompous man, and rather vain of his acquaintance with the lions who used to stop in his shop. Subsequently, being in Washington with a friend, he espied Randolph advancing towards him, and told his friend that he would introduce him to the "great man." His friend, however, knowing the waywardness of Randolph, declined. "Well," said Mr. ——, "I am sorry you will not be introduced. I'll go up and give him a shake of the hand, at any rate." Up he walked with outstretched hand, to salute the cynic. The aristocratic republican (by the by, how often your thoroughgoing republican is a full-blooded aristocrat in his private relations) immediately threw his hand behind him, as if he could not "dull his palm" with such "entertainment," and gazed searchingly into the face of the astonished bookseller. "Oh, ho!" said he, as if recollecting himself, "you are Mr. B——, from Baltimore." "Yes, sir," was the reply. "A bookseller." "Yes, sir," again. "Ah! I bought some books from you." "Yes, sir, you did." "Did I forget to pay you for them?" "No, sir, you did not."

"Good-morning, sir," said the orator, lifting his cap with offended dignity, and passing on.

This anecdote does not show either Randolph's goodness of head or heart, but it shows his character.

The other anecdote is as follows: The Honorable Peter ——, who was a watchmaker, and who had represented B—— County for many years in Congress, once made a motion to amend a resolution offered by Randolph, on the subject of military claims. Mr. Randolph rose up after the amendment had been offered, and drawing his watch from his fob, asked the Honorable Peter what o'clock it was. He told him. "Sir," replied the orator, "you can mend my watch, but not my motions. You understand tic-tics, sir, but not tactics!"

That, too, was a fine retort, when, after he had been speaking, several members rose in succession and attacked him. "Sir," said he to the Speaker, "I am in the condition of old Lear—

"'The little dogs and all,
Tray, Blanch, and Sweetheart—see, they bark at me.'"

All accounts agree in praising the oratorical powers of Randolph. His manner was generally slow and impressive, his voice squeaking, but clear and distinct; and, as far as it could be heard, what he said was clearly understood. His gestures were chiefly with his long and skeleton-like finger. The impressiveness with which he used it has been remarked by all who have heard him. When he was sarcastic, amidst a thousand it would say, stronger than language, to the individual whom he meant, "Thou art the man." In his choice of language, he was very fastidious, making sometimes a considerable pause to select a word. His reading was extensive, and in every department of knowledge—romances, tales, poems, plays, voyages, travels, history, biography, philosophy, all arrested his attention, and each had detained him long enough to render him familiar with the best works of the kind. His mind was naturally erratic, and his desultory reading, as he never devoted himself to any profession, and dipped a little into all, increased his natural and mental waywardness. He seldom reasoned, and when he did, it was with an effort that was painful, and which cost him more trouble than it was worth. He said himself, in one of his speeches in the Senate of the United States, "that he had a defect, whether of education or nature was immaterial, perhaps proceeding from both, a defect which had disabled him, from his first entrance into public life to the present hour, from making what is called a *regular speech*." The defect was doubtless both from education and nature; education might have, in some measure, corrected the tendencies of his nature; but there was, perhaps, an idiosyncrasy in the constitution of the man, which compelled him to be meteoric and erratic in mind as well as temper. He said that "ridicule was the keenest weapon in the whole parliamentary armory," and he learned all the tricks of fence with it, and never played with foils. He seems to have had more admiration for the oratory of Chatham than that of any other individual, if we may judge from the manner in which that great man is mentioned in his speeches. They were certainly unlike in character, very unlike. Chatham having had bad health, and it being well known that he went to Parliament and made his best efforts when almost sinking from sickness, Randolph might have felt that, as he had done the same thing, their characters were assimilated. Chatham was seized with a fainting fit when making his last speech, and died a short time afterwards. And probably it is not idle speculation to say that Randolph, with a morbid or perhaps an insane admiration of his character, wished to sink as Chatham did, in the legislative hall, and be borne thence to die.

However, there was enough in the character of Chatham to win the admiration of any one who loved eloquence, without seeking in adventitious circumstances a motive for his admiration; and Randolph appreciated such talents as his too highly not to have admired them under all circumstances; but his reverence was doubtless increased from the resemblance which he saw in their bodily conditions, and which, he was very willing to believe, extended to their minds. Chatham was bold, vehement, resistless, not often witty, but eminently successful when he attempted it; invective was his forte. In some of these points Randolph resembled him; but then Chatham's eloquence was but a means to gain his ends; his judgment was intuitive, his sagacity unrivalled; he bore down all opposition by his fearless energies, and he compelled his enemies to admit that he was a public benefactor in the very breath in which they expressed their personal dislike. Chatham kept his ends steadily in view, and never wavered in his efforts to gain them. Not so Randolph. He reminds us of the urchin in the "Lay of the Last Minstrel," who always used his fairy gifts with a spirit of deviltry, to provoke, to annoy, and to injure; no matter whom he wounded, or when, or where. Randolph did not want personal dignity, but he wanted the dignity which arises from consistent conduct, a want which no brilliancy of talent can supply. On the contrary, the splendor of high talents but serves to make such inconsistency the more apparent. He was an intellectual meteor, whose course no one could predict; but, be it where it might, all were certain that it would blaze, and wither, and destroy. As a statesman, it is believed that he never originated a single measure, though his influence often destroyed the measures of others. Some one observes "that the hand which is not able to build a hovel, may destroy a palace," and he seemed to have had a good deal of the ambition of him who fired the Ephesian dome. As a scholar, he left nothing behind him, though his wit was various and his acquirements profound. He seems not to have written a common communication for a newspaper without great labor and fastidious correction.

I have been informed by a compositor who set a part of his speech on "retrenchment," which he dedicated to his constituents, that his emendations were endless. I have a part of the MS. of this speech before me; it is written with a trembling hand, but with great attention to punctuation, and with a delicate stroke of the pen. It was as an orator he shone, and, as an orator, his power of chaining the attention of his audience has been, perhaps, never surpassed. In an assembly where Demosthenes, Cicero, Chatham, Mirabeau, or Henry spoke, Randolph's eloquence would have been listened to with profound interest, and his opposition would have been feared. As an orator, he felt his power—he knew that in eloquence he wielded a magic wand, and he was not only fearless of opposition, but he courted it; for who of his contemporaries has equalled him in the power of carrying on successfully the partisan warfare of desultory debate—the quick surprise—the cut and thrust—the arrowy aim—the murderous fire? Who could wield like him the tomahawk, and who of them possessed his dexterity in scalping a foe? His trophies are numberless, and he wore them with the pride of his progenitors, for there was truly a good deal of Indian blood in his veins. It is said that Randolph first signalized himself by making a stump speech in Virginia in opposition to Patrick Henry.

Scarcely any one knew him when he rose to reply to Henry, and so strong was Henry's conviction of his powers, on hearing him, that he spoke of them in the highest terms, and prophesied his future eminence. Randolph gloriously said of Henry, that "he was Shakspeare and Garrick combined."

Randolph's character and conduct forcibly impress upon us the power of eloquence in a republic. How many twists and turns, and tergiversations and obliquities were there in his course! Yet how much influence he possessed, particularly in Virginia! How much he was feared, courted, admired, shunned, hated, and all because he wielded the weapon that "rules the fierce democracy!" How many men, far his superiors in practical usefulness, lived unhonored and without influence, and died unsung, because they had not eloquence. Eloquence is superior to all other gifts, even to the dazzling fascinations of the warrior; for it rules alike in war and peace, and it wins all by its spell. Randolph was the very personification of inconsistency. Behold him talking of the "splendid misery" of office-holders; "what did he want with office? a cup of cold water was better in his condition; the sword of Damocles was suspended over him by a single hair," &c. &c.; when lo! he goes to the frigid north—for what? For health? No! for an outfit and a salary! and dies childless, worth, it is said, nearly a million.

Randolph's oratory reminds us forcibly of Don Juan; and if Byron had written nothing but Don Juan, Randolph might have been called the Byron of orators. He had all the wit, eccentricity, malice, and flightiness of that work—its touches that strike the heart, and sarcasms that scorn, the next moment, the tear that had started.

In a dying state, Randolph went to Washington during the last session of Congress, and, although not a member, he had himself borne daily to the hall of legislation to witness the debate. He returned home to his constituents, and was elected to Congress, and started on a tour to Europe, if possible to regain his health; he said, "it was the last throw of the die."

He expired in Philadelphia, where he had first

appeared in the councils of the nation, in the sixty-first year of his age, leaving a reputation behind him for classic wit and splendid eloquence which few of his contemporaries may hope to equal; and a character which his biographer may deem himself fortunate if he can explain it to have been compatible with either the duties of social life, the sacredness of friendship, or the requirements of patriotism, unless he offer as an apology partial derangement. In a letter, in which the deceased acknowledged that he had made a misstatement in regard to the character of Mr. Lowndes on the tariff, he assigned, as a reason for the error, the disordered state of his mind, arising from the exciting medicines which he was compelled to take to sustain life.

I have, perhaps, expressed myself harshly, inconsistently with that charitable feeling which all should possess who are "treading upon ashes under which the fire is not yet extinguished." If so, to express our conscientious opinions is sometimes to do wrong.

"Why draw his frailties from their dread abode?" Who can tell, in the close alliance between reason and madness, which were so strongly mixed up in his character, how much his actions and words partook of the one or the other? Where they alternated, or where one predominated, or where they mingled their influence, not in the embrace of love, but in the strife for mastery? Oh! how much he may have struggled with his mental aberrations and wanderings, and felt that they were errors, and yet struggled in vain. His spirit, like the great eye of the universe, may have known that storms and clouds beset it, and have felt that it was contending with disease and the film of coming death, yet hoped at last to beam forth in its brightness.

> "The day drags on, though storms keep out the sun,
> And thus the heart will break, and brokenly live on."

And so it is with the mind, and Randolph's "brokenly lived on" till the raven shadows of the night of death gathered over him and gave him to the dark beyond.

WILLIAM WIRT.*

PERHAPS there was no individual in our country more highly endowed with intellectual gifts than the late William Wirt, the greatest public blunder of whose career was that, late in life, and at the eleventh political hour, he suffered himself to be announced as a candidate for the presidency, by a party with whom he had not before acted. But, be this as it may, all must admit, who knew him, that whatever Mr. Wirt did he did conscientiously. We all know and feel "that to err is human," and we have yet to learn that error is a proof of selfishness. The Roman Cato, when he found that

"This world was made for Cæsar,"

fled to suicide. He might have shunned the deed, and outlived Cæsar, as Mr. Wirt did the excitement which made him a presidential candidate, and still,

* This sketch was written before the admirable Life of Wirt, by Hon. John P. Kennedy, had been issued.

like him, have served his country. "The post of honor is a private station" oftener than politicians are aware, but still, without guile, they have often quit it to return to it without reproach. Until this event, Mr. Wirt pursued the even tenor of his profession through a long life, dignifying it with the official statesmanship of Attorney-General of the United States, and not as a mere lawyer, who, like a drudge-horse, can only go in the gears of a particular vehicle, but adorning and illustrating it with literature and science. His knowledge of history and of the ancient and modern classics was as profound as his legal acquirements, while his political information and sagacity kept pace with his other improvements. His genius was of the first order, and he improved it with the most sedulous care. He exerted his mind at times as an author, then as an orator, and daily as a lawyer, while his efforts in each department improved his general powers, and gave him that variety of information and knowledge, which, when combined with genius, makes, what Mr. Wirt really was, a truly great man. Not great only in politics, literature, or law, but great in each and all, like Lord Brougham. Many of his countrymen were his superiors in some departments of learning, as they may be said to be his superiors in some natural endowments, but for universality and variety of talent perhaps he was not surpassed.

Mr. Wirt had none of the adventitious aids of

high birth, fortune, and connections, to assist him up the steep hill of fame. He was compelled to force his own way, unaided and unfriended, and, like many other great men of our country, he taught school for a maintenance while he studied law. It was during that time, while he was a student, or immediately after he was admitted to the practice, that he wrote the letters of the "British Spy." The description of the *novi homines*, the new men, which he so eloquently gives in one of those letters, applied aptly to himself. The eloquence with which he describes the elevated purposes of oratory exhibited his own devotion to the art, while it showed his capability of excelling in it.

It may be said to be almost the peculiar privilege of an American to win his own way, by the gifts nature has given him, with the certainty that success will wait on merit. Wealth and family influence, it is true, have great weight in the start of a young man; but, in the long run, superior talent will gain the prize, no matter what may have been the early disadvantages of their possessor, provided the resolution to be true to himself comes not too late. The history of almost every departed, as well as of almost every living worthy of our country, proves this remark; and it is right that it should be so. Perhaps this, more than any other feature in a republic, tends to its durability, while it renders it glorious. The great mass of the people are seldom wrong in their judgments, and therefore it is that with them talents meet with a just appreciation wherever they become known, at least talent for oratory.

Mr. Wirt had all the qualifications for obtaining the popular good-will. He possessed a fine person, remarkable amenity of manners, colloquial qualities of the first order, wit at will, and he abounded in anecdotes, which he related with remarkable pleasantness and tact. A stranger, on entering an assemblage where Mr. Wirt was, would immediately, on perceiving him, have supposed him to be a superior man.

His person was above the medium height, with an inclination to corpulency; his countenance was "sicklied o'er with the pale cast of thought;" his mouth was finely formed, and a physiognomist would have noted that the compression of his lips denoted firmness, and his smile good-humored irony; he had a Roman nose; an eye of cerulean blue, with a remarkably arch expression when he was animated, and of calm thoughtfulness when his features were in repose; his forehead was not high, but it was broad, with the phrenological developments strongly marked, particularly the poetic and perceptive faculties.

His hair was sandy, and his head bald on the top, which, with Byronian anxiety, he tried to hide by combing the hair over the baldness; and it was much his custom, when engaged in an oratorical display, to preserve its adjustment by passing his hands over it. He was much more careful in this regard than is the eloquent and chivalric Preston, who, though he wears a wig, seems not only indifferent as to who knows it, but of the wig itself; for, in a sturdy breeze which blew over the Canton Course, at the Baltimore Convention, it nearly left him, he the while apparently unconscious, as he fulminated to the vast and rapt multitude. Well! the Carolinian may not love the laurel as Cæsar did, because it hid his baldness, but he deserved to have it voted to him long ago for his eloquence.

General Harrison used to tell, as he gladdened the hearth at the Bend with stories of the past and the present, how he remembered to have seen Patrick Henry, in the heat of his glorious declamation, twist the back of his wig until it covered his brow; and any one who has heard the Senator from Carolina, would say that the resemblance between himself and his illustrious relative extended from great things to small.

On the first glance at Mr. Wirt's countenance, when he was not engaged in conversation or business, the observer would have been struck with the true dignity of the man, who seemed to hold all his energies in perfect control. His self-possession was great. When he arose to address the court or jury, there was no hurry, no agitation about him, as we perceive in many men; on the contrary, he stood collected, while his enunciation was deliberate and slow. He stated his proposition with great simplicity; in fact, it was generally a self-evident one, the applicability of which to the case, if it were intricate and doubtful, the hearer might in vain endeavor to trace; but when he had heard the orator to the conclusion, he would wonder that he had fancied any uncertainty about it—for Mr. Wirt would lead him by the gentlest gradations until he was convinced. It may be mentioned, too, that Mr. Wirt, like Mr. Clay, was a great taker of snuff, and he handled his box with a grace which would have rivalled even that of the Senator from Kentucky. Lord Chatham, it is said, made his crutch a weapon of oratory.

"You talk of conquering America, sir," said he; "I might as well attempt to drive them before me with this crutch."

And so Mr. Wirt made, and Mr. Clay makes, his snuffbox an oratorical weapon. Mr. Wirt's language was at times almost oriental; his figures being of the boldest, and his diction correspondent. His speeches in Burr's trial show this, though latterly he chastened somewhat his diction and his thoughts. He sustained himself well in the highest flight of eloquence, his hearers having no fear that he would fall from his eminence like him in the fable with the waxen wings. On the contrary, the hearer felt confident of his intellectual strength, and yielded his whole feelings to him without that drawback we experience in listening to some of the ablest speakers, who often have some glaring imperfection which is continually destroying their eloquence. Mr. Wirt studied oratory with Ciceronian care, and, in the recklessness with which he let fly the arrows of his wit, he much resembled the Roman. The power of ridiculing his adversary was Mr. Wirt's forte. The appropriate manner in which he applied an anecdote was admirable. After he had demonstrated the absurdity of his opponent's arguments, with a clearness which the most critical logician would have admired; after he had illustrated his position with all the lights of law, that law whose seat, Hooker said, "is the bosom of God, and whose voice is the harmony of the world," (and when Mr. Wirt had a strong case, he explored every field of literature and science, bringing their joint sanctions to his purposes;) after he had called up the truths of philosophy, the experience of history, and the beauties of poetry, all coming like spirits thronging to his call; after he had expatiated upon the cause, with such reflections as you would suppose Barrow or Tillotson to have used when speaking of the "oppressor's wrong;" after he had done all this, Mr. Wirt would, if the opposite party deserved the infliction, pour forth upon him a lava-like ridicule, which flamed while it burned, and which was at once terrible and beautiful—terrible from its severity and truth, and beautiful from the chaste language in which it was conveyed.

Mr. Wirt always struck me as being very much like the late Prime Minister of England, Canning, in his mind. Canning wanted, and Wirt in a degree, the power of calling up and controlling the stronger and deeper passions of our nature. He had not that withering scorn which Brougham possesses so strongly, nor could he rise above the tempest of popular commotion, as he tells us Patrick Henry could, and soar with "supreme dominion." He wanted deep passion. Comparing him with the leading orators of our country, it would be said that Clay far surpassed him in the power of controlling a miscellaneous assemblage, when the public mind was deeply agitated; that Pinkney on a question of feudal lore, Webster in profundity and on constitutional law, and Preston in the glare of vehement declamation, would have had the advantage over him; but before an auditory who loved to mingle wit with argument, and elegance with strength, who would make truth more beautiful by the adornments of poetry, and poetry useful as the handmaid of truth, adding to all those exterior graces which make oratory so captivating—before such an auditory, it may be said, without great hesitation, that Mr. Wirt would have surpassed either of them in general effect.

Mr. Wirt's gestures, too, gifts of which the Grecian thought so much, were in keeping with his other excellences. The fault was that they were studied—and yet the art with which he concealed his art was consummate. It was only by the closest observation that it could be detected. For a long time, Mr. Wirt's chief opponent at the Baltimore bar was Mr. Taney, the present Chief-Justice of the United States. Mr. Taney removed to Baltimore from Frederick, on the death of Pinkney, and there Mr. Wirt and himself were the great forensic rivals. No two men of the same profession could have been more different in their intellectual gifts than were these gentlemen. They were as unlike in these regards as they were in their personal appearance. Mr. Taney was then slim to feebleness (he looks now improved in health); he stooped, and his voice was weak, and such was the precarious condition of his health, that he had to station himself immediately before and near the jury, to make himself heard by them. Mr. Wirt always placed himself on the side of the trial table, opposite the jury, in oratorical position. Mr. Taney's manner of speaking was slow and firm, never using the least rhetorical ornament, but pressing into the heart of the cause with powerful arguments, like a great leader, with unbroken phalanx, into the heart of a besieged city. His style was plain, unadorned, and so forcible and direct, that it might be called palpable. With his snuffbox—for the Chief-Justice then, too, used snuff—compressed in his closed hands, he reasoned for hours without the least attempt at wit or eloquence. And yet, at times, he was truly eloquent, from his deep subdued earnestness. In a question of bail in the case of a youth who had shot at his teacher, I remember, though then a school-boy, attracted to the court-house in pity for the lad, that a crowded auditory were suffused in tears. It was the fervor of his own feelings, speaking right out, that made him eloquent. He did not appear to know that he was eloquent himself. It was an inspiration that came to him, if it came at all, unbidden, and which would no more answer to his call than Glendower's

"Spirits from the vasty deep."

One of the most interesting cases ever witnessed at the Baltimore bar, was a trial in a mandamus case, in which the right to a church was contested. Mr. Duncan had been established in the ministry in Baltimore, by a number of Scotch Presbyterians, in an obscure edifice. His talents drew such a congregation, that it soon became necessary to build a larger one. It was done; and in the progress of events, the pastor preached a more liberal doctrine than he had at first inculcated. His early supporters remained not only unchanged in their faith, but they resolved to have it preached to them by one with whom they could entirely agree upon religious matters. The majority of the congregation agreed with Mr. Duncan. A deep schism arose in the divided flock, which could not be healed, and which was eventually, by a writ of mandamus, carried before a legal tribunal. Mr. Taney was counsel for the Old School side, and Mr. Wirt for the defendants. The court-room, during the trial, was crowded with the beauty and fashion of the monumental city. It was such a display of eloquence, and a full appreciation of it, as is seldom witnessed. Mr. Wirt was always happy in making a quotation, and in concluding this cause he made one of his happiest. After alluding to the Old School members, who it has been said were Scotchmen, and after dwelling upon the tragedy of Macbeth, the scenes of which are laid in Scotland, he described their preacher as being in the condition of Macbeth's guest, and said, after a stern rebuke to them, that though they should succeed in their cause, which he felt confident they would not, they would feel like the guilty thane;

> "This *Duncan*
> Hath borne his faculties so meek, hath been
> So clear in his great office, that his virtues
> Will plead like angels, trumpet-tongued, against
> The deep damnation of his taking off."

This quotation, the name and circumstances being

so appropriate, was made with such oratorical effect that there was a deep silence when Mr. Wirt took his seat, which was succeeded by repeated outbreaks of applause. Mr. Wirt gained the case.

As an author, Mr. Wirt's merits are very high. His "British Spy" contains sketches of some of our first men, drawn with a graphic power, which makes us regret that he did not oftener direct his fine mind to the delineation of character. He was eminently calculated for a biographer. His high tone of moral feeling would have prevented him from becoming the apologist of vice, no matter how high were its endowments; while his great admiration of virtue and talent would have made him the enthusiastic eulogist of those qualifications which render biography so attractive and so useful. The great fault of his "Life of Patrick Henry" is exaggeration. His mind became heated and inflated as he contemplated the excellences of Henry as an orator and a man, and he overcolored that which, told with more simplicity, would have been more striking. The effects of Henry's eloquence being so wonderful in themselves, would, narrated in a plainer way, have more forcibly struck the mind. What they borrowed from the poetry of the biographer seems

> "Like gilding refined gold, painting the lily,
> Or throwing a perfume on the violet."

Mr. Wirt's "Old Bachelor" is deserving of high commendation. It is written in numbers, after the manner of the "Spectator," "Guardian," and "Adventurer," and has much of the eloquence of style which has contributed so largely to the popularity of those celebrated works. It treats of various subjects—oratory, poetry, morality, &c.—and abounds in reflections happily suited to the condition of young men who are entering the learned professions. It is not sparse of wit, while it shows the author's familiar acquaintance with the old worthies of English literature, those who drank of the "well of English undefiled."

It should not be neglected to be said of Mr. Wirt that he was one of those who, in early life, from the pressure of an unfriended condition upon a mind of excessive sensitiveness, fell for awhile into reckless despondency, alternated by wayward fits of intellectual energy, which had an unfortunate influence upon his habits. Such has been the situation of men like him, who had the "fatal gift," without any other gift—no friendly hand, no cheering voice. Alas! the records of genius, for wretchedness, are surpassed only by the records of the lunatic asylum; in fact, its history often illustrates and deepens the saddest story on the maniac's wall. But, to the glory of Mr. Wirt, it is known that his energies prevailed—that friends came—that religious trust, which had formerly visited him like the fitful wanderings of a perturbed spirit, at last made her home by his hearth, where a beautiful and gifted family grew up around him, until, full of years and full of honors, and the faith that is beyond them, he was gathered to his fathers.

When contemplating the moral and intellectual character of Mr. Wirt, it has been regretted that he did not turn away from the thorny paths of the law, and devote the whole force of his mind to general literature; but how could he, with the poor rewards of literature, support those nearest and dearest to him? Yet, had circumstances allowed him to do so, he would have been one of the first literary men of our country.

I have frequently heard Mr. Wirt when opposed to some of our eminent men, and this slight sketch is drawn from opinions then entertained and expressed. I presented, while he lived, the tribute of my admiration, not to the politician, not to the candidate for the presidency, but to the author of the "British Spy," "The Old Bachelor," "The Life of Henry," a great lawyer, an acute statesman, a consummate advocate, and last, though not least, an honest man; and, now that he is dead, I would fain garner a testimonial to his memory worthy of him, but the will must be taken for the deed.

REV. HENRY B. BASCOM.

WHEN this gentleman was in the full tide of his pulpit popularity in the West, a young lady friend of mine, in Kentucky, offered to take me in her carriage to a camp-meeting, a few miles from her residence, to hear the distinguished orator. I gladly consented, both for the sake of the company of my fair companion and for the pleasure of hearing Mr. Bascom.

When a lad, I had heard this gentleman and the lamented Summerfield, and I had been struck with the dissimilar but great powers of both preachers.

Summerfield's eloquence was the summer morning's sunshine, with its dew and flower; Bascom's the lurid light and flashings of the tempest. One preached the love and the other the terrors of the Gospel. Summerfield's attractiveness seemed that of another world, and his exceeding naturalness and the absence of all apparent effort were remarkable. Bascom was full of pith, and point, and preparation; he poured forth sentence after sentence of intense elaboration. To borrow, not incorrectly, a phrase from the theatre in relation to the stage efforts of Forrest, he "piled the agony up" fearfully—so fearfully as to make the hearer fear he would never get down, except by tumbling. It was whip and spur from the word go. His style and manner reminded one very much of Maryland's most distinguished orator, Pinkney.

The almost beardless chin and pallid countenance of Summerfield contrasted, again, with the flashing eye, the ruddy cheek, and the black beard of Bascom.

My lady friend, though a rigid Episcopalian, was a great admirer of Mr. Bascom. She thought he would look so well in the gown, and that he would read the service so eloquently. She said she felt like presenting him a gown, anyhow. Mr. Wesley and Mr. Whitefield always preached in a gown, and she could not see why he did not. She was warm in her eulogies of his personal independence, and dwelt particularly upon the fashion of his toilet, and how becomingly his apparel fit his manly form. She thought him the handsomest man she had ever seen, and wondered why he smoked so many cigars—and, above all, how he could chew so much tobacco! She said that, unlike every other popular preacher she had ever known, he seemed to be indifferent to the admiration of her sex, and that he certainly had no address in ladies' society. This she liked, as she thought it proved his sincerity. She then told the anecdote of some rich lady (she was rich herself, and wondered how any woman could so unsex herself), who offered him her purse, heart, and hand; and that his reply was, that "she had better give her purse to the poor, her heart to God, and her hand to him that asked for it." I told her that I had heard the same story of Summerfield and others. She replied that Summerfield had too little of this earth about him to inspire such an offer, and was too gentle ("gentlemanly?" some one asked; no, *gentle*, she repeated) to make such a reply, though she thought it the very one for the occasion—a Christian rebuke!

How she delighted to talk of the orator, and she was so proud that he was a Kentuckian. She said the Conference had kept him for years itinerating about in the "knobs" of Kentucky, to take the pride out of him, particularly the pride of dress, but that he would make his advent from the wilds into Frankfort or Lexington, with as exquisite a toilet, as if he had just left the shop of a fashionable tailor. She said he had been taken to task for his dress by some Quarterly Conference, and that he had replied to them that if they should cut a hole through a blanket, and put it over him, that he should still be Henry B. Bascom; that dress was no part of his religion, and if it was of theirs, it was well for them to look to their habiliments; that he had no idea of what a religious hat, or a religious pair of boots was. Here, again, he was in contrast with Summerfield, who, upon some "weak brother's" finding fault with a seal he wore, abolished it, and wore nothing but the ribbon.

In this pleasant chat, for the lady talked well, and in fact the Kentucky ladies generally have more conversational talent than any other ladies in the Union, we approached the camp. It was pitched on the gentle slope of a hill, at the foot of which a broad branch rippled, and the white tents and the crowd of people presented a most picturesque appearance. We were late, for we heard the bold tones of the orator ringing through the woods in the highest note of declamation. We thought we should have been early, for it was understood that it was at night the orator was to address the multitude. The sun was about half an hour from his setting, and we hurried from the carriage to the place of worship.

A dense crowd occupied the whole space, not only in front of the pulpit, but all around it, and, with my fair friend leaning upon my arm, we had to take a stand on the outskirts, and catch the intellectual manna, which fell in the wilderness, as we might. We, however, heard and saw the orator distinctly. His appearance, manner, and eloquence were magnificent and sublime, as, with the Bible raised aloft in his hand, he described the spread of the Gospel in heathen lands. We listened, like the rest of the audience, in rapt attention for ten or fifteen minutes, when, as he laid the Bible down and paused for a moment, my fair friend at my side exclaimed, in a glow of admiration:—

"He is, indeed, a prince in Israel."

And I thought so, too. In one bright spot the setting sun was flashing through the quivering leaves, throwing over his breast, and brow, and countenance, a halo of living light.

The orator gloriously alluded to the departing luminary, whose rising beams, he said, enabled the missionary to read the Word of God to the heathen of the farthest East in his own language, and whose setting beams flashed upon the blazonry of the Bible, bearing civilization and Christianity to the farthest West.

Mr. Bascom has been brought particularly to my mind in reading a volume of sermons which he has lately published. It appears, by his preface, that he "commenced preaching when he was but sixteen years old."

One would not think so, to read his sermons. He has none of the cant (I use the word not disrespectfully) of the trained preacher about him—nothing of "mere pulpit patois," to use his own phrase, in speaking in this connection. He seems studiously to avoid it. In his preface he says:—

"The author has long been impressed with the idea, perhaps he should say conviction, that the force and value of pulpit instruction are greatly lessened by the restraints and mannerism of pulpit style, arising mainly, perhaps, from undue attachments to creeds, confessions, and church formularies, as the tests and standards of truth and uniformity among different denominations of Christians, and the vicious standards of critical judgments already referred to. The natural, manly, and varied freedom of expression found in the Bible, and preserved, in greater or less degree, in all its translations into different languages, is laid aside, and gives place to the staidness and precision of an exclusive technical phraseology, and often having all the essential characteristics of a mere pulpit patois. And on this account alone, with or without reason, the pulpit too often becomes to the hearer a mere limbo of commonplace, from which he turns away with indifference, if not disgust."

These remarks are strong, but they are truthful, and Mr. Bascom has not certainly fallen into the error. With the hackneyed phrases too often heard in the pulpit, he has nothing to do whatever. Though he is often too ornate, and too fond of antithesis and alliteration, it is evident that the vast storehouse of literature, both sacred and profane, has furnished his supply. He makes few quotations, even from the Bible, except when he is establishing some very particular point by Divine authority; but he boldly and bravely expatiates upon the subject as it strikes his own mind. The volume before us is full of beauties, and it certainly has some startling defects. Almost all speakers have some pet words, which they drag in upon all occasions, and Mr. Bascom is no small transgressor in this way. He is fond, very, of the words "antagonism" and "adumbrating;" and he has taken the liberty of coining words, too, passing his counterfeits with the king's English, for which Dr. Johnson would find him guilty without benefit of clergy. Some of his phrases, too, are against all taste; for instance: "The smile of infidelity transformed to a groan in the very act of parturition," &c.

It is to be hoped that Mr. Bascom will never give birth to such a phrase as that again, but let it die like the "smile of infidelity" aforesaid. But away with fault-finding—this volume of "Sermons from the Pulpit" abounds with aphoristic thoughts and pages of burning eloquence. Speaking of the duties of the preacher, he says: "He should teach all, with unwearied urgency of appeal, that life is an orbit, through which mortality can pass but once; that it is but an hour-glass, and that every sand ought to be a pious deed or a virtuous thought."

Again, he says: "Honest severity in the pulpit is like the lightning of heaven—it makes holy what it scathes. It resembles the thunderbolt, passing through tainted exhalations but to purify them." "Every day you live without repentance, say, with the startled emperor of antiquity, 'I have lost a day,' and say, 'with the blessing of God, I will never lose another.'" Speaking of heaven, he says: "Ours may be the only prodigal in the great family of worlds; and, after due time and trial, all may meet in this vast region."

But I must not make this article too long. Pages of great beauty, as has been said, might be quoted from these "Sermons from the Pulpit," with the disfigurement here and there of a tortured phrase, or a noun pressed to do duty as a verb, "adumbrating" upon us in "antagonism" to all taste; but, after all, "de gustibus," &c. And, again, after all, the preacher has been one of the great lights of his church in his day, without one particle of cant in his conduct or character, and as little "pulpit patois" in his preachings. He is a frank, fearless, and consistent Christian, with this high praise, that his piety is commended most by those who know him best.

Possessing the power to draw the unthinking and the foolishly-fashionable to the Methodist meeting-house, with the learned and the pious of every shade of opinion and variety of creed, and of impressing multitudes, not only with the force of his talents, but with the truth of his faith, he has proved to the world that a preacher may present himself in society, in dress and address, an accomplished, high-toned, and high-bred gentleman, and yet be a Puritan in his morals and conduct; nay, more, a Methodist.

DEATH OF BISHOP BASCOM.

We learn with great regret the death of Bishop Henry B. Bascom, one of the Bishops of the Methodist Episcopal Church South, who died on Sunday last, at the residence of the Rev. Mr. Stevinson, in Louisville, Ky., where he had been a long time ill.

Bishop Bascom's illness arose from a bilious fever caught in Missouri some time since, while on his first tour of duty in his office of bishop.

Bishop Bascom's place in the Church South cannot easily be filled. He was a man of great energy, of great talents, of great fearlessness, and, in the matter of the church difficulty between the North and South, having taken sides with the South, he stood forth her admitted leader. The celebrated pamphlet on the subject, setting forth the grounds which the South meant to maintain in the premises, was from the pen of Bishop Bascom, and was full of point, argument, and energetic declamation.

Bishop Bascom was also editor of the *Review*, which was published under the auspices of the Methodist Church in the West, and he contributed many powerful articles to it. But it was as a pulpit orator that Bishop Bascom shone. His style as a writer was too stilty and too ornate; it wanted ease and naturalness. He was always for saying keen things, and wanted repose of style, if the expression may be used. This same fault, in a measure, followed him into the pulpit. He was never content unless he was in the upper region, like the spirit of the storm, wielding the lightning and speaking in the thunder. That varied gracefulness and self-command which distinguish his early and his fast friend, Mr. Clay, that gracefulness which, like the swallow, now skims the lake and now darts into the cloud, Mr. Bascom had not.

He wanted naturalness. He blazed, and corruscated, and startled, but he seldom melted his audience. Wonder and admiration often impressed them, but the tear seldom followed. But in denunciation, in scorn, in the terrors of the law, he was fearful. He could seize infidelity by the throat and shake the life out of it; or he could hurl against it the wrath of Divine vengeance until it would call on the mountains to cover it from an angry judge:

but he could not melt it into hopeful and penitent, yet trusting, tears. He had great elevation and expansion of mind, and delighted to expatiate with unfettered and uncircumscribed wing. He loved to dwell upon the beatitude of the saved, or the unutterable misery of the lost; and, in this last category, the heedless, and the reckless, and the criminal, would look as if the clinched fist of the preacher was stamping on their foreheads their inevitable doom.

Bishop Bascom was a man of remarkable personal beauty and manliness. He had the ample chest which almost all orators have; a rounded neck supported a head of classic mould; thin, dark hair, cut close, shaded not at all his ample forehead, which projected like a wall; his eyes were of dazzling blackness, and quailed not before power, position, or wealth; on the contrary, they quailed before him.

He has been heard to say that the only eye he ever met with, which made him feel its power, was that of Aaron Burr; that, on one occasion, when that fallen spirit was pointed out to him in New York, he stopped and gazed at him with a curiosity which forgot its courtesy, when the offended and piercing glance which Burr cast on him caused him to pass on, hurriedly and abashed. Bishop Bascom had a brilliant color, indicating the highest health, and, at the same time, a temperament of a bilious tendency. It has been often remarked that he looked very much like Mr. Webster, though he was a much handsomer man, without that look of massive intellectuality in which the great constitutional expounder surpasses all other men.

Bishop Bascom was remarkably fastidious in his toilet, and, like Whitefield, set off his person to advantage.

Many anecdotes are told of him, and some of the more rigid of his church, in this matter; but he did not obey the precept of St. Paul, and paid no respect to their "weakness." He was fond of telling the story that an old Dutch Methodist, who did not know him, and at whose house he was to stop on his way to fulfil his appointment, said to him, on learning who he was: "Well, if I had loaded my rifle to shoot a Methodist preacher, I never should have snapped at you!"

There was none of that preciseness about him which is so often remarked in the bearing of a minister; on the contrary, it almost seemed, so marked was his bearing to the contrary, that he somewhat affected a don't-care of manner. In his pulpit efforts he avoided everything like what is called cant, and what he called patois. All his life, he said, he had endeavored to avoid it; he certainly succeeded. He seemed like a statesman or lawyer, whom the stern reflection of Paul, "Woe is me if I preach not the Gospel of Christ," had driven, duty-called, into the pulpit. And there he stood, and there gloriously he fulfilled his mission. It was Methodism in earnest to hear Bishop Bascom preach, and Methodism which Chesterfield would have been compelled to respect, if but for the high and courtly, yet Christian bearing of its advocate. He was the son of thunder, and, like St. Paul, he bore himself to the enemies of his faith bravely, yet with a touch of consummate address, like the apostle before Festus. Bishop Bascom has fulfilled his mission; he has been true to himself and to his church, and to its Great Head, and it is earnestly hoped that some biographer may be selected by his friends, capable of doing justice to his memory.

A VISIT TO SIMON KENTON,

THE LAST OF THE PIONEERS.

> "An active hermit, even in age the child
> Of nature, or the man of Ross, run wild."—BYRON.

FALLING, the other day, accidentally upon Byron's beautiful lines in "Don Juan," on

> "General Boone, backwoodsman of Kentucky,"

I thought, as I dwelt upon their freshness—fresh as the forests and the character which is his theme—of a visit which I paid some years ago to Boone's contemporary and similar, Simon Kenton, who died shortly afterwards, and I determined to fill out a slight sketch then made of him. One bright morning in October, I think '34, after a hearty breakfast on venison, with the becoming appliances of cranberry-jelly, and all the et ceteras of a luxurious meal, such as you often get in the western country, and which our kind hostess of

West Liberty, Ohio, had, according to the promises of the previous evening, prepared for us by day-dawn, my friend and myself started from that village on our way to Bellefontaine, resolved to call and pay our respects—the respects of strangers and travellers—to the old pioneer, who, we were informed, dwelt some thirty miles from our whereabouts.

It was a glorious Indian-summer morning. The day was just dawning as we started, and the thick haze, which characterizes this season of the year, enveloped the whole landscape, but, without concealing, made it just indistinct enough for the imagination to group and marshal hill, prairie, tree, and stream, in a manner agreeable to our feelings. The haze rested on the face of nature like a veil over a sleeping beauty, disclosing enough of her features to charm, without dazzling us with the flash of her eye, which makes us shrink while we admire.

A vast prairie extended on our right, through which loitered a lazy stream, as if it lingered, loath to leave the fertile soil which embosomed it. A silvery mist hung over it, making it appear like a great lake. Here and there, arising from the immense body of the prairie, were what are called islands—that is, great clumps of trees, covering sometimes many acres, appearing just like so many islands in an outstretched ocean. One, I

6

observed, was peculiarly striking; it was a natural mound rising out of the prairie, and was covered with a dense wood, while around it the plain extended far and wide, and was as level as a floor.

As the day dawned, the scene became more and more enchanting. The sun blazed up through the forest-trees that skirted the prairie, like a beacon-fire. Those of the trees which were earliest touched by the frost, and had lost their foliage, seemed like so many warriors stretching forth their arms in mortal combat; while the fallen ones, which lay in their huge length upon the ground, might easily be fancied so many braves, who were realizing the poet's description of a contest:—

"Few shall part, where many meet."

Then my fancy caught another impression. I thought, as I looked upon the tranquil scene, the wide prairie, the sheep browsing on it, the gentle stream, the mist curling up, the towering trees, the distant hills, the blue smoke ascending here and there from a rustic dwelling, all looking tranquillity, that Peace had lighted her altar, and all nature was worshipping the Being whose blessings were upon all. The rich tint of those trees which still retained their foliage, added to the beauty and oneness of the scene, and, in gilding the picture, harmonized with it.

On our left, a hill ascended abruptly, covered

with tall trees, which, in some places, were remarkably clear of underwood, and in others choked up with it. The undergrowth, from its great luxuriance where it did appear, seemed emulous of the height of its neighbors. At the foot of the hill, and winding around it, lay our road; sometimes it would ascend the hill's side to the very summit, and then abruptly descend to the very foot. This gave us a full view of the surrounding scenery. It was beautiful. To me, like that of another world, coming, as I did, from the contagious breath of the city, where disease and death were spread, wide as the atmosphere, for I had just left Cincinnati, where the cholera was raging. The bustle of business; the hum of men; the discordant noises; the dusty streets; the sameness and dingy red of the houses; the smoky and impure atmosphere; the frequent hearse; the hurrying physician; the many in black; were all remembered in contrast with this bright scene of nature. I caught myself almost unconsciously repeating the lines of the poet:—

"Oh, how canst thou renounce the boundless store
Of charms, which Nature to her votary yields!
The warbling woodland, the resounding shore,
The pomp of groves, the garniture of fields;
All that the genial ray of morning gilds,
And all that echoes to the song of even;
All that the mountain's sheltering bosom shields,
And all the dread magnificence of heaven;
Oh, how canst thou renounce, and hope to be forgiven?"

I felt at once why I had been an invalid. I had been breathing an air pregnant with all sorts of sickness; was it any wonder I was sick? I had swallowed a whole drug shop—for what purpose? To be drugged to death!

Everything in this world takes the hue of our feelings. A few weeks previously I had been to a wedding in Lebanon, where I had enjoyed myself gloriously. We kept it up till "'tween the late and early," and all went off appropriately—

"As merry as a marriage bell."

The next morning I breakfasted with the bewitching bride and her generous lover, and then away from the bridal scene in a hazy rain, over horrible roads, tossed about in a trundlebed of a cariole, with no companion but my crutch, and a whole host of bachelor reflections. The scene was sad everywhere. I passed an old rooster by the roadside. He stood alone, dripping wet, with not a single hen near him—chick nor child—like a grand Turk who had been upset in an aquatic excursion, and had quarrelled with his whole seraglio. A dog skulked by me with his tail between his legs, looking, for all the world, as if he had been sheep-killing. How desolate the girdled trees looked! As the winds whistled through their leafless branches, they seemed the very emblems of aspiring manhood, deprived of all his honors, when he thought them greenest, yet still standing with the world's blight upon him. The road wound about, as if it had business all through the woods; and the long miry places were covered with rails, to prevent one from disappearing altogether! What jolting! zig-zag—this way, that way, every way. Why, Sancho Panza, when tossed in the blanket, enjoyed perfect luxury in the comparison. And when, at last, I did get upon a piece of road that was straight, it appeared a long vista leading to utter desolation. The turbid streams were but emblems of the lowering sky. They looked frowning on each other like foe on foe, while the autumn leaves fell thick around me like summer hopes. To-day is different—all is bright. To-morrow may be cloudy—and thus wags the world.

There is no nobler theme for the novelist and the poet than the stirring incidents of the first settlement of our country. The muse of Scott has made his country appear the appropriate place for romantic legend and traditionary feud, but it only wants his genius to make our country more than the rival of his in that respect. The field here is as abundant, and almost untrodden. However, I am not one of those who believe that legends of the olden time are the best themes for the novelist. If he would describe truly the manners, virtues, and vices around him as they are, he would win more applause than in the description of other scenes; because all would *feel* the truth of the portraiture. Scott failed in describing modern manners in "St. Ronan's Well." Why? Because his affections and feelings were with the past; and those ballads and romances in which his boyhood delighted, exercised over his imagination a controlling power; and when he came to give them a "local habitation and a name," that controlling power was manifest.

But who of Scott's readers has not regretted that he did not give us more of the men and manners of the day? If he had thought as much of them as of baronial and other periods; and, having studied, had attempted to paint them when his mind was in its vigor, he would have succeeded as well as in "Ivanhoe," "Rob Roy," or the "Crusaders." Fielding could describe only the manners around him, because he had thought only of them. Scott's imagination had a feudal bias, and, consequently, he painted that period best when, as he describes it—

"They laid down to rest,
With the corslet laced—
Pillowed on buckler cold and hard;
They carved at the meal
With gloves of steel,
And drank the red wine through the helmet barred."

How delightful if Scott had given us some of the scenes which he witnessed among the different circles with which he mingled. In such scenes he studied human nature, it is true, but he applied his knowledge in describing how men acted in other circumstances than those in which he saw them act, for he well knew that the truthful portraiture finds sympathy in every breast. He learned the whole history of the human heart, and then gave us volumes of the olden time, because there his imagination feasted. He should, sometimes, have shown us ourselves as we are. It seems to me that not only in our early history is there a wide field for the novelist, but that in our own times there is both a wider and a better. What a great variety of characters in our country! Men from all climes, of all opinions, parties, sects. The German, Frenchman, Englishman, Russian, the Backwoodsman, the Yankee, and the Southerner, are each and all often found in the barroom of a country tavern. To one who likes to observe character, what enjoyment! Why, as Falstaff would say, "it is a play extempore." And then to quit a scene like this, pass a few miles from one of these towns, and be right into the wilderness; for it seems a wilderness to look around on the deep woods, and the wild prairie, and see no marks of civilization but the road on which you travel. How the mind expands! You look up, and fancy some far-off cloud the Great Spirit looking down on his primeval world, in all the freshness and beauty of its first years. The imagination glows, the feelings freshen, the affections become intense. Rapidly, then, the scenes of our boyhood rush upon us—our early manhood, our hopes, our fears, the lady of our love, the objects of our ambition. We see some brilliant bird that we have started from its perch dart off in the blue ether, and thus before us seems the world, all our own. And then we enter the town, and behold the vast variety of human beings among whom and with whom we have to struggle. Here, too, we often find woman loveliest and most fascinating, a flower in the wilderness, and beautiful both in bud and in bloom. And here are generous and free spirits, who wear no disguise about them, whose feelings spring up, like the eagle from its eyry, in natural fearlessness. The change is enjoyment; one fits us for the other. In solitude, we think over, analyze, and examine what we see in the world; and, in the world, the reflections and resolutions of solitude strike us like a parental admonition.

That simplicity which Cooper has described so well in the character of Leatherstocking, seems to have been the characteristic of the early pioneers. It has been my good luck to meet with several of them. One, who is now a country squire, and of course far advanced in years, with whom I became acquainted in the interior of Ohio, frequently, in conversation with me, dwelt upon the peculiarities of the pioneers, lamenting with simplicity, energy, and natural eloquence, which told that he was one of them, the "falling off," as he called it, of the present times.

"Why," said he to me, "if you will believe me, there is not half the confidence between man and man that there used to be, when I was in the wilderness here, and used to travel to the different stations. It was a long tramp, I tell you; but you might rely on the man that went with you, to life and to death, just as you would on your rifle; and then you rested on your rifle, and looked upon the beauties of the wilderness—and the wilderness is beautiful to them that like it—and felt that you were a man. Why, I could do everything for myself, in those days—I needed no help, nohow. I tell you, I have a snug farm, and, may-be, some things that you call comforts, but I shall never be as happy as I was when here in the wilderness with my dog and rifle, and nothing else. No, I shall never be as happy again, and that's a fact. Mr. ——, our preacher, preaches a good sermon, bating a spice of Calvinism, that somehow I can't relish or believe natural; but he can't make me feel like I used to—I mean with such a reliance on Providence—as I did when I roused up in the morning, and looked out on the beauties of nature, just as God made them. You find fault with these roads

—and I know the travelling's bad—I thought so myself as I came to town—and yet I used to travel through the wilderness when there was no road or town. I sometimes felt tired, it's true; but it was not the weariness I feel now; no, no! I never shall be as happy as I was in the wilderness, and that's a fact."

I believe I have repeated the very words, as they fell from the lips of the fine old man. I was much amused with his opinion of novels.

"Why, I am told," he said, "that a man will write two big books, and not a word of truth in 'em from beginning to end. Now ain't that abominable? To tell a lie, anyhow, is a great shame; but to write, and then to print it, is what I never thought of. How can you tell it from truth, if he's an ingenious man? It looks just like truth when 'tis printed. It destroys all confidence in books. Judge Jones tells me that there was a man called Scott, who has written whole shelves of 'em—what do you call 'em?—novels? He tells me he was a pretty good sort of a man, too, with a good deal of the briar about him. I read one of them books once, that I liked, I suppose, from the name; they called it the 'Pioneers;' that's the reason I read it. I think there must be some mistake; you may depend on it, that man Leatherstocking never could have known so much about the wilderness and the ways of the Ingins, without being in it and among 'em."

What a fine compliment to the powers of Cooper! The scenery was striking, and, as we passed along, our conversation turned of course upon it, and from that to the dark forms that once flitted through it, and to those who had first struggled with the red man for its possession; and how naturally to him whom we were going to visit, who had been among the first and most fearless of the pioneers, and who was now lingering the last of them.

Simon Kenton's life had been a very eventful one—perhaps the most so of all the pioneers. Boone has been more spoken of and written about; but, in all probability, the reason is because he was the elder man, and had been then some time dead.

Kenton was a Virginian by birth, and, I believe, entirely uneducated. At a very early age he quarrelled with a rival in a love affair, and, after an unsuccessful conflict with him, Kenton challenged him to another, and was getting the worst of it, in a rough-and-tumble fight; being undermost, and subject to the full rage of his antagonist, he was much injured, when it occurred to him that if he could twist his rival's hair, which was very long, in a bush near by, he could punish him at his leisure. Crawling to the point, under the stunning blows of his antagonist, Kenton, with desperate energy, seized him by the hair, and succeeded in entangling it in the bush, as he desired. He then pommelled him with such right good-will, that he thought he had killed him. Kenton, fearing the consequences, instantly absconded, and changed his name from Simon Butler, which was his real name, to Simon Kenton. He pushed for the West. There he joined in several excursions against the savages, and was several times near being taken by them. He acted as a spy between the Indians and the colonies, in the war occasioned by the murder of Logan's family. After many adventures and hardships, he was taken by the Indians, in purloining some of their horses, which, in retaliation, he had led away in a night foray into one of their villages. He was treated with great cruelty; he ran the gauntlet thirteen times, and was finally saved from torture by the interference of Girty, a renegade white man who had joined the Indians, and was their leader in many of their attacks on the whites. Kenton and Girty had been friends, and pledged themselves so to continue, whatever changes might overtake them, before Girty apostatized. He, with all his savageness and treachery, was true to Kenton. This is but the caption of a chapter in Kenton's life.

After journeying for some time through thick woods, in which there were innumerable gray and black squirrels, we arrived at an angle of a worm-fence, and turned off into a swampy road, towards a log house, in which we were told the old pioneer lived. The house was comfortable and large for one of its kind. On stopping, a son-in-law of the old worthy met us at the bars; and, though he knew us not, with the hospitality of the country he insisted on putting up our horses, which kindness we were compelled to decline, as we could not tarry long. As we advanced towards the house, I observed everything about it wore the air of frugal comfort.

We ascended two or three steps, and entered the room, in which was a matron, who, we learned, was the wife of the pioneer, and, seated by the fire, was the old worthy himself. He rose as we entered. Advancing towards him, I said: "Mr. Kenton, we are strangers, who have read often of you and your adventures, and, being in your neighborhood, we have taken the liberty to call and see you, as we are anxious to know one of the first and the last of the pioneers."

The old pioneer was touched and gratified by the remark; and, while shaking hands with us, he said, "Take seats, take seats; I am right glad to see you."

We sat down, and immediately entered into conversation with him. He conversed in a desultory manner, and often had to make an effort to recollect himself; but, when he did, his memory seemed to call up the events alluded to, and, when asked anything, "Well, I'll tell you," he would say, and, after a pause, he narrated it. I have stood in the presence of men who had won laurels by field and flood, in the senate, at the bar, and in the pulpit, but my sensations were merely those of curiosity; a wish to know if the impressions which the individual made upon myself corresponded with the accounts given of him by others; if his countenance told his passions, and if the capabilities which he possessed could be read in him. This wish to observe prevents all other sensations, and makes one a curious but cold observer. But far different were my feelings as I looked upon the bent but manly form of the old pioneer, and observed his frank and fine features. Here, thought I, is a man who, if human character were dissected with a correct eye, would be found to be braver than many a one who has won the world's eulogy as a soldier. Who cannot be brave, with all the

"Pride, pomp, and circumstance of glorious war"

about him; with the neighing steed, the martial trump, the unfurled banner, the great army? In such a scene, the leader of so many legions finds in the very excitement bravery. The meanest soldier catches the contagious spark, and cowards fight with emulation. But think of a man alone in the wide, wild wilderness, whom a love of adventure has taken there, surrounded by wild beasts and savage foes, hundreds of miles from human aid; yet he sleeps calmly at night, and in the morning rises to pierce farther into the wilderness, nearer to those savage foes, and into the very den of those wild beasts. How calm must have been his courage! How enduring his spirit of endurance! In the deep solitude, hushed and holy as the Sabbath day of the world, he stands, with a self-reliance that nothing can shake; and he feels in the balmy air, in the blue heavens, in the great trees, in the tiny flower, in the woods and in the waterfalls, in the bird and in the beast, in everything and in all things, companionship. George Washington would have made such a pioneer.

Kenton's form, even under the weight of seventy years, was striking, and must have been a model of manly strength and agility. His eye was blue, mild, and yet penetrating in its glance. The forehead projected very much at the eyebrows (which were well defined), and then receded, and was not very high, nor very broad; his hair had been a light brown—it was then nearly all gray; his nose straight, and well shaped; his mouth, before he lost his teeth, must have been expressive and handsome. I observed that he had one tooth left, which, taking into consideration his character and manner of conversation, was continually reminding me of

Leatherstocking. The whole face was remarkably expressive, not of turbulence or excitement, but rather of rumination and self-possession. Simplicity, frankness, honesty, and a strict regard to truth, appeared the prominent traits of his character. In giving answer to a question which my friend asked him, I was particularly struck with his truthfulness and simplicity. The question was, whether the account of his life in "Sketches of Western Adventure" was true or not? "Well, I'll tell you," he said, "not true. The book says that when Blackfish, the Indian warrior, asked me, after they had taken me prisoner, if Colonel Boone sent me to steal their horses, that I said 'No, *sir*' (here he looked indignant, and rose from his chair); I tell you, I never said '*sir*' to an Ingin in my life; I scarcely ever say it to a white man."

Mrs. Kenton, who was engaged in some domestic occupation at the table, turned round and remarked: "When we were last in Kentucky, some one gave me the book to read, and when I came to that part, he would not let me read any more."

"And I will tell you," interrupted Kenton, "I never was tied to a stake in my life, to be burned; they had me painted black when I saw Girty, but not tied to a stake."

I mention this, not at all to disparage the book, but to show Kenton's character, for, though personally unacquainted with the author, I have a high respect for his talents; besides, Mr. McClung does not give the account of Kenton's adventures as narrated to himself by him, but as abridged from a MS. account given by the venerable pioneer himself, and now in the possession of Mr. John D. Taylor, of Kentucky. Kenton stated that he had narrated his adventures to a young lawyer (whose name I forget), and that all in the book was true. In answer to a question about Girty, he observed:—

"He was good to me. When he came up to me, when the Ingins had painted me black, I knew him at first. He asked me a good many questions, but I thought it best not to be too for'ard, and I held back from telling him my name; but, when I did tell him—oh! he was mighty glad to see me. He flung his arms round me, and cried like a child. I never did see one man so glad to see another yet. He made a speech to the Ingins—he could speak the Ingin tongue, and knew how to speak—and told them if they meant to do him a favor they must do it now, and save my life. Girty, afterwards, when we were at (I think he said) Detroit together, cried to me like a child, often, and told me he was sorry for the part he took against the whites; that he was too hasty. Yes, I tell you, Girty was good to me."

I remarked, "It's a wonder he was good to you."

"No," he replied, quickly but solemnly, "it's

no wonder. When we see our fellow-creatures every day, we don't care for them; but it is different when you meet a man all alone in the woods—the wild, lonely woods. I tell you, stranger, Girty and I met, lonely men, on the banks of the Ohio, and where Cincinnati now stands, and we pledged ourselves one to the other, hand in hand, for life and death, when there was *nobody in the wilderness but God and us.*" His very language, and a sublime expression I thought it.

He spoke kindly of the celebrated Logan, the Indian chief, and said he was a fine-looking man, with a good countenance, and that Logan spoke English as well as himself. Speaking of the Indians, he said: "Though they did abuse me mightily, I must say that they are as 'cute as other people—with many great warriors among them; they are as keen marksmen as the whites, but they do not take as good care of their rifles. Finding one's way through the woods is all habit. Indians talk much less than the whites when they travel, but that is because they have less to think about."

He spoke of Boone, and said that he had been with him a great deal. He described him as a Quaker-looking man, with great honesty and singleness of purpose, but very keen. We were struck with his acuteness and delicacy of feeling. He was going to show us his hand, which had been maimed by the Indians; he half drew off his mitten, and then pulled it on again.

"No," said he, "it hurts my feelings."

My friend observed that it was mentioned in the different accounts of him, that when himself and his companions arrived at the Ohio, with the horses of the Indians, they might have escaped if they had followed his advice.

"Understand, understand," said he, "I do not mean to blame them. The horses would not, somehow, enter the river. I knew the Indians were behind us, and told them so. They would not leave the horses; I could not leave them, so the Indians came yelling down the hills and took us."

I observed to him that I wondered, after his escape from the Indians, that he did not return to Virginia, and run no more risks of being taken by them.

"Ah!" said he, "I was a changed man; they abused me mightily. I determined, after that, never to miss a chance." (Meaning at the life of an Indian.)

He was very anxious that Clarke's life should be written — General George Rogers Clarke — who, he said, had done more to save Kentucky from the Indians than any other man. He told us that a gentleman from Urbanna, Ohio, had been with him two or three days, and that he had told him a good deal about himself. "But," said he,

"I am mighty anxious to tell what I know about Clarke. You may depend he was a brave man, and did much."

He then told us that not five miles from the place where we were, he had been a captive among the Indians, painted black, with his hands pinioned behind him, his body lacerated with the severest treatment; the bone of his arm broken, and projecting through the flesh, and his head shockingly bruised. I observed to him that he must have been a very strong and active man, to have endured so many hardships, and made so many escapes.

"Yes," said he, "I believe I might say I was once an active man. But," continued he, taking my crutch in his hand, as I sat beside him, and holding it, together with his staff—I could trace the association of his ideas—"I am an old man."

I observed, from his manner, that he wished to ask me about my crutch, but that he felt a delicacy in doing so. I explained it to him; after observing the fashion of it for some time—for I had a fashion of my own in my crutches—he looked earnestly at me, and said, with emotion, showing me his own staff—

"You see I have to use one, too; you are young and I am old; but, I tell you, we must all come to it at last."

Many, in their courtesy, have tried to reconcile

me to my crutch; but no one ever did it with so bland a spirit as this blunt backwoodsman, who never said *sir* to an Indian in his life, and scarcely ever to a white man.

True politeness is from the heart, and from the abundance of the heart it speaketh; the rest is but imitation, and, at best, the automaton *fashioned* to act like a man.

We arose twice to leave ere we did so, the old worthy pressed us so warmly "not to go yet." At last, after a hearty shake of the hand with him, we departed on our way to Bellefontaine. We were scarcely on the road before the rain descended fast upon us; but we went on, transacted our business, and returned to West Liberty to spend the night, unmindful of the heavy storm that poured down upon us in our open buggy, but full of the old pioneer, and the reflections which our visit had called up.

We looked around, and did not wonder that the Indians fought hard for the soil, so fruitful with all the resources and luxuries of savage life, redolent with so many associations for them, all their own —theirs for centuries—their prairies, their hunting-grounds, the places where their wigwams stood, where their council-fires were lighted, where rested the bones of their fathers, where their religious rites were performed. How often had they hailed the "bright eye of the universe!" as we hailed him that morning, almost with a Persian worship, and on that very spot. In a few hours, we beheld him sinking in his canopy of clouds. And thus they sink, and the shadows of their evening grow darker and darker, and they shall know no morrow. Happy for those who now possess their lands, if they cherish, and if their posterity shall cherish, the homely virtues, the simple honesty and love of freedom of the early pioneers—of him with whom we shook hands that morning, on the brink of the grave. If they do, then, indeed, may their broad banner, with its stars and stripes trebled, be planted on the far shores of the Pacific, the emblem of a free and a united people.

OLD NAT.

A FACT.

In my boyhood, while dwelling at my uncle's, about three miles from Baltimore, on the York turnpike road, I remember to have been deeply grieved by the invitation to our household to attend the funeral of our neighbor and friend, Mr. Richardson. The deceased dwelt about half a mile from my uncle's, between the Falls and York turnpike roads, in a broad strip of bottom-land, where he cultivated a farm and carried on a mill. The mill-dam, to my boyish ideas, was an ocean! How rankly the weeds and long grass grew upon its sides. The water-snakes therein were only outnumbered by the bull-frogs thereof, while the mud-turtles, like a neutral party, with the assistance of the floating chips that looked like them, would have polled somewhat more than either. The summer barks that I have set afloat there, and which the sweeping breeze bore to a returnless distance, and which went down, like Tom Moore's (though not "at sea"), when heaven was all tranquillity—well do I remember them! Often have my schoolmates and I there proved Cardinal Wolsey's illustration of "Little wanton boys that swim on bladders." By the mill-race, how it delighted me to loll and throw chips into the rushing waters! I thought then, and the simile came to me from nature, as it has many times since from books that were a thousand years older than either myself or the mill-race, that, like those pent-up waters breaking forth, was the outbreak of human passions.

The house stood on a gentle knoll beside the dam, and multitudinous were the numbers of geese, ducks, chickens, and turkeys, which the frugal housewife exulted in raising. Here the two latter races wandered and worried, when the two former paddled and plashed in the mill-dam. And while chickens and hens, with the rooster in their midst, or at their flank, or in their rear, and the turkeys with their grand seignior, the gobler, in similar fashion, would take up a scattering trail for the barnyard or the woods—it was amusing to observe with what regular solemnity, in contrast, the ducks, with the drake at their head, but more especially the geese with the truculent and burly gander in advance, would parade in Indian file, along the devious, narrow race-path to the mill-dam. In my mind's eye I "see them on their winding way," now. Well may I remember the first time I saw them. I was then but a child, and was sent on the farthest adventure I had ever made from home alone, on an errand to Mr. Richardson's. I passed the graveyard tremulously; the rustling leaves whispered ghost stories to me, and the booming beetle struck against me, like a rushing train of funeral spirits met in mid career, but I got safe through the bars which inclosed the dam. There I thought I might be lost in the hazel-bushes, or that some Georgia man, as the negroes then called the slave-dealers—for to Georgia many of the negroes were then sold, and it was their horror—would leap upon me from the woods, paint me black, and forthwith sell me into slavery. But the bushes were passed safely, though an old stump, which glanced at me on the side of the road, had hastened me through them. I had now but to turn a sudden angle in the race-path, and the house of Mr. Richardson would be full in view and near by. I trod upon it, with my little crutch under my arm, bravely. Lo, as I turned the angle, I beheld, not ten feet from me, the old gander, at the head of a considerable troop, making a dignified descent on the mill-dam. The path was of the narrowest, made by the footsteps of those who attended to the dam, and it was closely girt by high thick grass and alder-bushes; it was evident that either the gander and train or myself must turn out into them. Numbers were against me; but I, who had passed graveyard and Georgia men all alone, I, it was certain, could not nor would not be such a goose as to give way to a gander. Through the trees I saw the slaves of Mr. Richardson at play about the house, and I resolved, notwithstanding the democracy of numbers was against me, to maintain my path. The gander condescended not to notice me until we had got within five feet of each other. He then raised his head with a hissing sound; I waved my hand mechanically, and ejaculated "shoo!" The gander stood for a moment at bay, expanding his wings and protruding his neck, then, with a hiss, hiss, hiss, malignant as a viper's, he made right at me. The suddenness, and, I may say, the unexpectedness of the assault, rather than fear, caused me to recoil, and, as I did so, my crutch slipped, and I tumbled on my side and rolled over on my face on my way down the hill. In that position I seized an alder-bush, with the intention of maintaining my ground and regaining an upright position, when, just as I did so, the gander's hiss ceased, and for a good reason. On the skirt of my jacket the gander seized murderously—over and upon me he flapped his wings with diabolical energy, tightening, as he did so, his grapple, while his whole bevy raised such a clatter that I felt myself in a whirlwind of unappeasable wrath, and thought my death hour had come. Oh, the agony of dying away from home! I lifted my voice and screamed aloud. The progenitors of this race saved Rome, but they certainly would have done for me, had not "Old Nat" arrived at this instant, and most valorously rescued me.

This was my first acquaintance with old Nat. He wiped the dust and dirt from my face and hands, readjusted my disordered habiliments, and led me to the house. I delivered my message, and departed for home, where I arrived in safety, but not by the mill-race path.

I never saw Nat after this until I saw him at his master's grave. My uncle had been down to Mr. Richardson's, offering all the consolation and assistance in his power. It was rather late for us to get to the dwelling of the deceased before the funeral-train should leave it, when my relative returned for us; and, as the ceremony was to be performed at the grave, which was between Mr. Richardson's and our residence, it was agreed that we should go directly to the graveyard. In fact, it lay on the side of the road which communicated between the two estates. As it was not more than a quarter of a mile off, my uncle took me by the hand, and, with his wife on his arm, we repaired thither. We found ourselves somewhat late when we approached the graveyard, for the coffin had been lowered into its earthly receptacle, and the clergyman was performing his last offices. The widow did not attend, but the children of the deceased stood weeping over him, and the grief of one of them, John, a playmate of mine, was touching in the extreme.

That we might not disturb the hallowed feelings of the mourners, my uncle stopped with us on the outskirts of the group. I saw him directing the attention of my aunt to Nat, and my eye followed hers. Nat's mother was a dark mulatto, and his father a negro; there was, therefore, a slight admixture of the races in his veins.

He was tall, raw-boned, and erect, with very long arms. His mouth was small, considering the predominance of his African blood, and his nose straight, but with very big nostrils; and he had a quick, shrewd eye, which wore generally any but a sad expression.

Now it was far different; and any one who might have looked at him, would have known, at a glance, that the deceased was a kind master, for Nat leaned with both hands upon his spade, with which he was to throw the earth upon the coffin, while the big round tears gushed down his cheeks. He looked at my schoolmate, and then into the grave, and, stepping to his side, said:—

"Oh, Master John, look here, now; don't take on so."

"Susan," said my uncle to my aunt, as he dashed a tear from his eye, "Mr. Richardson's servants are to be free after they have served a certain time for which they are to be sold, according to his will, and I shall certainly buy Nat."

On the day of sale, in fulfilment of the purpose which my uncle expressed at the grave, he attended, taking me with him in his gig. Nat was forty years of age, and was sold for five years, at the expiration of which he was to be free. He expressed great gratitude when my uncle told him he meant to purchase him, saying that he was glad he was not to leave the neighborhood where he had worked so long with his old master.

As soon as the bidding had ceased, and Nat was struck down to my relative, a broad grin broke over his countenance, and, stepping up to him, he said: "Master, I'll go to my new home now, if you say so."

My uncle nodded assent, and, after shaking hands all around with his fellow-slaves, he departed with alacrity. Having no other purpose at the sale but the purchase of Nat, my uncle soon followed that worthy homeward. Our route lay directly by the graveyard where Mr. Richardson was buried, and, as we approached it, we beheld Nat, leaning with his arms on the top of the fence, and gazing wistfully at the grave. As soon as he saw us, he took a by-path to my uncle's, where we found him on our arrival.

My uncle's dwelling was a long one-story mansion, with immense windows, that made it look, at a distance, like a large country church, for which, in fact, it has been more than once mistaken. It had a basement story, where were the sleeping apartments of many of the slaves, together with the kitchen. As soon as I had finished my tea—for the sale took place in the afternoon, and we found the table set when we got home—I descended into the kitchen, with the wish to see my old acquaintance, Nat, and, by recognizing him, do my boyish best to make him feel at home in his new quarters.

Nat needed not my welcome to place him at home. He was seated quietly in the chimney-corner, smoking a pipe with the ease of a Turk in his own especial *sanctum*. The cook, Viney, who had a race of nearly a dozen about her, was listening respectfully to the new-comer, as was also Cuffy, an African, whom my uncle's brother had purchased in one of the slave-markets of the West Indies. One day my uncle's brother was passing through the slave-market in Cuba, I think, when the poor fellow sprang from among the gang, and, throwing himself on his knees before him, implored him, by signs most impressive, to become his purchaser. Touched by the scene, he purchased him, and a deep attachment had grown up between the master and the slave. "Master John," as Cuffy always called him, was now on a visit to the United States, and had brought Cuffy with him.

Lem, or, as he preferred being called, in full, Lemuel, the coachman, was pretending to busy himself with something or other by the dresser, as it was called, in which the dishes were spread out on shelves; but he was evidently listening to, and scrutinizing Nat, with the desire of not being observed.

Lem wore livery, drove the carriage, and waited on the table, and, of course, held himself in aristocratic elevation above the field-hands. He was a short, duck-legged negro, with a forehead slanting directly back from his eyebrows. It was short, and, to make the most of it, Lem combed, with much care, every bit of wool back from it. His nose turned up, as if to take a view over the top of his head, or, perhaps, to avoid the chasm of his immense mouth, which was garnished with two rows of dusky teeth, that were not half as white as Cuffy's, though Lem, every morning, in imitation of his master, used a toothbrush. My uncle was a dyspeptic, and Lem was a dyspeptic, too. He was an envious, conceited fellow, and nothing would have pleased him more, had he been farther south, than to have been placed, whip in hand, as a driver over his fellows. "Sarvant, master William," said Nat, offering me a chair, and taking a seat on a stool that stood beside him. "I hope old master's things sold well, for missus and the children's sake. I suppose you didn't notice, though."

"Uncle says they did, Nat," I replied. "What were you talking about?"

"Whether or not spirits walk, sir; an' I maintains it as how they does, sir."

"Why?" asked I, with boyish fear, approaching nearer to him.

"Because I seed my old master the other night as plainly as I see you. I had been sent in town by missus, to market, the Saturday master died, and, feeling sad like, I had to take my bitters pretty often. I felt something was going to happen to me; and that night, after I got home, I spent mighty uneasy. The next day, being Sunday, I had to myself, and, by way of breaking the spell, I goes down on to the road, right by here, and spent my time with the boys. I stayed there all day, and just after night-time I starts for home. I had always tried to do what was right by old master, so I took my way by the graveyard, a kind o' sorrowing for him, but not afeard for myself, though I felt rather awful for all. You know the graveyard comes right to a pint as you are agwine down the hill. I kind of looks over at the grave, and there, after I looked steady a moment, something white rises. I knew it must be old master, for right at once it come over me that I had been taking too much lately, and he always 'posed it in everybody, might and main. I tell you, my hair riz as straight as yourn. I walked right on, as hard as I could go; it followed. You know the fence leads right straight down to the barn, by the big grape-vine, whar' you go into the mill; it followed to thar. I couldn't look round—I heer'd it; but, as I got over the fence, I looked, an' I saw master. It was him. I saw him, as plain as I see you, turn into a little white dog, an'—"

"It was the dog that followed you," said Lem, from the graveyard; "you must have been intoxhacated."

"Intoxhacated!" re-echoed Nat: "I thanks you, sir, for your manners to a strange gentleman. If it had been a dog," resumed Nat, turning to me, but answering Lem, "how comes I to hear it walk with two heavy feet, like master used to walk afore me, and hear nothing when it walked away?"

Lem's interruption discomposed Nat's dignity, and he resumed his pipe and quitted his story. Lem's notion was no doubt, however, correct, for Nat, who was given to the bottle, was a great seer of sights when he had over-indulged himself. Nat and Lem never became friends, and I always attributed it to this little circumstance.

Lem, as I have said, imitated his master in everything, even in his complaints.

My uncle was very dyspeptic; he took a great many nostrums, without their producing any good effect upon him (of course). At last, however, he fancied that old Doctor Mann, a French physician, who kept at the corner of Calvert and Market streets, had compounded certain pills which gave him relief. My uncle generally obtained them through Nat, whom he sent into the city to market regularly twice a week, and who hauled at other times wood to the city, and manure for the farm from it. The coach was not often used, except on Sundays, when the family went to church, so that Nat went much oftener to the city than Lem. Lem though was quite a moneyed man, for he was always in waiting to hold the horses of the friends of my uncle when they visited us, and he was sure to obtain a piece of silver when they remounted.

One day I overheard Lem say very pompously to Nat (slaves with each other generally bear the names of their masters, as the servants in the admirable farce of "High Life below Stairs," become dukes and lords with each other, and Nat retained his old master's name), "Mr. Richardson, you would obligate me if with this money," putting a twenty-five cent piece into Nat's hand, "you would obtain for me from Doctor Mann a box of his dispeptus pills. My bowels is terribly disordered, and there's nothin' that takes me to town to-day.

Master says them pills helps him, and I think they'll help me too."

Nat took the money, and said he would do so. About half an hour afterwards he came to me and said,

"Master William, if you will give me some of them old pill-boxes of master's, what I seed you have, I'll get you all the chestnuts you want."

That I esteemed a most liberal offer on the part of Nat, and I was not slow in closing the bargain, by handing him several of the empty boxes. I heard no more about the pills for three or four weeks, during which time Nat had obtained several boxes of them for Lem, until one day Nat asked him how they operated.

"To a fraction," replied Lem, with dignity, "and they am not hard to take, only they 'casion a little nauseum on account of their tasting a leetle fishy."

"Master William," said Nat, slyly to me, when Lem was out of hearing, "I tells you something if you says nothing about it."

"Not a word."

"Them old pill-boxes of master's you got for me, I rubs mackerel eyes in flour—them's the pills, and I spends Lem's quarters drinking his health, and a hoping they may do him much good."

Nat was an active muscular fellow, and a great walker. I was passionately fond of attending husking matches; so was Nat. I had accompanied him to several, and whenever I got tired of walking, and I could not go far at night on my crutch, unless I knew the road, and not even then if the ground was soft, Nat would stoop down, and placing his hands for stirrups, with the left arm shorter than the other, I would mount, and he would jog along as easily as if I were not heavier than his axe—in truth, I was not much heavier. In this way I have gone with him five or six miles to a husking frolic, and back again the same night. There was one stipulation between us always upon these occasions, namely, that Nat was not to get drunk, which would have prevented my getting home, and that I, when we got home, was to supply him with as much whiskey as he wanted. This I could easily do, as the keys of the storeroom, which was in the basement, were, when not in use, always hung up in the sitting-room, and my uncle and aunt indulged me in everything.

One night, though Nat religiously kept his promise with me, I broke mine with him. He revenged himself. We were late on the next occasion in starting to the husking, which was some five miles off. I walked about a hundred yards, and then mounted on Nat's back. Away we went, over meadow and ploughed land, and through the woods. Who more full of fun than I? With my handkerchief around Nat's neck, for the rein, sometimes I would lean away back, and press my feet in his palms, like a rider who restrains the impatience of his fiery steed, while Nat, humoring the notion, would prance, caper, neigh, and play the Bucephalus entirely to my admiration. Then again I would be seized with the fear that he would throw me, and would pat his big ears and cheeks, and coax him into a walk. I even went so far on this occasion as to introduce two large pins into the heels of my shoes, spur-like; but, upon my applying them, my steed, like Balaam's ass, not only became endowed with speech, but laid me right flat down upon my back in the woods, nor would he suffer me to remount until I had placed my evidences of knighthood in his possession. After this, we got to the husking-match safe, and Nat showed forth conspicuously. His companions pressed him over and over to drink, and, amidst the uproarious conviviality, he laid no restraint upon himself, and soon broke loose from the bounds of sobriety.

When I again mounted for home, I found that no spur was necessary. I tied my crutch with my handkerchief, so as to fix it to my arm, and seized with both hands the collar of Nat's linsey-woolsey jacket, in right-down earnest. It was necessary, for Nat pitched and heaved like a war-steed when stricken a desperate blow by the foe. It was quite natural, for Nat was combating his worst enemy. We got in this way into the woods. He staggered fore and aft, brought up against a huge tree, with an oath, and, expanding his palms, gave me a tumble into the leaves at his feet, while he grasped the trunk. Steadying himself thereby, he looked down at me, and hiccoughed out—

"You sees the konsekense, Master Billy, of breaking bargains. I kept every word of my word to you on drinking, refusing the fellows, and awaiting till we got home, and there was no liquor. I've got my liquor now, because I could not get it at home, and you knows whose fault it is."

So speaking, the old fellow tumbled down in the leaves at my feet, and, all I could do, I could not rouse him, except to an inarticulate remark. In two minutes he was fast asleep.

Though I felt provoked, I reflected that old Nat had served me right, and I sank down by his side, hoping that in a half hour or so he would recover. While waiting for that event, I changed my sitting to a recumbent position, and was soon as fast asleep as himself. I did not awake until he himself aroused me at daybreak, and hurried with me off home. After that I broke no bargains with Nat.

Nat was a lover of the sex, a kind of colored Lothario. One day, as I was playing in front of the house, I cast my eyes down the road, and beheld Nat seated on a board in front of the cart, returning from town, with a perfect specimen of one of Africa's daughters beside him. She was a likely slave of some eighteen or upwards, whom my uncle had purchased. It was a sight, that pair. Nat was seated bolt upright beside her, with an inclination of his person towards the damsel, after the fashion which he had witnessed in the most splendid vehicles of the city, as their lords drove out with the fair. The damsel, whose name was Becky, had less of art, and more of nature in her manner. She was dressed in her best, which was a spotted-muslin gown, with an old lace cape, that her former mistress had given her. A flaming bandanna was tastefully tied round her head, and she looked tidy, attentive, and neat, but not without a consciousness. Nat was explaining the localities of the farm to her, having no doubt previously satisfied her of the kind qualities of her new master. I had certainly come in for a share of panegyric, for I saw him point me out to her, and a broad grin of satisfaction broke over her countenance.

At the back door Nat descended first from the cart, according to fashion, and then handed down Miss Becky. From the side door my aunt spoke to her kindly, and desired her to hand some of the bundles into the house. When they were disposed of, Nat resumed his seat, and I took Becky's beside him, for the purpose of riding to the stable, and hearing his opinion of the newcomer. To my inquiry he replied—

"Master bought her to-day, from the widow Bushrod, Master William. She is a likely colored person. I have been telling her all about our folks, and a kind of eased her mind as to her new master and mistress. She is not married, quite a gal like, an' I s'pose the next thing we shall know, Mr. Lem will be dodging round, and axing old master for her for a wife."

"Nat, as you are not married either, why don't you get uncle to give her to you?"

"Master William," replied Nat quickly, "I have been thinking of that; but in course old master will give her to the one she likes, an' you know what a fooling way Lem has. I'm a getting on to the outskirts of the vale of years, as the preacher says, an' Lem's not twenty-three. Anyhow, I'm a free man in six months from this; my time will be out then, for which my first master sold me. My master, that's now, may-be though would hire me, if I was to get Becky, so I could stay about the place."

"You knew Becky before?" I remarked.

"Yes, slightly, as you'd say, Master William; an' Lem never seed her before."

A fierce rivalry forthwith commenced between Lem and Nat for Miss Becky's favor. Well do I remember the tactics practised by either party, and many a lover whom I have met in society practised his arts with not half the tact of these colored gentlemen. As for Becky, she proved that the gift of coquetry was not confined exclusively to the fairer portion of Adam's race of her sex.

It was my wont to go into the kitchen on winter evenings, to discourse with Nat upon the intricate subject of bird and rabbit-catching; and there I witnessed man-catching practised with equal adroitness. Lem was coachman; so he considered himself Nat's superior. Nat was possessed of a great deal of ingenuity, could do almost anything about a farm, and often, when Lem was otherwise employed, drove the coach; therefore he was disposed not at all to yield to Lem on the score of personal pretension, except as regarded years, and they, Nat said, when not conversing with me on the subject, but to his fellows, entitled him to the greater respect; a consideration which a prudent personage would not certainly press upon the sex in a love-affair. In the progress of events, it appeared certain that Lem was about to be victor. He had greater facilities for obtaining money than his rival, from the fact that he held the horses, and waited on my uncle's visitors; and much of it he spent in making propitiatory sacrifices to the goddess of his idolatry. While affairs were in this posture, the time for which Nat was sold expired. He was a free man. Struck with jealousy at the success of his more fortunate rival, he determined, like Ernest Maltravers, the Bulwerian hero, when he thought Vasgrave about to be the happy man, to exile himself from the presence of the charmer. Accordingly, Nat announced his determination to my uncle to go back to Harford County, where he was raised. Now, Nat was my uncle's man-of-all-work, his man Friday, and my relative felt that he should be at great loss without him. Besides, my uncle was much older than my aunt, and, notwithstanding this, and in spite of many rivals, he had succeeded in his suit. He was aware of the rivalry which existed between Lem and Nat, and, I believe, from a fellow-feeling, he entertained a sly wish that Nat should outgeneral his compeer. Controlled, I think, by these feelings, my uncle offered Nat fifteen dollars a month to stay with him, which our colored worthy most thankfully accepted.

A few days after Nat's first monthly payment, Lem's star paled, for Nat was as generous as a prince, and rivalry, as well as love and generosity, combined to make him open his purse-strings to Miss Becky.

My uncle paid Nat his fifteen dollars in silver one Saturday night, no doubt with a purpose, for he was full of sly humor, and was fond of observing the characters of those about him. Becky had been engaged to go with Lem to the country Methodist Church on Sunday, but she suddenly declined, and was all smiles upon Nat during the day. The next Sunday she appeared at church, attended by Nat, in habiliments that far outshone the gorgeous daughters of Africa in the throng. From that day forth, Lem's case was hopeless.

It had a speedy termination in despair, for the following Sunday Nat and Becky appeared together at church as man and wife, after the fashion of their people.

By way of revenge, Lem broke open a blacksmith-shop down on the road, stole the tools, and buried them in a patch of ground which my uncle allowed Nat to cultivate for himself. Search was made for the tools, and Lem, with an accomplice and backer, named Toney, who belonged to a neighbor, asserted that they had seen Nat secreting them in the patch, one night. Luckily, Nat proved an *alibi* conclusively. Alas for Lem! it was decided that he should receive thirty-nine lashes on the bare back, and, by way of preventing mistakes, he was compelled to count them himself. This was not all; he was degraded from the coach-box into the field-service, in which he speedily recovered of his dyspepsia, and became a hale, hearty fellow. And yet this circumstance, which placed Nat in the ascendant, was, after all, his ruin. He was elevated to the coach-box. As my cousins were growing up, the carriage was called into frequent requisition, and Nat was driving to and from town constantly. His opportunities for the obtaining of liquor were frequent, and also, like many a better man, he not only availed himself of every opportunity to drink, but he exhibited a great deal of tact in making them. No matter how drunk, he could drive; and his constitution was one of those hardy ones, in which the vital powers hold on to the last, and the extremities yield first. Gradually his left foot increased to double its size, became misshapen like a club-foot, and the old fellow had to have a shoe made expressly for it. Still he sat on the coach-box. But this was not all. One Christmas eve, returning from a shooting-match down on the road, and supplying himself from a flask of whiskey which he had stowed away in his pocket, he became so drunk as to be unable to proceed, and pitched down into the snow, where he remained all night.

The consequence was that old Nat became a martyr to the rheumatism, which not only rendered him incapable of service, but an expense to my relative, for medical attendance. It was two months before the old fellow could crawl out, and then he made his appearance on crutches.

When Nat was first taken, Becky's attentions to him were unremitting; she was so anxious to restore him to the field, and thereby prevent the abatement of his wages; but, as his prospects of future labor diminished, and his medical expense to my uncle increased, Becky became indifferent to him.

The great minstrel of the North, after speaking of the general waywardness of woman, says, in that hackneyed quotation (hackneyed, we suppose, because true):—

> When pain and anguish wring the brow,
> A ministering angel thou!

Becky might have been a ministering angel to old Nat, but she removed her quarters from his room, and made her visits, like other "angel visits," a good distance apart.

Almost by miracle Nat's rheumatism left him for a season, and Becky lighted the torch of hymen anew, but the flames had scarcely ascended when the old fellow had a relapse. In this way for years Nat lingered along, at times apparently well except his lameness, but with relapses that, at each recurrence, were at lesser intervals and more severe. Becky's attentions to him graduated accordingly.

At last Nat's wages were reduced one-half, and her complaints against his habits were loud and frequent; but old Nat was sincerely attached to her, and bore them after the manner of Socrates. Becky made meanwhile a less brilliant appearance at church, though her domestic qualities gathered no new energy.

Years slipped away, and I approached man's estate. Nat eked out now what my uncle allowed him, which was but a few dollars a month, for he had become almost useless, by setting traps for rabbits and partridges, and selling them to the neighbors or at market. Almost every cent he received was transferred to Becky ere it touched his pocket.

I was a good deal amused one day, poor fellow, at his lamentation over his lame leg. He said—

"Master William, I don't care for the looks of the thing, but for the thing itself. You see Becky will dress, and old master has docked my wages on account of my rhumatiz, and my not being able to work as I did, and now when I expected to make a catching of rabbits and partridges, the niggers all about here track me through the snow by my lame leg, and steals everything. There's Bryant's Toney, I suspects him strong. Master William, suppose you walks down with me to-morrow morning to the clump of trees next to Bryant's. Right in the sheep-track, there I've set my gun (a trap made out of a hollow log), and by hokey I know we'll catch that Toney stealing my rabbit out if there's airy one in."

"Agreed," said I, and the next morning bright and early, for the purpose of defending the old fellow's rights, I attended him to the clump of trees. There stood the trap with the fall-down about ten feet from us.

"We 're afore the tarnal rabbit thief this morning, Master William," exclaimed Nat, stepping up to the trap, and preparing to take from it the live captive; "every morning afore this, for these three mornings past, there's been somebody here, and helped themselves, and then set the trap again, for I has a 'tickler way of setting my traps, and can tell."

By this time, *secundum artem*, Nat had extracted the rabbit from his trap, and with the affrighted animal under his arm, was proceeding to set it again, when he looked up and observed—

"See! Master William, yonder! that's Toney Bryant's. Toney, he's the thief, you may depend on it. He's coming this way; he's looking out for other traps, but he ha'n't seed me yet; let's hide, Master William, behind the trees, and catch the varmint."

We accordingly hid, and in a whisper, Nat pointed Toney out to me at some distance off on the skirts of the woods, closely eyeing the ground as he walked on in search of traps. With an eye glittering through the bushes at him, Nat said,

"That agravating varmint 'll find the trap down, and think there's a rabbit in—he, he."

Toney walked directly to Nat's trap, and, finding the fall down, concluded, of course, that the game was there. Accordingly he got down on his knees, for the purpose of purloining it, muttering to himself, as he did so, "I'll save old Nat the trouble again."

Nat, meanwhile, was not an uninteresting picture.

He stood in a stooping attitude, glaring at the thief, while he held the rabbit by the hind legs, with its head under his arm. Every now and then the animal gave a convulsive start, in its efforts to escape, at which the old fellow would grasp it harder, and gaze the keener at Toney, who, on finding the trap empty and down, concluded that some other poacher had been there before him. He therefore determined, it seemed, to remove it to some place where he could make sure of its contents, and accordingly he very deliberately lifted it up and adjusted it under his arm.

At this instant Nat stepped forth, and confronted him, saying, with great dignity—

"You've no 'casion to take that trap."

Toney started, and dropped the trap, but, in an instant, recovered himself, and, putting his foot on it, he said—

"The trap's mine."

Nat, full of courage from my presence, though I was unobserved by Toney, exclaimed—

"You lie, you thief!" And forthwith he slung (forgetting in his passion what would be his loss) the rabbit full in his face.

Toney had the reputation of being a dexterous fellow, and amply proved it on this occasion, for he caught the rabbit as it struck him, and, bursting into a loud laugh, he held it over his head a moment, in derision, and then darted off like a deer with it into the woods.

Matters were in this state with Nat when I left my uncle's, and domesticated myself in the city, as a student of the law.

In due time I was admitted to practice, and did so for nearly twelve months, when increasing indisposition compelled me to repair to the country for my health. There I found old Nat a hanger-on about the farm, incapable of doing anything but feed the poultry, or some such light service. He earned no wages now, and, as a matter of kindness, my uncle supported him. Meanwhile a stout, black, free negro, named Joe Mooney, of about Becky's age, and a preacher withal, made his appearance at my uncle's, as a visitor of Becky. Nat hated him from the first, for he was fond of discoursing against intemperance, and doubtless did so intentionally, aiming his shafts at Nat in the presence of Becky. She was held a beauty by her race. She was now reduced to the plain habiliments of a servant, and could no more make the display on Sundays at the meeting-house which was her wont in the days of Nat's prosperity. If we could dissect human motives to their first mainspring, I have no doubt we should find Becky's first partiality to the preacher arose from his complimenting her upon the plainness of her attire, with well-directed observations upon the impropriety of appearing in gayer habiliments, for she was anxious to make it known that choice, not necessity, had caused the change. The result was, Becky joined the church under Mooney. The next thing, her conscience was troubled about the unceremonious manner in which she had become Nat's wife, so she discarded the old fellow eventually. She and Mooney held long conversations together, and the issue was that she determined to be married over again, as she expressed it, but not to Nat.

The old negro plainly proved that the demon jealousy is not confined to its habitancy of a white bosom. He was now old and decrepit, but he remembered well, and it made his age the more desolate, that all his means, when he had any, were given, without scarcely a cent's expenditure upon himself, to one who now, from compunctions of conscience, spurned him from her bed and board.

He advised with me about speaking to my uncle on the matter, but I told him it would be of no use; for he well knew, as his own case proved, that my relative never interfered in such matters among his slaves.

Nat's only resource now was in the bottle, and he thanked his stars that I was near by, from whom he could obtain the needful "bit." I could not find it in my heart to refuse to add a dram or two to the daily one my uncle allowed him, which was always sent down to him at dinner time. In the morning early it was that the old fellow said he most needed his "bitters," and then it was that I used to start one of the little black boys off to the tavern on the road for a pint for Nat. How the old toper's eyes gloated on it when it came! In fact, his long habits of intemperance had made stimulus necessary to his existence. At least so the country doctor said, who was given to stimulus himself.

As soon as Nat had his bottle filled in the morning, he would repair instantly to the barn-yard, where, after having poured into a tin cup a considerable portion of "old rye," he would fill from the glowing udder of the cow the remainder up to the brim with the warm milk, and take it down as a Virginian or Kentuckian takes his "mint juleps" at rising, with a gusto, a lighting up of the eye, followed by an immediate tendency to loquacity.

Alas for old Nat, it was then that he would come and take a seat by me, and live his life over again. How he would chuckle as he reminded me of the time I had to sleep out all night, and how he would laugh over Lem and his "dyspeptus pills."

After taking his morning bitters, Nat touched not again through the day except at dinner, when he disposed of the dram which my uncle sent him. But at night, and particularly if "Parson Joe" came over to see Becky, he was sure to have recourse to the black bottle, which was as sure to be ready for my "bit" in the morning.

Besides the pocket-money that Nat gathered between my uncle and myself, my relative frequently gave him vegetables, fruits, &c., which he sold to the neighbors. After my relative had set out his early York cabbages, he told Nat that he might have all the "plantings" that were left, which amounted to a thousand or more, and were selling at twenty-five cents per hundred. Happy in the opportunity of putting so much "grog-money" in his pocket, Nat went forth among the neighbors to effect sales. There was an old man near by named Tatem, who was always called Squire Tatem, from the fact that the governor had given him a commission in the magistracy. This commission brought Tatem little more than the dignity, for there were squires enough before he was made one. He had kept an extensive shoe-store in Baltimore, and failed. He lived at this time on a little farm of few acres, which previous to his failure he had deeded to his wife. The front of Tatem's barn bounded on the opposite side of the road from my uncle's, about a quarter of a mile below the termination of his estate. As Tatem had been used to a town life, and liked company, it was his custom, whenever the weather permitted, to leave his house, which was situated a hundred or more yards off of the road, and take his station by the road fence, leaning thereon, and stopping whatever passengers he chanced to know in their way to and from town, to learn the news.

Nat had sold four hundred of his early York "plantings" to Squire Tatem, but on their delivery the Squire had failed to make payment, and had put Nat off from time to time, whenever the old negro had requested him thereto. One day Nat came to me and stated his grievance, saying,

"You must know, Master William, that I sold him, that Squire Tatem, the four hundred early York plantings at twenty-five cents a hundred. You can see how good they was, for look at old master's and look at the Squire's or mine, for mine they are, when you pass by his place. Finer early Yorks the hand of black or white man never planted. Well, after I handed 'em to him, he said he had no change then, an' that he would pay me the first time he seed me. I let him, Master William, see me every time I had a chance for a full month afterwards, but he never said a word. So one day I meets him down at the tavern on the road, where there was a quantity of gentlemen, an' I says to him as purlite as possible, taking off my hat at the same time, 'Servant, Squire,' says I. 'Nathaniel, my worthy,'—he called me at full length, Nathaniel—'Nathaniel, my worthy,' says he, very kind, 'how's your health?' Says I, 'I thanks you, Squire, very kindly, my rheumatiz is better—how does 'em early Yorks come on?' 'Early Yorks,' says he, snapping his eye quickly at me. 'Oh, my fine fellow, near the road? Admirably. Your master never had any like them, hey?' 'Yes, Master Squire,' says I, 'them ere come from old master's; they're growing first rate, and, Squire,' says I, making a low purlite bow, 'Nat would be your 'bedient servant, if you would let him have that change for 'em!' 'Change,' said he; 'them few plantings I got from you wasn't worth a snap; it's my opinion you stole 'em from your master, you drunken vagabond; I shall call and see him; but for my respect for him I should commit you to jail right off.' Then Bob Hollands told him that the receiver was as bad as the thief. How everybody did laugh; but the Squire looked so angry at me that I thought it best to leave, so I did."

"Have you ever spoken to him since about the matter?" I asked.

"Yes, Master William; the other day I finds him leaning over the fence; and he told me if I ever spoke to him in the company of gentlemen about such things again, that he would cowhide me the first time he caught me on the road. He said when he had any change he'd let me know, without my axing for it. Now, Master William, you knows the law; what are a colored man to do under them circumstances?"

"Was there no white person by," I asked, "when you sold the cabbages to the Squire?"

"Not a soul, black or white, Master William."

"It's a pity, Nat," I replied, "that he did not confess the debt in the presence of some of those gentlemen at the tavern. You are now a free man, and you could sue him for the amount, and bring one of those gentlemen to prove that he confessed the debt."

"Ha, now I understand it, Master William. That's the reason why the Squire didn't want to hear anything of it before them are gentlemen; he knew I could make him pay. So, if he was to confess, in the presence of a white person, as how he owed me the money, then I could sue him, and make him pay."

"Precisely so, Nat," I replied. Nat chuckled to himself, and then said: "The Squire'll find I'm not such a cabbage-head as he takes me for."

A week or so after this, and when I had forgotten the circumstance, Nat was one day driving me into the city in the carriage. As we approached Squire Tatem's, Nat turned round, and said quickly to me:—

"Master William, there's the Squire now. Don't let him see you, and just mark, now, how I'll tickle him along about the cabbage. If I stops, he'll think of a konsekence there's nobody in." Accordingly, with great respect, Nat spoke to the

Squire, and was immediately asked by him what the news was."

"Nothing 'tickler, Squire. I hopes you is well to-day, sir."

"Very well, Nathaniel; how's your master?"

"Well, I tanks you, Squire. How nice your place looks! You beats up the whole of us all hollow, Squire, a-gardening."

"Yes, the place looks pretty well. What do you think of those cabbages, you rascal, hey?" and the Squire spoke half humorously.

"That is a great soil, yours, Squire; ours is nothing like 'em."

"Why didn't you say so, then, the other day, you black scamp, when I asked you?"

"I didn't like, Squire, to run down things at home before company."

"Ha, ha! you don't, hey? But you come dunning before company, do you?"

"You wouldn't hear me through, then, Squire; I was gwine to say, when you stopped me, that master talked about buying that cider-press of yourn, to get all ready for the cider season."

"That was it, hey? I have said I would sell it to a neighbor, so I will."

"Master wants me to look at it, Squire."

"Ay, come and do so, Nathaniel, as you come out, and we'll talk about that little change I owe you. How much was it?"

"Four hundred, Squire, at twenty-five cents a hundred," replied Nathaniel.

"Yes, yes, so it is exactly right. I owe you one dollar, Nathaniel, and when your master buys the cider-press I'll pay you."

"Squire," exclaimed Nat, in a changed tone, "whether master buys that press or not, you've got to pay me. I just tell you I have a white gentleman in here, an' he'll prove it." And before, between indignation and surprise, the Squire could reply, Nat put whip to his horses, and away he went.

Nat informed me, a few days afterwards, that he had met the Squire on the road since; that the Squire "gave him a hard cussing, but chucked the dollar at him."

"Who can control his fate?" as Othello says. Nat struggled in vain against his. Becky, after she had discarded Nat, and the formalities of a courtship were gone through with, married "Parson Joe." I must do Joe, too, the justice to state, that by hard labor he obtained the means, before the birth of her first child by him, of buying her from my uncle. The old gentleman let him have her at half her value, and rented cheaply, to her husband, a cabin and lot on the road-side. Joe treats her well, and is doing well. Joe never entertained any ill-feeling towards Nat, but, on the contrary, treated him with kindness—with much more than Becky, whom I have seen stand in great dignity at the door of her own household, and offer Nat three cents to split wood for her, and rate him soundly for not splitting the money's worth!

I had made up my mind to push my fortunes in the West, and, on the eve of my departure, I left the city, to which I had again returned, for the purpose of spending a week with my kind uncle and aunt. My cousins had all married off, and they were the only white persons on the farm. There was old Nat, and right glad was he to see me, and have his bottle filled; but he felt desolate and deserted, and could not get over Becky's treatment of him. Sad, sad was my parting with my relatives. Nat had not driven the carriage for some time, but he asked permission to drive me into the city, on my leave-taking, and I could not refuse him. Just as we reached Barnum's steps, we saw the stage in which I had taken my seat turn from Market (now Baltimore) Street into Calvert Street. "Master William," said old Nat, with heart so full that he could hardly speak it, "you'll never see Nat any more. We'll never have any more talks together. Though you're gwine far over the mountains, you must think of old Nat when you're there; an' when you write home, you must name me in black and white, an' old master'll read it to me. If old master lives, I shall have a good home as long as I wants one;

but, if he dies afore me, I shall end my days in the poorhouse. But it is no matter where old Nat dies; he's old, now, and of no account nohow to nobody. Master William," and here the old fellow's voice grew firm and admonitory, "remember this what I tell you at our last parting. Master William, arter the experience of sixty years, a woman can deceive any man."

"The stage waits, sir," exclaimed the driver to me. Old Nat assisted me in, grasped my hand convulsively, but had no words. The tears down his dusky cheek spoke for him. Away we dashed, and the last sight I caught of my humble friend was as we whirled around the corner; he was gazing after me with a full heart. I am still a bachelor. Nat's advice certainly has not confined me to my present solitary state; yet it is as certain that on many a night of festivity in lighted hall, and on many a moonlight ramble, his words have crossed me like the disenchanting power of some ugly old elf o'er the wanderer in fairy land.

"OLD KENTUCK."

A TRUE STORY.

> "O! Kentucky,
> The hunters of Kentucky."—WESTERN SONG.

SOME years since I left Pittsburg in a first-rate steamer, on my way to New Orleans. I was bound upon a rare trip of pleasure, and, full of health and the excitement consequent upon it, was alive to every scene around and every character about me. And the characters upon our western waters, fifteen years ago, had more *character* in them; just as the scenes around one had more of nature in them than now, inasmuch as art had not displayed as much of her power there as she has since; a power which, with enlightened laws and republican institutions, is destined, as I believe, to make the West the model land of the world.

One day, I think it was the day after we left Pittsburg, we saw a white man, with a black boy beside him, evidently designing to take passage, as the boy was waving, with might and main, a large handkerchief on the end of a stick. Impatient that the steamboat, by her movements, indicated no notice, on the part of her officers, of the signal aforesaid, the white man took the stick, which proved to be a ramrod, from the hand of the negro, and, leaning on a rifle which he held in his hand, waved it, with a good deal of emphasis in his manner, while we could hear his stentorian voice (it was indeed stentorian, to reach us at that distance), exclaiming: "Hello!"

"Hello!" replied a voice from the upper deck of our steamer, the Fort Adams.

"It's Samson," exclaimed the captain, who was standing on the guards beside a crowd of us; "round to."

No sooner said than done. As the boat approached the parties, Samson exclaimed: "Why, you are blind as a horse-blanket—blind as your boat. I don't stand so low that you can't see me, do I? I! I stand six feet four inches in my stocking feet, and I waved this handkerchief as many feet over my head besides."

"Who do you think is looking out for you from the wheelhouse?" replied the pilot. "You're big enough to look out for yourself, and you're big enough to be a snag, old fellow—but I'd rather see you on the shore than in the river. But I am keeping a sharp lookout ahead, here—we hit a snag somewhere about here last time. How would you like to hire out to Uncle Sam for a light-house? A little more liquor, and your face would go without any other light."

"Ha, Rogers, is that you, you thief you? That's a Joe Miller—you stole it from old Falstaff in the play, about that chap whose nose lit him up the hill at night. I hope you don't extend your thieveries to other matters."

"It's no thievery, Kentuck," replied Rogers—"it's only like a parson's text, which anybody has the right to apply—well applied, I drawed the inference, old boy."

"Yes," replied old Kentuck, as he was called, "you'll have a bee line drawed upon you some of these days, in consequence of that tongue of yours—everybody that knows you, knows that yours is no slander—but never mind, you'll meet with a stranger, some of these short days, and that will be like a snag to your boat." By this time our yawl had received old Kentuck, and I saw the black boy deposit the traveller's trunk in it, while that individual deposited a piece of silver in his hand, which glittered like the ivory the darkey exhibited on the occasion.

"Take care of yourself, Pomp, and mind what I told you."

"Yes, Master Samson, you 'pend 'pon me; there's no mistake in this nigger."

"That's a tall man," I said to the captain, as Old Kentuck sprang upon the deck, rifle in hand.

"Tall," rejoined the captain; "well, he's tall in a good many ways; he's what we call a "case." He's a pilot going down to New Orleans, to bring the Emperor up, as he wrote me. I've been expecting to find him somewhere along shore here."

Soon the Kentuckian was up stairs, shaking the captain by the hand in the most cordial manner. Old Kentuck was certainly a character. He wore a pair of pants, with enormous stripes in them; a most preposterous pattern! his vest was of rich silk, of a gorgeous fashion, while around his neck he had a cross-barred neckcloth of black and red, tied in a curious kind of knot, in which he seemed to pride himself. A loose frock-coat, brown, and with a brown velvet collar thrown back, covered his body, while his head was adorned with a huge foxskin cap, with the tale of Reynard fantastically curled above it. But the face of the stranger was certainly attractive. Across the "broad Atlantic of his countenance," as some one said of Charles James Fox, there played a continued sunshine of cheerfulness and good-nature; at the same time that his clear blue eye and the occasional compression of his well-defined lips, showed a nature that might be waked up to desperate deeds.

"Samson, does that Pomp belong to you?"

"Yes, sir-ee—why?"

"I want a hand."

"Well, you can take him, and give me what's right—ha! ha! Capting, do you know Pomp's father, old Dave?"

"Yes."

"Well, the old rascal has turned Mormon; he sees sights and has visions, and talks about another book of Mormon. He's great on foreknowledge. The other day, Dave comes to me with the most awful face you ever saw a nigger carry, and said he wished to speak to me apart. Apart I went with him, and after glancing around fearfully and with an ominous look, he said: 'Master, I'se got something of highest consekence to tell you.' 'What's that, Dave?' 'Why, master, you don't believe in the book of Mormon and visions, but my duty to you is nevertheless my duty.'—'That's good, Dave,' I replied; 'there's Christianity in that! 'Master, there's Mormon in it, and the truth is, I've had a dream now for the third night in secession—and being, as you always have been, a good master to me, and kind, I thought I ought to tell you that, according to them three dreams, dreamed three nights in secession, I shall die next Sunday night, and see Joe Smith to a certainty.' 'Well, Dave,' says I, 'I am very much obliged to you—seeing that your end's so near, it's a gratification for me to know that I have been a good master to you—a great gratification, as you are near your end; and being, Dave, as, you know, you cost me six hundred dollars, and I can't afford to lose you, as it is a-going to please the Lord to take you on Sunday, I shall, the Lord willing, put you in my pocket in the shape of seven hundred dollars next Saturday. Old Bowler will give that for you, for he told me so—and though he is a hard master, you can escape him, at least for one day, especially as he belongs to church, and never flogs on Sunday, and you'll have your clearance that night."

"Whew," ejaculated the captain, "ha! ha! ha!"

"Yes—I come it, didn't I? Dave called on me the next morning early—he had been watching to see me come out, thinking that I might slip over the back way to Bowler's, and told me that he had had seven dreams that very night, assuring him that he should live a very long time, and that it was very wrong anyway to believe in dreams. Pomp said his daddy was a fool; the old man overheard it and licked him for it—so Pomp was the fool after all. What's the news, captain—anything up stream?"

"Nothing," replied the captain.

"Any boats up?"

"No—did you see the Shelby."

"Yes, she's just below here in the bend, getting her shaft mended."

"I'll pass her, then," said the captain; and he proceeded below.

Soon the accelerated speed of our boat showed that the captain had ordered a press of steam, and we were dashing gallantly through the beautiful Ohio, while the heavy waves on either side of us ran rippling to the shore.

In the bend, sure enough, we soon discovered the Shelby, on board of which boat it was evident our appearance created some commotion. It appears that she had just finished the repair of her shaft, and was about leaving the shore as we drew in sight.

"Ha, ha," said Old Kentuck, leaning on his rifle, which was as long as he was tall, "she looks like trying if she can beat you."

"Don't know," said the captain quickly. "They've made big bets on her up at Pittsburg, and I can't stand everything. I say, Samson, I am opposed to racing, but I can't stand everything."

"Sometimes I won't stand anything," replied Samson.

"Is the Shelby a fast boat?" I asked of the Kentuckian; "I hope we shan't have racing."

"Racing! why, don't you like excitement, stranger—what's life without excitement?" replied old Kentuck; "a mud-puddle to Niagara. I tell you, stranger, in dull times, and when a man don't choose to take liquor, and sometimes I don't choose—I go and sleep over the boiler, by way of excitement."

"Do you? That's a tall rifle," I said.

"Tall—it's just as tall as I am. You've hearn tell of Capting Scott, who was such a tall shot that the coon came down as soon as he saw him and give in—haven t you?"

"I have," replied I, laughing.

"Well, this is the rifle that did it—Capting Scott wouldn't have been anything without the rifle, would he? I don't say I ever had a talk with a coon, but I do say that this rifle can talk to them, and that I can bring one down from just as big a distance as he can."

I took the Kentuckian's rifle in my hand, and after feeling the weight of it, handed it back to him.

"Love me, love my dog!" said he—"ha! ha! I had a hearty laugh to myself the other day. Them Frenchmen, you don't think they are civilized, stranger, do you?"

"Civilized—why, they think themselves the most civilized nation in the world."

"Well, they're mistaken, that's all—it's confounded easy for a man or men to get mistaken in themselves. I was reading the other day how some Frenchmen tried to blow Napoleon up with what they called an "infernal machine."—Bah, it's the most foolish contrivance I ever heard of; it put me in mind of the Irishman now who went to spear a fish with a scythe, and cut his own head off. Ha, but let them put me anywhere in a fifth or tenth story, just where I can see his majesty's nose as he goes by in his carriage, I don't care if fifty horses are going it at a leap, and he behind them —it ain't as fast as a bird on the wing is it, or worse than a squirrel on the top of a tree? Well, just let him show his nose, and I'd put a bullet between the peepers of the Lord's anointed certainly."

"Yes, I expect you could."

"And no mistake.—No, sir, because Frenchmen teach dancing, you call them civilized. Why, stranger, I've been among various folks, and the Indians dance more than the French do. Firearms is the invention of civilization, ain't it?"

"Yes, I understand so."

"Well, the rifle is the best kind of firearms—it's the highest point of civilization, I maintain.—Ha! there she comes—this boat can't stand it with the Shelby." By this time all was excitement on board the Fort Adams. The Shelby was a larger and faster boat, and she was pressing us hard. I could hear the barkeeper calling out to the steward for more ice—and, as I glanced towards the bar, I discovered a crowd of persons in excited talk, drinking; among them was the captain.

"Come, let's go on the hurricane deck," said Kentuck, "and see how matters look."

As we entered the cabin to go forward and ascend to the hurricane deck that way, a number of ladies rushed from their cabin towards us, exclaiming—

"Gentlemen, they are racing; they'll blow us all up, gentlemen."

"Ladies, don't be frightened," said old Kentuck, in a manner of exceeding courtesy, at the same time taking off his fox-skin.

"Oh! sir," exclaimed a beautiful, delicate looking lady to him in an agony of terror, "don't let them race; I had a brother and sister lost on the Mozelle."

"Don't be frightened, my good lady, don't be frightened," rejoined the Kentuckian; and, shaking her hand, he proceeded to the hurricane deck.

The Shelby was "barking" after us like a bloodhound from the slip. There was quite an expanse of water in this place, but, as I learned from the Kentuckian, who was an old pilot, and acquainted with every foot of the river, the channel here was very devious and dangerous. The captain came to the Kentuckian's side with a flushed cheek, and asked,

"What do you think of it, Samson?"

"If I had the strength of my namesake," replied the Kentuckian, "I'd swim out and chuck that boat, cargo, passengers and all ashore; as it is, she is too fast for us, and I always knew it. I told you Bob Albert, the pilot there, has been on a bust for this week past; they sent their yawl ashore when they saw me this morning, wanting to learn something about another pilot. Beattie's sick; and I saw then Albert was tight; he swore you should not beat them if they blew everything up. I tell you, capting, it's my opinion they'll be into us; the channel is too narrow here for them to pass us; and they're got such a head of steam on, and they are so much bigger than we are, that if they come agin us, we are gone."

"Kentuck," called out Rogers from the wheel-house, "just step here a moment. You know the channel better than I do. I wonder what those rascals mean?"

The meaning seemed to be to my eye a resolve to run us down; the smoke ascended black and sulphury from her chimneys, with occasional flashes of volcanic fire, that showed he had all the steam on possible. He gained on us evidently, while the excited crowd on her hurricane deck and guards repeatedly hurrawed, as, by the orders of the mate, they stepped to the centre of the boat, to keep her righted.

The noise they made and their evident approach, with the fearful trembling of our boat, for we had all steam on, too, so alarmed the ladies that, following impulse rather than reason, for they would have been safest perhaps in the cabin, they hurried on to the hurricane deck, and the one that I have before spoken of rushed to Samson, who was at the wheel, and begged him not to race any more.

"Kentuck," said Rogers, "they'll be into us—it's my opinion they mean to run us down—they must be all drunk there."

"Pretty much so," replied the Kentuckian; "Bob Albert was in for it early this morning; he's the only pilot on board; that is, Beattie is down with a fever mighty low—Bob hates your capting here, and when he's tight he's perfectly crazy."

"We shall all be lost—we shall all be lost," exclaimed the young lady, "O! Mr. Old Kentucky save us."

"Old Kentucky will do that, my dear young lady, if he has to shoot the rascal at the wheel; they're bent on running us down—self-preservation is the first law of nature—if two men are grappling for the same plank at sea, which will hold but one, each has the right to push the other off if he can—that's law I'm told, though I never thought it was exactly fair, especially if the weaker man had got the plank first—however, if these fellows run into us it will be a clear case of murder, and they are hardly six lengths off. Hang it, these boats bark so that you can hardly hear yourself talk. Halloo, there, what are you after? Look out! Here, Rogers, you take the wheel a moment, and hand me my rifle—you see it's necessity."

"Don't kill him," exclaimed Rogers, nevertheless complying with his request.

"Kill him! no, but I'll just break that right arm of his between the wrist and elbow, the first time he shows it fairly."

So saying, the Kentuckian deliberately lifted his rifle to his shoulder. We all felt our danger too much to interfere or even to say a word. In a moment more the sharp report of the rifle was heard, all eyes were fixed upon the pilot of the Shelby. In an instant his arm fell lifeless to his side, and the Shelby, uncontrolled, rushed on to a shallow bar just beside her, and in another moment was fast aground.

A FROLIC AMONG THE LAWYERS.

CHAPTER I.

I WAS born in the South. I had very bad health there in my early childhood, and a maiden aunt took a voyage by sea, from Baltimore to my birth-place, for the purpose of returning with me to a climate which the physician had said would strengthen my constitution.

She brought me up with the greatest kindness, or rather, I should say, she kept me comparatively feeble by her over-care of my health. When I was about fourteen years of age my father brought my mother and my little sister Virginia from Charleston to see me. My meeting with my kind mother I shall never forget. She held me at arm's length for a instant, to see if she could recognize in the chubby boy before her, the puny sickly child with whom she had parted with such fond regret on board the Caroline but a few years before; and when, in memory and in heart, she recognized each lineament, she clasped me to her bosom with a wild hysteric joy which compensated her—more than compensated her—she said, for all the agony which our separation had caused her. I loved my mother devotedly, yet I wondered at the emotion which she exhibited at our meeting; and child though I was, a sense of unworthiness came over me, possibly because my affections could not sound the depths of hers.

My father's recognition was kinder than I had expected from what I remembered of our separation. He felt prouder of me than at our parting, I presume from my improved health and looks; and this made him feel that being tied to the apron-strings of my good old aunt, would not improve my manliness. A gentleman whom he had met at a dinner party, who was the principal of an academy, a kind of miniature college, some distance from Baltimore, had impressed my father, by his disquisitions, with a profound respect for such a mode of education.

"William," said my father, in speaking on the subject to a friend, "will be better there than here among the women; he'll be a baby forever here. No, I must make a man of him. I shall take him next week with me, and leave him in charge of Sears."

My mother insisted upon it that I should stay longer, that she might enjoy my society, and that my sister and myself might become more attached to each other ere they returned to Carolina. But my father said, "No, my dear; you know it was always agreed between us, that you should bring up Virginia as you pleased, and that I would bring up William as I pleased."

"Let us take him, then, back home," exclaimed my mother; "he is healthy enough now."

"But he would not be healthy long there, my dear. No, I have made inquiry; Mr. Sears is an admirable man; and under his care, which I am satisfied will be paternal, William will improve his mind, and learn to be a man—will you not, William?"

I could only cling to my mother without reply.

"Here," exclaimed my father exultingly, "you see the effect of his education thus far."

"The effect of his education thus far!" retorted my aunt, who did not relish my father's remark; "he has been taught to say his prayers, and to love his parents, and to tell the truth. You see the effects in him now," and she pointed to me, seated on a stool by my mother.

All this made no impression on my father. He was resolved that I should go to Bel-Air, the county town of Harford County, Md., situated about twenty-four miles from Baltimore, where the school was, the next week, and he so expressed himself decidedly.

The condemned criminal, who counts the hours that speed to his execution, scarcely feels more horror at the rush of time than I did. One appalling *now* seemed to possess me. I was deeply sensitive, and the dread of my loneliness away from all I loved, and the fear of the ridicule and tyranny of the oldsters, haunted me so that I could not sleep, and I laid awake all night picturing to myself what would be the misery of my situation at Bel-Air. In fact, when the day arrived, I bade my mother, aunt, and my little sister Virginia farewell, with scarcely a consciousness, and was placed in the gig by my father, as the stunned criminal is assisted into the fatal cart.

This over-sensitiveness—what a curse it is! I lay no claims to genius, and yet I have often thought it hard that I should have the quality which makes the "fatal gift" so dangerous, and not the gift. My little sister Virginia, who had been my playmate for weeks, cried bitterly when I left her. I dwelt upon her swimming eye with mine, tearless and stony as death. The waters of bitterness had gathered around my heart, but had not as yet found an outlet from their icy thrall, 'neath which they flowed dark and deep.

Bel-Air, at the time I write of, was a little village of some twenty-five or more houses, six of which were taverns. It was and is a county town, and court was regularly held there, to which the

Baltimore lawyers used to flock in crowds; and many mad pranks have I known them to play there for their own amusement, if not for the edification of the pupils of Mr. Sears.

My father drew up at McKenney's tavern, and as it was about twelve when we arrived, and the pupils were dismissed to dinner, he sent in his card to the principal, who in a few minutes made his appearance. Talk of a lover watching the movements and having impressed upon his memory the image of her whom he loveth!—the school-boy has a much more vivid recollection of his teacher. Mr. Sears was a tall, stout man, with broad, stooping shoulders. He carried a large cane, and his step was as decided as ever was Dr. Busby's, who would not take off his hat when the King visited his school, for the reason, as he told his Majesty afterwards, that if his scholars thought that there was a greater man in the kingdom than himself, he never could control them. The face of Mr. Sears resembled much the likeness of Alexander Hamilton, though his features were more contracted, and his forehead had nothing like the expansion of the great statesman's; yet it projected similarly at the brows. He welcomed my father to the village with great courtesy, and me to his pupilage with greater dignity. He dined with my father with me by his side, and every now and then he would pat me on the head and ask me a question. I stammered out monosyllabic answers, when the gentleman would address himself again to his plate with renewed gusto.

Mr. Sears recommended my father to board me at the house of a Mr. Hall, who had formerly been the Sheriff of the county, and whose wife and daughters, he said, were very fine women. He regretted, he said, when he first took charge of the academy, that there was not some general place attached to it, where the pupils could board in common ; but after-reflection had taught him that to board them among the towns-people would be as well. He remarked that I was one of his smallest pupils, but that he would look upon me *in loco parentis*, and doubted not that he could make a man of me.

After dinner he escorted my father, leading me by the hand, down to the academy, which was on the outskirts of the town, at the other end of it from McKenney's. The buzz, which the usher had not the power to control in the absence of Mr. Sears, hushed instantly in his presence, and as he entered with my father, the pupils all rose, and remained standing until he ordered them to be seated. Giving my father a seat, and placing me in the one which he designed for me in the school, Mr. Sears called several of his most proficient scholars in the different classes, from Homer down to the elements of English, and examined them.

When a boy blundered, he darted at him a look which made him shake in his shoes; and when another boy gave a correct answer and took his fellow's place, and glanced up for Mr. Sears's smile, it was a picture which my friend Beard, of Cincinnati, would delight to draw. The blunderer looked like one caught in the act of sheep-stealing, while the successful pupil took his place with an air that might have marked one of Napoleon's approved soldiers, when the Emperor had witnessed an act of daring on his part. As for Mr. Sears, he thought Napoleon a common creature to himself. To kill men, he used to say, was much more easy than to instruct them. He felt himself to be like one of the philosophers of old in his academy; and he considered Dr. Parr and Dr. Busby, who boasted that they had whipped every distinguished man in the country, much greater than he of Pharsalia, or he of Austerlitz.

When the rehearsal of several classes had given my father a due impression of Mr. Sears's great gifts as an instructor, and of his scholars' proficiency, he took my father to Mr. Hall's, to introduce us to my future host.

We found the family seated in the long room in which their boarders dined. To Mr. Sears they paid the most profound respect. Well they might, for without his recommendation they would have been without boarders. Hall was a tall, good-humored, careless man. His wife was older than himself, tall too, but full of energy. He had two daughters, Harriet and Jane.

Harriet was a quick, active, lively girl, and withal pretty; whilst Jane was lolling and lazy in her motions, and without either good looks or smartness. The matter of my boarding was soon arranged, and it had become time for my father to depart. All this while the variety and excitement of the scene had somewhat relieved my feelings, but when my father bade me be a good boy, and drove off, I felt as if the "last link" was indeed broken; and though I made every effort, from a sense of shame, to repress my tears, it was in vain, and they broke forth the wilder from their previous restraint. Harriet Hall came up instantly to comfort me. She took a seat beside me at the open window at which I was looking out after my father, and with a sweet voice whose tones I remember yet, she told me not to grieve because I was away from my friends; that I should soon see them again, and that she would think I feared they would not be kind to me if I showed so much sorrow. This last remark touched me, and whilst I was drying my eyes, one of the larger boys, a youth of eighteen or twenty, came up to the window (for the academy by this time had been dismissed for the evening), and said :—

"Ah, Miss Harriet, is this another baby crying for home?"

In an instant my eyes were dried. I cast one glance at the speaker; he was a tall, slim, reckless-looking fellow, named Prettyman, and from that day to this I have neither forgotten it, nor I fear, forgiven him.

In the night, when we retired to our rooms, I found that my bed was in a room with two others, Prettyman and a country bumpkin by the name of Muzzy. As usual on going to bed, I kneeled down to say my prayers, putting my hands up in the attitude of supplication. I had scarcely uttered to myself the first words, "Our Father," but to the ear that heareth all things, when Prettyman exclaimed—

"He's praying! 'By the Apostle Paul!' as Richard the Third says, that's against rules. Suppose we cob him, Muzzy?"

Muzzy laughed and got into bed; and I am ashamed to say that I arose with the prayer dying away from my thoughts, and indignation and shame usurping them, and sneaked into bed, where I said my prayers in silence, and wept myself in silence to sleep. In the morning, with a heavy heart, and none but the kind Harriet to comfort me, I betook myself to the academy.

Parents little know what a sensitive child suffers at a public school. I verily believe that these schools engender often more treachery, falsehood, and cruelty, than exist in West India slavery; I was about saying even in the brains of an abolitionist. Most tenderly nurtured under the care of an affectionate old aunt, who was always fixing my clothes to keep me warm, coddling up something nice to pamper me with, watching all my out-goings and in-comings, and seeing that everything around me conduced to my convenience and comfort, the contrast was indeed great when I appeared at the Bel-Air Academy, one of the smallest boys there, and subjected to the taunts and buffetings of every larger boy than myself in the institution. My father little knew what agony it cost me to be made a man of.

I am not certain that the good produced by such academies is equal to their evils. I remember well for two or three nights after Prettyman laughed at me, that I crept into bed to say my prayers, and at last under this ridicule—for he practised his gift on me every night—I not only neglected to say them, but began to feel angry toward my aunt that she had ever taught them to me, as they brought so much contempt on me. Yet such is the power of conscience, at that tender age, that when I woke in the morning of the first night I had not prayed, I felt myself guilty and unworthy, and went into the garden and wept aloud tears of sincere contrition.

Too often, in public schools, the first thing a youth learns from his elders, is to laugh at parental authority, and to exhibit to the ridicule of his fellows the letter of advice which his parent or guardian feels it his duty to write to him, taking care, with a jest upon them, to pocket the money they send, with an air of incipient profligacy, which any one may see will soon not only be rank but prurient. Such a moral contagion should be avoided; and I therefore am inclined to think that the Catholic mode of tuition, where some one of the teachers is with the scholars, not only by day but by night, is preferable. And in fact any one, who has witnessed the respectful familiarity which they teach their pupils to feel and exhibit towards them, and the kindness with which it is met, cannot but be impressed with the truth of my remarks.

There were nearly one hundred pupils at Bel-Air, at the period of which I write, and the only assistant Mr. Sears had, was a gaunt fellow named Dogberry. Like his illustrious namesake in Shakspeare, from whom I believe he was a legitimate descendant, he might truly have been "*written down an ass.*"

The boys invented all sorts of annoyances to torture Dogberry withal. A favorite one was, when Mr. Sears was in the city, which was at periods not unfrequent, for them to assemble in the school before Dogberry came, and, setting one by the door to give notice when the usher was within a few feet of it, to begin as soon as he appeared in sight, to shout as with one voice—first "*Dog*," and then, after a pause, by way of chorus, "*berry*."

As soon as notice was given by the watcher, he leaped to his seat, and every tongue was silent, and every eye upon the book before it.

The rage of Dogberry knew no bounds on these occasions. He did not like to tell the principal; for the circumstance would have proved not only his want of authority over the boys, but the contempt in which they held him.

A trick which Prettyman played him, nearly caused his death, and, luckily for the delinquent, he was never discovered. Dogberry was very penurious; he saved two-thirds of his salary, and as it was not large, he had of course to live humbly.

He dined at Hall's and took breakfast and supper in his lodgings, if he ever took them, and the quantity of dinner of which he made himself the receptacle caused it to be doubted. His lodgings were the *dormant* story of a log-cabin, to which he had entrance by a rough flight of stairs without the house and against its side. Under the stairs was a large mud-hole, and Prettyman contrived one gusty night to pull them down, with the intention of calling the usher, in the tone of Mr.

Sears (for he was a good mimic), and causing him to fall in the mud. Unluckily, the usher heard the racket without, and not dreaming it was the fall of the stairs, he leaped from his bed, and hurried out to see what caused it. He fell on them; and though no bones were broken, he was laid up for several weeks. The wind always had the credit of this affair, and Prettyman won great applause for his speedy assistance and sympathy with Dogberry, whom he visited constantly during his confinement.

The night of the adjournment of court, the lawyers, and even the judges, had what they called a regular frolic. Mr. Sears was in Baltimore, and the scholars were easily induced to join in it—in fact, they wanted no inducement. About twelve o'clock at night, we were aroused from our beds by a most awful yelling for the ex-sheriff. "Hall! Hall!" was the cry. Soon the door was opened, and the trampling of feet was heard; in a minute the frolickers ascended the stairs, and one of the judges, with a blanket wrapped around him like an Indian, with his face painted, and a red handkerchief tied round his head, and with red slippers on, entered our room, with a candle in one hand and a bottle in the other; and, after making us drink all round, bade us get up. We were nothing loath. On descending into the dining-room, lo! there were the whole bar dressed off in the most fantastic style, and some of them scarcely dressed at all. They were mad with fun and wine. The ex-sheriff brought forth his liquors, and was placed on his own table a culprit, and tried and found guilty of not having been, as in duty bound, one of the originators of the frolic. He was, therefore, fined glasses round for the company, and ordered by the judges to pay it at Richardson's bar. To Richardson's the order was given to repair. Accordingly, they formed a line without, Indian-file. Two large black women carried a light in each hand beside the first judge, and two smaller black women carried a light in their right hands beside the next one. The lawyers followed, each with a light in his hand; and the procession closed with the scholars, who each also bore a light. I being the smallest, brought up the rear. There was neither man nor boy who was not more or less intoxicated, and the wildest pranks were played.

When we reached Dogberry's domicil, one of the boys proposed to have him out with us. The question was put by one of the judges, and carried by unanimous acclamation. It was farther resolved, that a deputation of three, each bearing a bottle of different liquor, should be appointed to wait on him, with the request that he would visit the Pawnee tribe, from the far West, drink some firewater with them, and smoke the pipe of peace.

Prettyman, whose recklessness knew no bounds,

and who, as I suppose, wished to involve me in difficulty, moved that the smallest and largest person in the council be of that deputation. There happened to be by Dogberry's a quantity of logs, which had been gathered there for the purpose of building a log-house. Mr. Patterson (I use here a fictitious name) was at this time the great lawyer of Maryland. He was dressed in a splendid Indian costume, which a western client had given him, and he had painted himself with care and taste. He was a fine-looking man, and stretching out his hand, he exclaimed:—

"Brothers, be seated; but not on the prostrate forms of the forest, which the ruthless white man has felled, to make unto himself a habitation. Like the big warrior, Tecumseh, in a council with the great white chief, Harrison, we will sit upon the lap of our mother, the earth; upon her breast will we sleep; the Pawnee has no roof but the blue sky, where dwelleth the Great Spirit; and he looks up to the shining stars, and they look down upon him; and they count the leaves of the forest, and know the might of the Pawnees."

Every one, by this time, had taken a seat upon the ground, and all were silent. As the lights flashed over the group, they formed as grotesque a scene as I have ever witnessed.

"Brothers," he continued, "those eyes of the Great Spirit"—pointing upward to the stars—"behold the rushing river, and they say to our fathers, who are in the happy hunting-grounds of the blest, that, like it, is the might of the Pawnee, when he rushes to battle. The white men are dogs; their carcasses drift in the tide; they are cast out on the shore, and the prairie-wolf fattens on them.

"Brothers! the eyes of the Great Spirit behold the prairies and the forest, where the breath of the wintry wind bears the red fire through them; where the prairie-wolf flies and the fire flies faster. Brothers, the white man is the prairie-wolf, and the Pawnee is the fire.

"Brothers! when the forked fire from the right arm of the Great Spirit smites the mountain's brow, the eagle soars upward to his home in the clouds, but the snake crawls over the bare rock in the blast, and hides in the clefts, and hollows, and holes. Behold! the forked fire strikes the rock and scatters it, as the big warrior would throw pebbles from his hand; and the soaring eagle darts from the clouds, and the death-rattle of the snake is heard, and he hisses no more.

"Brothers! the Pawnee is the eagle, the bird of the Great Spirit; and the white man is the crawling snake that the Great Spirit hates.

"Brothers! the shining eyes of the Great Spirit see all these things, and he tells them to our fathers, who are in the happy hunting-grounds of the blest; and they say that some day, wrapped in the clouds, they will come and see us, for our land is like theirs."

This was said with so much eloquence by the distinguished lawyer, that there was a silence of nearly a minute when he concluded. In the company was a lawyer named Short, who, strange to say, was just six feet three inches and a half high, and he had a client, which is stranger still, named Long, who was but five feet high.

"Who has precedence, Judge Williard?" called out some one in the crowd, breaking in upon the business of the occasion, as upon such occasions business always will be broken in upon—"Who has precedence, Long or Short?"

"Long," exclaimed the Judge, "of course. It is a settled rule in law, that you must take as much land as is called for in the deed; therefore, Long takes precedence of Short. Maybe, Short has a remedy in equity; but this court has nothing to do with that; so you have the *long* and the *short* of the matter."

"Judge," cried out the ex-sheriff, "we must go to Richardson's; you know it is my treat."

"The Pawnee, the eagle of his race," exclaimed Patterson; "the prophet of his tribe; he who is more than warrior; whose tongue is clothed with the Great Spirit's thunder; who can speak with the eloquence of the spring air when it whispers among the leaves, and makes the flowers open and give forth their sweets; he, the Charming Serpent, that hath a tongue forked with persuasion; he, even he, will go in unto the white man, and invite him to come forth and taste the fire-water, and smoke the pipe of peace with the Pawnee. Then, if he come not forth when the Charming Serpent takes him by the hand and bids him, the Pawnees shall smoke him out like a fox, and his blazing habitation shall make night pale; and there shall be no resting-place for his foot; and children and squaws shall whip him into the forest, and set dogs upon his trail; and he shall be hunted from hill to hill, from river to river, from prairie to prairie, from forest to forest, till, like the frightened deer, he rushes panting into the great lakes, and the waters rise over him, and cover him from the Pawnee's scorn."

This was received with acclamation. Mr. Patterson played the Indian so well, that he drew me one of the closest to him in the charmed circle that surrounded him. His eye flashed, his lips quivered with fiery ardor, though but in a mimic scene. He would have made a great actor. I was so lost in admiration of him, that I placed myself beside him without knowing it. He saw the effect he had produced upon me, and was evidently gratified. Taking me by the hand, he said:—

"Warriors and braves, give unto me the brand, that the Charming Serpent may light the steps of the boy to the hiding-place of the pale-face. He shall listen to the eloquence of the Charming Serpent when he takes the white man by the hand—he shall learn to move alike the heart of the pale-face and the red man."

"Brothers: the Charming Serpent to-night," said he, handing me the candle, and placing himself in an oratorical attitude, while every man lifted his candle so that it shone full upon him—"Brothers, the Charming Serpent to-night could speak unto the four winds that are now howling in the desolate Pawnee paths of the wilderness, and make them sink into a low moan, and sigh themselves into silence, were he to tell them of the many of his tribe who are now lying mangled, unburied, and cold, beneath the shadow of the Rocky Mountains—victims of the white man's treacherous cruelty.

"Brothers! O! that the Great Spirit would give the Charming Serpent his voice of thunder—then would he stand upon the highest peak of the Alleghanies, with forked lightning in his red right hand, and tell a listening and heart-struck world the wrongs of his race. And when all of every tribe of every people had come crouching in the valleys, and had filled up the gorges of the hills, then would the Charming Serpent hurl vengeance on the oppressor. But come," said he, taking the candle in one hand and myself in the other, "the

Pawnee talks like a squaw. The Charming Serpent will speak with the pale-face, and lead him forth from his wigwam to the great council-fire."

CHAPTER II.

ACCORDINGLY the Charming Serpent, holding me by the hand, led me up the stairs. His steps were steady. It was evident that his libations had excited his brain, and instead of weakening gave him strength.

"What's your name," said he to me kindly.

"William Russell, Sir."

"Do you know me, my little fellow?"

"Yes, sir, you're Mr. Patterson, the great lawyer."

"Ah, ha! they call me the great lawyer! What else do they say?"

"That you're the greatest orator in the country," I replied, for what I had drank made me bold, too.

"They do—I know they do, my little fellow—I believe, in fact, that I could have stood up in the Areopagus of old, in favor of human rights, and faced the best of them. Yes, sir, I too could have fulminated over Greece. But we are not Grecians now—we are Pawnees."

"Stop, stop, Mr. Pawnee," called out some one from the crowd; "Short was to go, he is the tallest man."

"The tallest man!" re-echoed Patterson, speaking in his natural tone. "The judge, sir, has already decided that by just legal construction Short is short, no matter how long he is, and if he claims to be long, sir, I can just inform him that Lord Bacon says, 'that tall men are like tall houses, the upper story is the worst furnished.'" Here every eye was turned on Short, and there was a shout of laughter.

"If," continued Patterson, and it was evident his potations were doing their work—"if it be true, I will just say to you, sir, Dr. Watts was a very small man, and he said, and I repeat it, of all small men—

'Had I the height to reach the pole,
Or mete the ocean with my span,
I would be measured by my soul—
The mind's the standard of the man.'

"There, gentlemen of the jury, if that be true, I opine that the tallest man in the crowd is addressing you. But I forget, I am a Pawnee.

"Brothers: the tall grass is swept by the fire, while the flint endureth the flames of the stake. The loftiest trees of the forest snap like a reed in the whirlwind, and the bird that builds there leaves her eggs unhatched. The highest peak of the mountain is always the bleakest and barest; in the valley are the sweet waters and pleasant places. Gentlemen," said he, speaking in his proper person, for he began to forget his personation, "why do we value the gem—

> 'Ask why God made the gem so small,
> And why so huge the granite?
> Because he meant mankind should set
> The higher value on it.'

"That's Burns, an illustrious name, gentlemen. When I was minister abroad, I stood beside the peasant-poet's grave, and thanked God that he had given me the faculties to appreciate him. Suppose that he had been born in this land of ours, sirs, all we who think ourselves lights in law and statesmanship would have seen our stars paled—paled, sirs, as the fire of the prairie grows dim when the eye of the Great Spirit looks forth from its eastern gates—ba! that's Ossian, and not Pawnee—upon it in its fierceness.

> 'Thou the bright eye of the universe,
> That openest over all, and unto all
> Art a delight—thou shinest not on my soul.'

That's Byron—I knew him well—handsome fellow. 'Thou shinest not on my soul'—no, but thou shinest on the prairie."

"The usher!—Dogberry—let's have Dogberry!" called out several of the students.

"Ha!" exclaimed Patterson, "Dogberry! He's Goldsmith's village teacher. that caused the wonder—

'That one small head could carry all he knew.'

Dogberry!—Dogberry!—but that sounds Shakspearian. 'Reading and writing come by nature.' Those certainly are not his sentiments, I mean the defendant's; were they, he should throw away the usher's rod, and betake himself to something else; for if these things come by nature, then is Dogberry's occupation gone. Yes, he had better betake himself to the constableship—the night watch. Come, my little friend—come, son of the Pawnee, and we will arouse the pale-face." Obeying Mr. Patterson, we ascended to the little platform in front of Dogberry's door, at which he rapped three times distinctly. "Who's there?" cried out a voice from within. Dogberry must of course have been awake for at least half an hour.

"Pale-face," said the Pawnee chief, "thou hast not followed the example of the great chief of the pale-faces; the string of thy latch is pulled in. Upon my word, this is certainly the attic story," he continued in a low voice, "are you *attic*, too, Dogberry?"

"No, sir, I am *rheumatic.* Gentlemen, unless your business be pressing—"

"Pressing! Pale-face, the Pawnees have lighted their council-fire, and invite thee to drink with them the fire-water, and smoke the pipe of peace."

"Thank you, gentlemen, I never drink," responded Dogberry, in an impatient tone.

"Never drink! Pale-face, thou liest! Who made the fire-water, and gave it to my people, but thee and thine? Lo! before it, though they once covered the land, they have melted away like snow beneath the sun."

"I belong to the temperance society," cried out Dogberry from within.

"Dogberry," exclaimed Patterson, whose patience like that of the crowd below, who were calling for the usher as if they were at a town meeting, and expected him to speak, was becoming exhausted; "Dogberry, compel me not, as your great namesake would say, to commit either 'perjury' or 'burglary,' and break the door open. You remember in 'Marmion,' Dogberry, that the chief, speaking of the insult that had been put to him, said:—

> 'I'll right such wrongs where'er they're given,
> Though in the very court of heaven.'

Now I will not say that I would make you drink wherever the old chief would 'right his wrongs,' but this I will say, that whenever I, Burbage Patterson, get drunk, I think you can come forth and take a stirrup cup with him; he leaves for the Supreme Court to-morrow, to encounter the giant of the North."

"Mr. Patterson," said Dogberry, coming towards the door, "your character can stand it; it can stand anything; mine can't."

"There's truth in that," said Mr. Patterson aside to me.

"Gentlemen, let us leave the pedagogue to his reflection; and now it occurs to me that we had better not uncage him, for, boys, he would be a witness against you; more, witness, judge, jury, and executioner; by the by, clear against law. Were I in your place I would appeal, and for every stripe he gives you, should the judgment be reversed, do you give him two."

Here a sprightly fellow, one of the scholars named Morris, from Long Green, ran up the steps and said to Mr. Patterson:—

"Do, sir, have him out; for if we get him into the frolic too, we are as safe, sir, as if we were all in our beds. He has seen us all through some infernal crack or other."

"Ah!" exclaimed Patterson, in a low tone to Morris, "he has been playing Cowper, has he; looking from the loop-holes of retreat, seeing the Babel and not feeling the stir?"

"Yes, sir, but he'll make a *stir* about it to-morrow."

"He shall come forth, then," said Mr. Patterson; "Dogberry, open the door; they speak of removing Sears, and why don't you come forth and greet your friends? We have an idea of getting the appointment for you."

This flattery took instant effect; for we heard Dogberry bustling to the door, and in a moment it was opened about half-way, and the usher put his head out, and said, but with an evident wish that his invitation should be refused, "Will you come in, sir? Why, William Russell!" to me in surprise.

"Pale-face, this is a youthful brave, to whom I want the pale-face to teach the arts of his race. Behold! I am the Charming Serpent. Come forth and taste of the fire-water."

As Mr. Patterson spoke, he took Dogberry by the hand and pulled him on the platform. The usher was greeted by loud acclamations and laughter. He, however, did not relish it, and was frightened out of his wits. He really looked the personification of a caricature. His head was covered with an old flannel nightcap, notwithstanding it was warm weather, and his trowsers were held up by his hips, while his suspenders dangled about his knees. On his right leg he had an old boot, and on his left foot an old shoe; he was without coat or vest. As Mr. Patterson held up the light, so that the crowd below could see him, there was such a yelling as had not been heard on the spot since those whose characters the crowd were assuming had left it.

Dogberry hastily withdrew into his room, but followed by Mr. Patterson and myself, each bearing a light. When we entered, the crowd rushed up the steps.

"For God's sake, sir, for the sake of my character and situation, don't let them come in here."

"They shall not, if you will promise to drink with me. Pale-face, speak, will you drink with the Pawnee?"

"Yes, sir," said Dogberry, faintly.

The Charming Serpent here went to the door, and said—

"Brothers, the Charming Serpent would hold a private talk with the chief of the pale-faces. Ere long, he will be with you. Let the Big Bull (one of the lawyers was named Bull, and he was very humorous) pass round the fire-water and the calumet, and by that time the Charming Serpent will come forth. Brothers, give unto the Charming Serpent some of the fire-water, that he may work his spells."

A dozen handed up bottles of different wines and liquors. The Charming Serpent gave Dogberry the candles to hold, took a bottle of Champagne, and handed me another. Then shutting the door he said, "This is the fire-water that hath no evil in it. It courses through the veins like a silvery lake through the prairie, where the wild grass waves green and glorious, and it makes the heart merry like the merriment of birds in springtime, and not with the fierce fires of the dark lake, like the strong fire-water, that glows red as the living coal. Brothers, we will drink."

Dogberry's apartment was indeed an humble one. Only in the centre of it could you stand upright. Over our heads were the rafters and bare shingles, formed exactly in the shape of the capital letter V inverted. Opposite the door was a little window of four panes of glass, and under it, or rather beside it, in the corner, was a little bedstead, with a straw mattress upon it. A small table, with a tumbler and broken pitcher, and a candle in a tin candlestick, stood opposite the bed. A board nailed across from rafter to rafter, held a few books, and beside it, on nails, were a few articles of clothing. There were besides in the apartment two chairs, and a wooden chest in the corner by the door.

"Come, drink, my old boy," exclaimed Patterson.

"Thank you, Mr. Patterson; your character can stand it, I tell you, but mine can't."

"Friend of my soul, this goblet sip," reiterated Patterson, offering Dogberry the glass.

"Thank you, Mr. Patterson, I would not choose any," said he.

"You can't but choose, Dogberry; there is no alternative. Do you remember what the poet beautifully says of the Roman daughter, who sustained her imprisoned father from her own breast?

'Drink, drink and live, old man;
Heaven's realm holds no such tide.'

Do you remember it? I bid you drink, then; and I say to you Hebe or Ganymede never offered to the immortals purer wine than that; I imported it for my own use. Drink; here's to you, Dogberry, and to your speedy promotion;" and Mr. Patterson swallowed every drop in the glass, and refilling it handed it to the usher.

"How do you like the letter, Mr. Dogberry?" asked Patterson of the pedagogue.

"What letter, sir? I must say this is a strange proceeding; I don't know, sir, to what you allude."

"Don't know to what I allude! Why the letter wishing to know if you would take the academy at the same price at which Sears now holds it."

"Sir, I have no such letter. I certainly would, sir, if it was thought that I was—"

"Was competent. Merit is always modest;

you're the most competent of the two, sir—take some."

So saying, Mr. Patterson filled up the tumbler, and Dogberry swallowed the wine and the compliment together, and fixed his eyes on the rafters with an exulting look.

While he was so gazing, the lawyer filled his glass, and observed, "Come, drink, and let me open this other bottle; I want a glass myself." Down went the wine, and, with a smack of his lips, Dogberry handed the glass to Mr. Patterson.

"Capital, ain't it, eh?"

"Capital," re-echoed Dogberry. The wine and his supposed honors had roused the brain of the pedagogue in a manner which seemed to awake him to a new existence.

While Mr. Patterson was striking the top from the other bottle, Dogberry handed me the candle which he held, the other he had put in his candlestick, taking out his own candle, when he first drank, and lifting the tumbler he stood ready. Again he quaffed a bumper. The effect of these potations on him was electrical. He had a long face, with a snipe-like nose, which was subject to a nervous twitching, whenever its owner was excited. It now danced about seemingly, all over his face, while his naturally cadaverous countenance, under the excitement turned to a glowing red, and his small ferret eyes looked both dignified and dancing, merry and important. "So," he exclaimed, "I am to be principal of the academy; ha-ha-ha! O Lord! William Russell, I would reprove you on the spot, but that you are in such distinguished company."

Whether Dogberry meant only Mr. Patterson or included himself, I do not know; but as he spoke he arose, and paced his apartment with a proud tread, forgetting what a figure he cut, with his suspenders dangling about his knees, and his night-cap on, and forgetting, also, that his attic was not high enough to admit his head to be carried at its present altitude. The consequence was that he struck it against one of the rafters, with a violence which threatened injury to the rafter, if not to the head. He stooped down and rubbed the injured part, when Mr. Patterson said to him, "'Pro-di-gi-ous,' as Dominie Sampson, one of you, said, ain't it? Hang Franklin's notion about stooping in this world. Come, we'll finish this bottle and then go forth. The scholars are all rejoiced at your promotion, and are all assembled without to do you honor. They have made a complete saturnalia of it. They marvel why you treat them with so much reserve."

"Gad, I'll do it," exclaimed Dogberry, taking the tumbler and swallowing the contents.

"Just put your blanket around you," said Patterson to him, "and let your nightcap remain; it becomes you."

"No, it don't indeed, eh?"

"It does 'pon honor. That's it. Now, pale-face, come forth; the eloquence of the Charming Serpent has prevailed."

So speaking, Mr. Patterson opened the door, and we stepped upon the platform.

The scene without was grotesque in the extreme. In front of us, I suppose to the number of a hundred persons, were the frolickers, composed of lawyers, students, and town's people, all seated in a circle; while Mr. Patterson's client from the West, dressed in costume, was giving the Pawnee war-dance. This client was a rough uneducated man, but full of originality, and whim. Mr. Patterson had gained a suit for him, in which the title to an estate in the neighborhood was involved, worth sixty thousand dollars. The whole bar believed that the suit could not be sustained by Patterson, but his luminous mind had detected the clue through the labyrinths of litigation, where they saw nothing but confusion and defeat. His client was overjoyed at the result, as every one had croaked defeat to him. He gave Mr. Patterson fifteen thousand dollars, five more than he had promised, and had made him a present of the splendid Indian dress, in which, as a bit of fun, before the frolic commenced, he had decked himself, under the supervision of his client, who acted as his costumer, and afterwards dressed himself in the same way. The client had a great many Indian dresses, which he had selected with a great deal of care, and on this occasion he had thrown open his trunks, and supplied nearly the whole bar.

The name of Mr. Patterson's client was Blackwood, and the admiration which he excited seemed to give him no little pleasure. Most of the lawyers in the circle had something Indian on them, while the boys, who could not appear in costume, and were determined to appear wild, had turned their jackets wrong side out, and swopped with each other, the big ones with the little, so that one wore his neighbor's jacket, the waist of which came up under his arms, and exhibited the back of the vest, while the other wore a coat, the hip buttons of which were at his knees.

On the outskirts of the assembly could be seen, here and there, a negro, who might be said at once to contribute to the darkness that surrounded the scene, and to reflect light upon it; for their black skins were as ebon as night, while their broad grins certainly had something luminous about them, as their white teeth shone forth.

We stood about a minute admiring the dance; when it was concluded, some one spied us, and pointed us out to the rest. We, or rather, I should say, Dogberry was greeted with three times three. I have never seen, for the size of the assembly, such an uproarious outbreak of bacchanalian merriment. After the cheers were given, many of the boys threw themselves on the grass and rolled over and over, shouting as they rolled. Others jerked their fellow's hats off and threw them in the air. Prettyman stood with his arms folded, as if he did not know what to make of it, and then, deliberately spreading his blanket on the ground, he took a seat in the centre of it, and, like an amateur at play, enjoyed the scene. Morris held his sides, stooped down his head, and glancing sideways cunningly at Dogberry, threw himself back every now and then, with a sudden jerk, while loud explosive bursts of laughter, from his very heart, echoed through the village above every other sound.

"A speech from Dogberry," exclaimed Prettyman.

"Ay, a speech!" shouted Morris, "a speech!"

"No, gentlemen, not now," exclaimed Richardson, the proprietor of one of the hotels; "I sent down to my house an hour ago, and have had a collation served. Mr. Patterson, and gentlemen, and students all, I invite you to partake with me."

"Silence!" called out Mr. Patterson. All were silent. "Students of the Bel-Air Academy, and citizens generally, I have the honor to announce to you, that my friend, Mr. Dogberry, is about to supersede Mr. Sears. We must form a procession and place him in our midst, the post of honor, and then to mine host's." So speaking, Mr. Patterson descended, followed by Dogberry and myself. The students gave their candles to the negroes to hold, joined hands, and danced round Dogberry with the wildest glee, while he received it all in drunken dignity.

When I have seen since in Chapman's floating theatre, or in a barn or shed, in the far West, some lubberly, drunken son of the sock and buskin enact Macbeth, with the witches about him, I have recalled this scene, and thought that the boys looked like the witches, and Dogberry like the Thane, when the witches greet him—

> "All hail, Macbeth, that shall be king hereafter!"

The procession was at length formed. Surrounded by the boys, who rent the air with shouts, with his nightcap on his head and his blanket around him, with one boot and one shoe, Dogberry, following immediately after the judges, proceeded with them to Richardson's hotel. Whenever there was a silence of a minute or two, some boy or other would ask Dogberry not to remember on the morrow that he saw them out that night.

"No, boys, no, certainly not; this thing, I understand, is done in honor of me. I shan't take Sears in, even as an assistant. Boys, he has not used me well."

We arrived at Richardson's as well as we could, having business on both sides of the street. His dining-room was a very large one, and he had a very fine collation set out, with plenty of wines and other liquors. Judge Willard took the head of the table, and Judge Noland the foot. Dogberry was to the right of Judge Willard, and Mr. Patterson to the left. He made me sit beside him. The eating was soon dispatched, and it silenced us all a little, while it laid the groundwork for standing another supply of wine, which was soon sparkling in our glasses, and we were now all more excited than ever. It was amusing to see the merry faces of my schoolmates twinkling about among the crowd, trying to catch and comprehend whatever was said by the lawyers, particularly those that were distinguished.

Songs were sung, sentiments given, and Indian talks held by the quantity. Dogberry looked the while first at the boys, then at the lawyers, and then at himself, not knowing whether the scene before him was a reality or a dream. The great respect which the boys showed him, and Patterson making an occasional remark to him, seemed at least, not only fully to impress him with the reality, but also with a full, if not a sober conviction of his own importance.

"A song! a song!" was shouted by a dozen of the larger students; "a song from Morris. Give us 'Down with the pedagogue Sears.' Hurrah for old Dogberry! Dogberry forever!"

"No," cried out others, "a speech from Mr. Patterson—no, from the Pawnee. You're finable for not speaking in character."

Here Prettyman took Mr. Patterson courteously by the hand, and said something to him in a whisper.

"Ah, ha!" exclaimed Mr. Patterson, "so it shall be; I like Morris. Come, my good fellow, sing us the song you wrote; come, Dogberry's star is now in the ascendant. 'Down with the pedagogue Sears'—let's have it."

Nothing loth, Morris was placed on the table, while the students gathered round him, ready to join in the chorus. Taking a preparatory glass of wine, while Mr. Patterson rapped on the table, by way of commanding silence, Morris placed himself in an attitude and sang the following, which he had written on some rebellious occasion or other:—

SONG.

You may talk of the sway of imperial power,
And tell how its subjects must fawn, cringe, and cower,
  And offer the incense of tears;
But I tell you at once that there's none can compare

With the tyrant that rules o'er the lads of Bel-Air;
So down with the pedagogue Sears.
Chorus—Down, down,
So down with the pedagogue Sears.
Down, down, &c.

The serf has his Sunday: the negroes tell o'er
Their Christmas, the Fourth, ay, and many days more,
When they feel themselves fully our peers;
But we're tasked night and day by the line and the rule,
And Sunday's no Sunday for there's Sunday-school;
So down with the pedagogue Sears.
Down, down,
So down with the pedagogue Sears.

So here's to the lad who can talk to his lass,
And here's to the lad who can take down his glass,
And is only a lad in his years:
Who can stand up and act a bold part like a man,
And do just whatever another man can;
So down with the pedagogue Sears.
Down, down,
So down with the pedagogue Sears.
Down, down, &c.

"Hip, hip, hurrah—once more," shouted Morris. "Now then—"

While the whole room was in uproarious chorussing, who should enter but Sears himself. He looked round with stern dignity and surprise, at first uncertain on whom to fix his indignation, when his eye lit on Dogberry, who, the most elated and inebriated of all, was flourishing his nightcap over his head, and shouting at the top of his voice,

"Down with the pedagogue Sears."

As soon as Sears caught a view of Dogberry, he advanced towards him, as if determined to inflict personal chastisement on the usher. At first, Dogberry again prepared to vociferate the chorus, but when he met the eye of Sears his voice failed him, and he moved hastily towards Mr. Patterson, who slapped him on the shoulders and cried out,

"Dogberry, be true to yourself."

"I am true to myself. Yes, my old boy, old Sears, you're no longer head devil at Bel-Air Academy. You're no devil at all; or if you are, old boy, you're a poor devil, and be hanged to you?"

"You're a drunken outcast, sir," exclaimed Sears. "Never let me see your face again; I dismiss you from my service, from Bel-Air Academy;" and so speaking he took a note-book from his pocket, and began hastily to take down the names of the students. The Big Bull saw this, and caught it from his hand.

"Sir, sir," exclaimed Sears, enraged, "My vocation, and not any respect I bear you, prevents my infliction of personal chastisement upon you. Boys, young gentlemen, leave instantly for your respective boarding-houses."

During this, Patterson was clapping Dogberry on the shoulder, evidently to inspire him with courage.

"Tell him yourself," I overheard Dogberry say.

"No, no," replied Patterson, "it's your place."

"Well, then, I'll tell you at once; Sears, you're no longer principal of this academy; you're dished. Mr. Patterson, sir, will tell you so."

"Mr. Patterson!" exclaimed Sears, for the first time recognizing in the semblance of the Indian chief the distinguished lawyer and statesman. "Sir, I am more than astonished."

"Sir," rejoined Patterson, drawing himself up with dignity, "I am a Pawnee brave; more, a red-man eloquent, or a pale-face eloquent, as it pleases me; but, sir, under all circumstances, I respect your craft and calling. What more dignified than such? A poor, unfriended boy, I was taken by the hand by an humble teacher of a country school, and here I stand, let me say, sir, high in the councils of a great people, a leader among leaders in the senate hall of nations; and I owe it to him. Peace to old Playfair's ashes. The old philosopher, like Porson, loved his cups, and like Parr, loved his pipe; but, sir, he was a ripe scholar, and a noble spirit; and I have so said, sir, in the humble monument which I am proud, sir, I was enabled, through the education he gave me, to build over him—

'After life's fitful fever, he sleeps well.'

Yes, as some one says, he was 'my friend before I had flatterers.' How proud he was of me. I remember well catching his eye in making my first speech, and the approving nod he gave me had more gratification to me than the approbation of bench, bar, and audience. Glorious old Playfair! Mr. Sears, you were his pupil too. Many a time have I heard him speak of you; he said, of all his pupils you were the one to wear his mantle. And sir, that was the highest compliment he could pay you—the highest, Mr. Speaker, for he esteemed himself of the class of the philosophers, the teachers of youth. Sir, Mr. Sears, I propose to you that, in testimony of our life-long respect for him, we drink to his memory."

This was said so eloquently, and withal so naturally, that Sears, forgetful of his whereabouts, took the glass which Mr. Patterson offered him, and drank its contents reverently to the memory of his old teacher.

"Sir," resumed Patterson, "how glorious is your vocation! But, tell me, do you subscribe to the sentiments of Don Juan?

"'O, ye! who teach the ingenuous youth of nations—
Holland, France, England, Germany, or Spain,
I pray ye, flog them upon all occasions—
It mends their morals—never mind the pain.'"

The appropriate quotation caused a thrill to run through the assembled students, while they cast ominous looks at each other. For the life of him, Sears could not resist a smile.

At this, Mr. Patterson glanced at us with a quiet meaning, and turning to Mr. Sears, he continued: "The elder Adams taught school—he whose eloquence Jefferson has so loudly lauded—the man who was for liberty or death, and so expressed himself in that beautiful letter to his wife. Do you not remember that passage, sir, where he speaks of the Fourth being greeted thereafter with bonfires and illuminations? His son, Johnny Q., taught school. My dark-eyed friend Webster, who is now figuring so gloriously in the halls of Congress, and in the Supreme Court, and whom I meet to-morrow, taught school. Judge Rowan, of Kentucky, a master-spirit too, taught school. Who was that

"'Who passed the flaming bounds of time and space
The living throne, the sapphire blaze,
Where angels tremble as they gaze;
Who saw, but, blasted with excess of light,
Closed his eyes in endless night—'

Who was he?—Milton, the glorious, the sublime; who, in his aspirations for human liberty, prayed to the great Spirit, who, as he himself says, sends forth the fire from his altar, to touch and purify the lips of whom he pleaseth. Milton, the schoolmaster.

"'If, fallen in evil days on evil tongues,
Milton appealed to the avenger, Time:
If Time, the avenger, execrates his wrongs,
And makes the word 'Miltonic' mean 'sublime.'

"'He deigned not to belie his soul in songs,
Nor turn his very talent to a crime;
He did not loathe the sire to laud the son,
But closed the tyrant-hater he begun.

"'Think'st thou, could he—the blind old man—arise
Like Samuel, from the grave, to freeze once more
The blood of monarchs with his prophecies,
Or be alive again—again all hoar,
With time, and trials, and those helpless eyes
And heartless daughters, worn, and pale, and poor'—

"Would he not be proud of his vocation, when he reflected how many great spirits had followed his example? The schoolmaster is indeed abroad. Mr. Sears, let us drink the health of the blind old man eloquent."

"Thank you, Mr. Patterson, thank you; but before my scholars, under the circumstances, it would be setting a bad example, when existing circumstances prove they need a good one. Sir, it was thought I should not return from Baltimore until to-morrow, and this advantage has been taken of my absence. But, Mr. Patterson, when such distinguished gentlemen as yourself set the example, I know not what to say."

"Forgive them, sir, forgive them," said Mr. Patterson, in his blandest tones.

"Let them repair to their homes, then, instantly. Mr. Patterson, your eloquent conversation has made me forget myself; I don't wonder they should have forgotten themselves. Let them depart."

"There, boys," exclaimed Mr. Patterson, "I have a greater opinion of my oratorical powers than ever. Be ye all dismissed until I again appear as a Pawnee brave, which I fear will be a long time, for 'tis not every day that such men as my western client are picked up. But, Mr. Sears, what do you say about Dogberry? He must be where he was; to-morrow must type yesterday. Dogberry, how is Verges?"

"I don't know him," said Dogberry, doggedly.

"Why, sir, he is the associate of your namesake in Shakspeare's immortal page. Let this play to-night, Mr. Sears, be like that in which Dogberry's namesake appeared—let it be 'Much ado about Nothing.'"

Sears smiled, and nodded his head approvingly.

"Then be the court adjourned," exclaimed Mr. Patterson. "Dogberry, you and my friend Sears are still together, and you must remember in the premises, what your namesake said to Verges. 'An' two men ride of a horse, one man must ride behind.'"

Giving three cheers for Mr. Patterson, we boys separated, and the next day found us betimes in the academy, where mum was the word between all parties.

THE MISSIONARY'S CONVERT.

CHAPTER I.

I HAVE always had a peculiar respect for the Methodists. My grandfather was a rigid member, and one of the first proselytes in Baltimore. I have heard it said that he stood within the door of an humble dwelling, I think in Tripolet's alley, where he could see what was going on without, as well as listen to the preacher, in order to give notice of any contemplated intrusion, while Bishop Coke, the friend of Wesley, expounded his faith to his then few followers. He was at that time a man of ample means; a leading member of the city council, many of whose ordinances he framed; charitable and public spirited, and, withal, a local preacher, for which he received no salary. The good he strove to do, was performed for its own sake. He "coveted no man's silver, nor gold, nor apparel." One Sabbath, while administering the sacrament, he was stricken with a paralysis, from the effects of which he never recovered. I have often heard him speak of Coke, and the little flock who then worshipped with him.

We all know what a strong hold the Methodist faith has on the public mind. I should not, however, omit to notice one trait in my grandfather's faith. He was sternly opposed to what are called "shouting meetings." He held, however, that Christianity inculcated, in all its precepts, republicanism; and that Methodism conformed more strictly to it than any other Christian creed. Though not myself a member of any church, I remember with deep respect and reverence, the manner in which he would open the "big ha' Bible," and say, while the family were all assembled round him, before retiring for the night, "let us worship God!"

In "the monumental city" I read law, and before I was nineteen, was admitted to its practice. I had some little business, particularly in defending criminals; and I was wont to exercise my lungs in crazy declamations at political meetings.

I had not been a "lawyer at law" quite a year, when ill health compelled me to renounce the profession, and I became domiciliated at the residence of my uncle, who rejoiced in a delightful farm a few miles from town. A kinder spirit never illumined mortal clay, or left it for a fitter sphere.

But for his attention, and that of a beloved aunt, "life's fitful fever," would have ended with me but a few years after it commenced.

While practising my profession, I defended a schoolmate of mine under the following circumstances: His father was a Methodist, a peace-loving man, who had been converted under the preaching of my grandfather, for whom he had a profound respect, and more than a brotherly regard. The fraternal hand extended beyond this world, and, I believe, binds them in another and a better.

This worthy gentleman, who was named Godfrey, acquired a handsome fortune, and purchased a large estate a few miles from my uncle's. His son Adam, who was named after my grandfather, was a roystering, reckless blade, but his character was dashed with the noblest impulses, which would flash forth like the play of the lightning in a darkening cloud. He had a lovely sister, named Jane, whom I have always deemed to be one of the most enchanting women I ever beheld; and it was not more her peerless beauty, than her angelic purity, which impressed you. A young lawyer, of feeble mind, but malignant heart, was assiduously attentive to her. I knew him slightly before I knew her; and he was wont to remark to me, in reply to some jest or other of mine, with regard to the report of an engagement existing between them, that he "never could get that far, until he turned religious, and that he was waiting on the 'anxious seat' of hope, for the first favorable opportunity."

I did not relish this jest at the religious views of a sect which I respected; and I told him so, with a bluntness that ever afterward prevented anything between us but a salute in passing.

Jane, at first, rather encouraged his attentions; but certain developments in his character, together with her father's wishes, caused her to reject him. Perhaps the advice of Adam influenced her as much as anything; for he despised my brother limb, and she loved her brother with a devotedness I have never seen surpassed. Upon this, the rejected suitor, in a disguised hand, wrote an infamous anonymous letter to her father concerning her. It was shown to Adam, who had then left school, and was living with his widowed father and his sister, in the country, where they generally passed the summer.

Without saying a word, Adam mounted his horse, repaired to town, and sought the office of the lawyer, whose door he entered and locked, and whom, in his rage, he would have beaten to death with no other weapon than his horsewhip and fist, in spite of the superior size of his antagonist, and his liberal use of the chairs and table, if persons without, attracted by his cries of "murder!" and "help!" had not rushed in, and with much difficulty rescued him.

Our lawyer, whose skull was as brainless as that of his dead brother, whose

"Dome of thought and palace of the soul,"

was rid of its tenant when Hamlet picked it up in the graveyard, where they laid Ophelia in the earth; would, nevertheless, not be knocked about the sconce, without complaining of his "action of battery!" Adam was immediately indicted for the offence. He employed me as his counsel, and this renewed an old acquaintance. I had no doubt who wrote the letter, but the point was to prove it, in mitigation of damages; for although weeks elapsed before the trial, my brother limb still bore, on that day, like the veteran of a worthier field, convincing evidence of stern encounters.

I obtained many of the lawyer's letters, and several legal instruments which he had drawn up; but he had so well disguised his hand in this outrageous communication, that it could not be said that any similarity existed between them. Butler remarks, in commenting upon "Junius Identified," a work which assumes to prove that Sir Philip Francis was the author of these celebrated letters, that the *external* evidence was sufficient, he believed, to satisfy a jury of the fact, but that the *internal* evidence proved the contrary; that

Sir Philip's mind was not capable of the authorship. Our evidence was quite the opposite of this —the internal evidence; the mind and heart of the party were quite capable of the act; but the external proof was wanting.

I knew, if I were to ask him if he wrote the letter, the court would not require him to answer the question, should he or his counsel object to it, as no one is bound to criminate himself. But, I thought, from what I knew of his character, that he would not employ any aid, and I did not believe that the prosecuting attorney, who knew him well, would be over anxious to shield him from the inquiry. I therefore believed that, by suddenly producing the letter, and asking him the question, boldly: "Did you write that?" I might extort the confession from his conscious guilt. It was optional with my client, either to have a jury trial, or to submit the case to the court. I advised the latter. I knew the judge to be a man of sterling integrity, who from his heart would despise such an act as I intended to charge upon the prosecuting witness.

The witnessing lawyer, who was large enough to have swallowed my little friend Adam, entered with great minuteness into the aggravations, horrors, and death-purpose of the assault. He told how he was seated in his office, busily engaged in professional business, when my client entered, locked the door, and knocked him down, and, before he was enabled to defend himself, horribly blackened his eyes. "*Ecce signum*," said his glance at the court, as plainly as ever glance said it. He was thus prevented, he said, from seeing anything distinctly that afterwards occurred; my client, he declared, took advantage of this, and attacked him with a chair; with the intention of murdering him.

"It's a lie!" shouted Adam, oblivious of his whereabout, and advancing toward the witness with the evident intention of "deepening the combat" and the "black and blue" of his eye. His honor ordered silence, looking sternly at Adam, as if with the purpose of reprimanding him; when I took advantage of the occasion, and suddenly opening the letter to the confused gaze of the witness, demanded, "Did you write that?" "I must do my duty," I added, "I have specimens of your handwriting in court."

The guilty victim started, and scarcely knowing what he did, confessed the fact. I asked no more questions, but handing the letter to the judge, explained, in a sentence, the relation the witness had sought to establish for himself in the family of Mr. Godfrey, and his failure; which, I stated, I could prove by persons then in court, if the witness denied it. He replied to me—

"I don't deny it, and that will prove that I meant no harm in writing the letter."

The judge thought otherwise. I never saw his countenance assume such an expression of displeasure as on this occasion, although he was a stern man, and had long presided in a criminal court, which had made him familiar with every species of depravity. He imposed but a nominal fine upon my client, and seemed to regret that it was made his duty to impose any; and then read the lawyer a lecture, which I am persuaded he will never forget. He said, he had doubts whether it was not his duty to exclude him altogether from the bar. This remark operated as an effectual expulsion, for the letter-writer left the city a few weeks after; and if he has not materially mended his ways, he has certainly ere this appeared as a prisoner, instead of a practitioner.

Shortly after this trial, in midsummer, I repaired to the country, obtained a Rosinante, and, as far as my health would permit, amused myself —when I left my books, which was very often— with the little incidents and adventures in the neighborhood, not forgetting an occasional attendance at the political meetings. My indisposition spread a gloom over everything. My father's family had departed for the West. For many years they had occupied an estate adjoining my uncle's; and, with a feverish, morbid fondness, I delighted to visit the scenes of my boyhood, and dwell upon every rivulet, and rock, and hill, and tree that had been familiar to my earliest memory. How often, in the hush of night, when returning from town, have I taken a by-way through the woods, that I might call up old, thick, clustering associations! With feelings so different from a child's, when, benighted by the old graveyard, I have stopped my horse, and tried to recall the sensations of indescribable awe with which my schoolmates and myself hurried past, in solemn silence, when the evening sun had gone down, and left us lingering in our playful stroll home from school.

Near by was our parting place; and well do I remember the echoing shout, or the whistle dying away in the woods, with which the lonely little wayfarers beguiled their fears, as they took their separate paths to their homes. More than one bonny face was in the group, from which I was here wont to part, the black or blue-eyed daughters of our neighbors around. They are mothers now; and most of them have seen, ere this, the grave inclose their gray-headed sires, who were wont to pat me on the head, and promise to vote for me, if I took the right side in politics, when I grew to be a man. They are resting in that old graveyard; and although it is not many years ago, more than one of their fair-haired daughters are sleeping their last sleep beside them—stem and flower together! Twice, with my frail literary attempts, have I sought the shrine of the autocrats of literature in the East; the publishers, who drink their wine, it is said, out of the skulls of authors; but wide and far, I turned from the monumental city; for well I knew, I could not bear to call up old associations to sunder them again. The final leave-taking, if I die away from these haunts, cannot give me half the sorrow; I must wait until the ice grows a little harder around my heart, before I revisit the home of my childhood. It will be hard, indeed, even then, if it be not melted by the memory of "auld lang syne" in the scenes "where memory first began."

A day or two after I had settled myself in the country, my friend Adam, who had been amusing himself in travelling from village to village with an itinerant juggler, returned, and called to see me.

I observed, with deep regret, that he had not only fallen into the habit of occasional wild intoxication, but he had also acquired a passion for gaming, which had already lost him large sums of money. While he was absent, I had visited his family frequently, and was delighted with the beauty, intelligence, and almost angelic purity of his sister.

With the good old gentleman, I was wont to

hold long discourses upon freewill, predestination, Wesley, Summerfield, Bascom, and Adam Clarke's Commentaries. I ventured to remonstrate frequently with Adam upon his habits; but he always turned it off with a laugh or joke, or left me without saying a word. I saw he deeply distressed his father and sister.

After this, I seldom accompanied him anywhere, or knew much of what he did, except from a common friend, whom I shall call Harry, who was attached to his sister, and who was doing everything in his power to reclaim her brother and his friend. I began to fear his efforts were hopeless.

One day Harry came from the city, where they had been together for a week, and told me that Adam was with a nest of gamblers; that he had raised every cent he could control, and lent it to him; but that he had no doubt he would lose it all. "They are cheating him foully!" said Harry. "I told him if he would suffer himself to be made a dupe of in that way, I would not stand by and see it, and so I left him."

That night Adam returned home. He was silent and sad. A camp-meeting was to commence next day, and an eloquent and aged missionary, a celebrated minister, was to deliver a discourse. I had been all the evening talking with him. His silver locks parted over his high, calm forehead; his fine features, the simplicity of his dress and manners;

the naturalness of his conversation, and his gushing, heartfelt piety, impressed me with feelings of profound respect. It was a beautiful summer moonlight night, when the family were all called together to prayers. Adam was seated moodily apart, on the porch, and entered the room doggedly. The missionary addressed us upon the joys of home, and the homely virtues; told us how they solaced the cares of life, and prepared us, in our contemplation of them, for the "home of homes." The pathetic tenderness of his language and manners stole over the heart like the strains of some touching melody, which the affections seem to recognize, yet wonder over.

It was like a song of home, heard in a far land; a memory of the past, which something undefinable has linked, by an electric chain, with the future. It was, in fact, the piety of a better world, calling down blessings, like sunlight, upon the rugged pathway and weary wanderer of this; cheering him, the while, to lift his moral eye above the mists that enshroud him here, to the light that would lead him to its holy home. He concluded with a prayer as impressive as his remarks, and bade us good-night.

As we left the room, Adam said, with an oath, "that's a good man; don't you think so?"

"I do," I replied, emphatically.

CHAPTER II.

We all took a seat at the end of the porch in silence, which was interrupted by my inquiry of Adam "as to how he came on with those fellows?"

"Badly, in their opinion," replied Adam. "I knew they were cheating me, and I waited to catch them at it. I was alone with them, and presently saw one plainly hide a card. There were three in the room. I had no friend by, but I was desperate. I sprang to the door, locked it, drew my pistols, and told them that I had detected them in the act of cheating; that I knew there was a combination among them for that purpose; and," said I, presenting my pistols, "you must refund every cent I ever lost to you, or take your *chances!* Two of you I can kill instantly, and the other must take it 'rough and tumble' with a desperate man!" You know them—Bowling, Jackson, and Sharp. They tried to laugh it off, but I stood on the other side of the table, and, drawing out my watch, gave them just one minute. Bowling blustered, and swore he'd have the law on me; but asked me, nevertheless, how much I claimed?

"Fifteen hundred and fifty dollars," said I. He's the leader, you know, and he shelled it out.

I pocketed my watch and my money, opened the door, and left the room. As I passed, I heard Bowling whisper to the others: "Let's follow him out, brain him, and get back the money?" as he said this, all three followed me out. I warned them to return; they would not, and I fired at the foremost."

"Did you kill him?" we all exclaimed at once.

"No; I may have hit him, though I believe they all returned to their room, and I left the house unmolested. I am told they mean to get me indicted for shooting with intent to kill. I don't care for myself; but the disgrace, let such a trial end as it may, to the old gentleman and Jane! Bradshaw, what do you say about it?"

"Why," said I, plainly, "to tell you the truth, if you had not been associating with these men so much lately, your character, and the respectability of your family, would bear you through with a grand-jury, and prevent them from finding a bill. As it is, though they should indict you upon the false swearing of these men (for from your statement there would be no grounds), they could not, in my opinion, possibly obtain a conviction. Did any one overhear Bowling's remark, about braining you?"

"Yes; Whelan, the bar-keeper, was in the next room. It is separated only by a thin board partition, full of chinks, from the other, and he overheard it. I have done him some favors; and as I was leaving the house, we talked the matter over, and he told me what he had heard. But his testimony is no better than theirs; he's a gambler, himself, and they are three to one."

"I think," said I, "I can manage it, if they have not gone too far to retreat. I'll ride in to-morrow."

"*Do*, Bradshaw," said he, grasping my hand; "and you will do me a service I shall never forget. I do not care for myself, but the old gentleman and Jane! He paid a large debt for me, yesterday, and this, *this!* That old missionary," said he, abruptly interrupting himself, "prayed with great feeling."

"Yes, he did!" I replied.

"Adam," exclaimed Harry, "with not half the feeling of a prayer I heard this morning. I walked leisurely out, and arrived here before breakfast. When it was over, your father and sister followed me out of the room, and asked for you. I told them I believed you were in town. Your sister burst into tears, but said not a word. I was tired, and going into the front room, I threw myself on the sofa, behind the folding-doors. I was lost in thought, and don't know how long it was before your sister entered the back room, alone. She kneeled down and prayed aloud; thinking that no one heard her but the Being to whom her supplication was addressed. I wish you could have heard her. She was praying for *you*."

Adam sprung to his feet, struck his clenched hand against his brow, and, rushing from the porch, passed into an adjacent grove.

I stayed all night, but saw no more of Adam until the next morning, when he made his appearance at the breakfast-table, and announced his intention of accompanying his sister to the camp-meeting.

I mounted my horse, rode into the city, and proceeded directly to the hotel at which I knew the gamblers, at least Bowling, stopped. Though gaming is not among my vices, since I never played for a cent in my life, yet I knew Bowling well. We agreed in politics, and he was a great better on elections; one who gained his point by indirection, and who, though not so depraved as he was thought to be, was more vicious than bold. Once, when he was indicted for gambling, I defended him.

I asked for him, and was told he was in his room. Not being disposed to stand upon ceremony, save when it is required, I asked the number, and forthwith proceeded thither. I rapped. A husky voice called, "come in!" I entered. The gambler had evidently just arisen, late as it was, for his bed was unmade; and with his coat off, and in his stocking feet, he was gathering into a pack a number of cards that were scattered on the table and floor. On the table, also, were a couple of empty decanters, and several half-filled glasses, from the different colored contents of which it was evident that, though the gamblers might have agreed as to their game, they had that variety which is the spice of life in their choice of liquors. The ends of cigars, which had been thrown, with an unsteady hand, toward the fireplace, were scattered around. Bowling appeared a little confused when he recognized his visitor, but he immediately rallied. His brow was flushed, and he threw upon me an inquiring glance, as he said—

"Walk in, Mr. Bradshaw; I am glad to see you. Anything stirring?"

"Nothing remarkable, that I know of, Bowling; how is it with you?"

"I am glad to see you, Squire. I was asking, just now, after you. I have been robbed, sir, of three thousand dollars?"

"Ah!" said I.

"I'll tell you; you havn t quit the practice, have you? They told me you were living in the country. I want your advice. Yes, sir, take a seat; robbed of three thousand dollars. That infernal blackleg, Adam Godfrey; I won some money from him; he drew a pistol on me, swore he'd kill me, if I did'nt give him three thousand. I can prove it, both by Jackson and Sharp. Not only that, but after I paid him the money, as I was leaving the room, he shot at me. There, sir, look at that hat; that bullet-hole tells the story. I'll go the whole law against him. I want you to go with me to the magistrate's; I must have out a writ. Nothing less than an attempt to murder! Simbo'll cool him! You must resist bail, save the highest. There, sir, that bullet-hole tells the tale."

I thought it would have been well, could Adam have escaped, if the bullet had gone a little lower.

On discovering what his feelings were, I thought myself justified, in defending Adam, to practice a little artifice, for I knew that they would swear anything against him; this was sufficiently evident, indeed, from what I now heard; I therefore remarked—

"Bowling, it is proper that I should tell you, that I am employed by Godfrey against yourself, Jackson, and Sharp."

"Against *me!* for what?"

"Why, he says that you, and the rest, cheated him out of fifteen hundred dollars, which he made you refund; that after he left the room, you followed him out, agreeing to beset him, 'brain him,' and take back the money."

"Ha! can he prove it?—can he *prove* it?"

"Yes; he says that a person in the next room, I

believe, through a thin partition, overheard you, as well as himself; and that on your following him out, to put your threat into execution, he fired to defend himself. I shall be sorry to appear against you, but a lawyer must go for his client. The truth is, you are well known to be gamblers; and with this proof, if he should bind you over, the court would require enormous security. Besides, I should not be surprised if he could prove that you, together with Jackson and Sharp, were overheard conspiring to cheat him, and boasting afterward that you had succeeded."

Bowling looked exceedingly black at this. Oh, what an advantage innocence has over guilt!

"Squire," said he, in an altered tone, approaching close to me, "as you say, the hounds are always after us. If ever there were persecuted men, we are. Thunder! I'll tell you—"

"Stop, Bowling; remember I am, in this case, Mr. Godfrey's counsel. Don't tell me anything against yourself; for I should be sorry to be compelled to use it."

"You're right. He's combining with a set of rascals to put us down; that's it. He knows that the court and jury will be against us, and after he has obtained, by threatening our lives, money we won fairly from him, he wants more; I suppose to try his luck somewhere else. How much more does he claim, Squire?"

"I don't know," I replied, "that he is entirely certain how much you got from him; but I speak candidly to you—"

"Do, do; I don't think you have any cause for being an enemy of mine."

"None whatever. I appeared for Godfrey once, when he was charged with an assault and battery. He nearly beat a doctor to death."

"He'll die with his shoes on, yet," interrupted Bowling.

"I defended him, as I said, since then; I have known him well, and his family, who have wealth, and are of the first respectability. On their account, I don't think, when his temper cools, he will be very anxious to appear in this business; for if he should, it would be evident to all that he had been gambling himself."

"That's a fact! Gambling?—he's *always* gambling; he's one of the biggest blacklegs I ever knew."

"His father, I am sure, would object to anything of the kind, on his part; and I think I have some influence with the old man."

"Then, Squire, let's have it hushed up. You shan't lose by it. But that Godfrey is a perfect devil! Nobody can do anything with him. He was once near throwing Jackson, big as he is, out of a third story window. Do you think he'll cool off?"

"He wouldn't, if it were not for the exposure. I'll advise with him."

"Do—*do!* Stop, won't you take something to drink?"

"No, I thank you."

"When shall I see you, Squire?"

"In a day or two; in the mean time, keep dark."

"I will—depend on me; I'll go immediately and see Jackson and Sharp," said he, hurrying on his coat. "Squire, I may depend on you now?" he continued, offering me his hand.

Taking the proffer, I replied: "The matter shall be hushed up, Bowling, or it will be your fault. Forthwith see Jackson and Sharp."

So saying, I departed, leaving Mr. Bowling in quite a ruminating mood.

The camp-meeting, which we were about to attend, was not more than five miles from the residence of Mr. Godfrey. He did not, therefore, pitch a tent on the ground, but, accompanied by the missionary and his daughter, rode over every day, and as it was moonlight, stayed until after the evening service. The first day, in consequence of my visit to Bowling, the blackleg, I did not attend the camp, but met the family, together with A'dam, who had been with them, at night. I communicated to the latter what had occurred between Bowling and myself, at which he was greatly relieved. I never heard a word more on the subject, except from the gamblers themselves in their anxious inquiries to know whether it would be hushed up? Such a coward is guilt!

That evening we kept our steps from bedward until much after the usual hour for retiring, employing the time in agreeable conversation. Adam sat by, an attentive listener. The missionary rehearsed to us many scenes in the far West, in which he had been an actor, of deep interest. He regretted much that he had never heard Summerfield.

It so happened that I was the only one present who had heard him; and notwithstanding I told the venerable minister I was but a child at the time, yet such was his admiration for that most eloquent and apostolic man, that he questioned me over and over again touching my impressions of him; and I seemed to gain an interest in his eyes, from the fact that I had looked upon and listened to that gentle spirit of his church, now "inheriting the promises."

The missionary had known my grandfather, and he spoke of him in terms that greatly gratified me. "My son," said he, "your grandfather was a truly good man. I was with him when he died; and though it is many years ago, the scene lives in my heart and memory more vividly than the events of the hour that have just passed. I was kneeling by his bedside, and I knew the hour had come, for I have witnessed many such an hour, my children; and, O, it is a fearful one to him who is not prepared! He was perfectly conscious, but the lamp of life was flickering fast. As he closed his eyes, apparently in prayer, I said to him: 'Brother, tell me at this earthly parting, are you convinced of the great principles of our faith?' He opened his eyes and looked upward, with the calmness and trust with which a child, when resting in its mother's arms, will look up into her face, as slumber steals over it, and said: 'I know that my Redeemer liveth!' It was his last breath that uttered these words, but his spirit passed away so gently, that I was not convinced it had departed until I felt his hand grow cold in mine. I said, then, my children, to the bystanders, and after long experience of the world, I say now to you, that I would rather have been that humble Christian, on his lowly bed of death, than Napoleon at the head of his devoted and victorious legions, the conqueror of the world. The true Christian is a greater conqueror; he conquers himself. The greatest eulogy that was ever pronounced on Washington, was made by his biographer, Ramsay, who in speaking of the strength of his passions, says: 'With them was his first contest, and over them his first victory.' This, his first victory, saved our country; for it enabled him to curb, like an obedient child, that ambition which, in another heart, might have gained a giant's strength and prompted its possessor to grasp at empire. It was this, his first victory, that illustrated, in his last moments, the lines of the poet:—

> 'O grave, where is thy victory!
> O death, where is thy sting!'

It enabled him calmly, on his death-bed, to review the great events of his varied existence, and to say to his physician, who stood beside him: 'Doctor, I am not afraid to die.' How beautiful! There is in such a scene a philosophy beyond the stoic's, for it expresses a hope beyond the grave. How different the earthly parting of Napoleon, chained on his ocean-washed rock, with a mind as wild as the waves dying in the hour of the storm, and mistaking the war of the elements for the thunders of the battle-field. 'Head of the army!' he exclaimed, in that mad moment, with his last breath, and his soul took its flight to meet, at the dread tribunal, the hundreds of thousands whom he had hurried to their long account, unconscious, unrepentant, unredeemed."

Stirred by the tones of the old man, but not catching his spirit, I exclaimed.

> "Charge, Chester, charge!—on, Stanly, on!
> Were the last words of Marmion!"

He smiled at my enthusiasm, and then said, gravely—

"But what were his *last hopes?*"

"True," said I:—

'Shame and dishonor sit
By his grave ever!
Blessings shall hallow it,
Never, oh, never!'

"God's mercy is boundless," said the missionary. "He is merciful, not only to his dutiful and lovely child, but the mightiest, the most rebellious, and the most sinful."

We had a touching prayer from the missionary, before we separated. I took a seat on the porch, and Adam, after pacing to and fro for some time, at last paused before me, and said—

"'A high-heeled Shoe for a Limping Christian;' 'Hooks and Eyes for Unbelievers' Breeches.' Confound those books! I read them in my boyhood, and they gave me a disrespect for the Methodists, which I never could surmount, until I heard this good old missionary. I ought to have reflected that my father and sister at least try to practice what I believe he both practices and preaches."

CHAPTER III.

WHEN we left the room, after the missionary, who had gone up stairs, I heard Adam order his horse. I asked him if he was going to town.

"No," said he, "a black boy has come over to say, that Mr. Jones, who has been ill for some time, is worse. The missionary is going to see him to-night, and I think I ought to accompany him, and not leave him to the guidance of the negro."

In a few moments the good old man came out, the horses were brought, and they departed together. It was after midnight when he and Adam returned. They reported that Jones died about an hour after they arrived.

The next day we all proceeded together to the camp-meeting. I was surprised when Adam again expressed his determination to attend. We all rode on horseback. My friend Harry, and I, by the side of the gentle Jane, and Adam—it was a little singular—on one side of the missionary, and his father on the other. The suspicion crossed my mind more than once, that he was meditating some mad prank or other.

"No," thought I, "it cannot be, after such an

occurrence as has just happened, and in the presence of his father and the clergyman."

The morning was beautiful. Not a cloud appeared in the heavens, although the early warmth threatened a noon of sultriness. We rode up the turnpike about a mile, and then struck off into what was called an "old field," an uninclosed place, where tobacco had been tilled, until the soil was exhausted. This was bounded on one side by a deep ravine, which was bridged over, in which flowed a stream called Mad Run. A comparatively slight rain would swell it to a great depth and wideness, owing to the fact that the country immediately around its source, and for a long way beside it, was very hilly, and fed it, particularly during a rain, with innumerable torrents. As we were crossing the bridge, I could not but observe that it was a very slight one, and I lingered behind my companions, to admire the wild channel, which the perpetual wear of the waters had made through the very hills. About twelve or fifteen feet below the bridge, the waters splashed over a rocky bed, and, chafed like human beings by resistance, rushed on like them to the goal.

A pleasant ride over hill and dale, from this spot, brought us to a place where a hill, covered with the highest and most luxurious trees, gently sloped down a crystal brook that wound round its base, and then meandered on to the Mad Run.

On the side of the hill was the camp-meeting. Curving up from the brook, the tents were pitched in the form of a half moon, extending about half-way up the side of the hill. Midway, between the extreme tents, under the clump of noble trees, a temporary pulpit, or rostrum, was erected, from which the preacher addressed the multitude.

The missionary preached, and most movingly. As I glanced at a group of fashionable loiterers, who had been sauntering through the camp, with easy indifference, uttering witless jests upon the scene, listening to him with attention, I thought of the line of the poet:—

"And fools who came to scoff, remained to pray."

He spoke of the sustained contentment of the good man, amid all the ills of life, because of the heavenward hope, and contrasted his feelings with that of the wrong-doer, who, however well situated, in a worldly point of view, doubts and yet fears the great results beyond the grave. In speaking of the immortality of the soul, and the shrinking which it feels on leaving its earthly tenement, he employed an illustration which it strikes me I have heard before, but certainly never so impressively expressed.

He compared the soul, about to take its upward flight, to an eagle, which, after long confinement, finds its prison-door open. "How fearfully," he said, in a faint voice—and he seemed to fear to raise his hand above the pulpit—"how fearfully it looks forth at first, and then shrinks back! How, when it ventures forth, it gazes round and round with a dazzled eye, and casts a wondering glance upon the day-god above!" Here the speaker looked timidly at the sun, which, through the trees, threw a tremulous ray upon him. "How feebly it essays a little circle, with wing but half expanded; then it feels its strength of pinion, and takes a broader sweep, yet casts a longing, lingering look upon its earthly tabernacle. Then," continued he, while the wave of his arm waxed eloquent, and his tones heart-stirring, "it circles wider and wider, farther and farther, higher and higher; its impulses lose their earthliness; it bathes and gladdens its outstretched wing in the refulgent beam; it feels the glory more and more, and its strength is renovated beyond the might of its prime, until, fixing its unwinking eye on the glorious orb, it darts upward to the sources of everlasting light." As he said this, he advanced, with upturned hands and eyes, while the rays of the sun, through an opening in the trees, flashed upon his long and silvery locks, and threw a halo around him, that made the man, like the sentiment, sublime. Methought I saw the heavens open, and the winged messenger pass the everlasting skies. The speaker had scarcely concluded, when the sultriness, which had succeeded the warmth of the morning, became intense. For some minutes, not a breath of air stirred, not a leaf moved. Then the heavens became suddenly overcast; the clouds floated together in dark masses, like the gathering of armies; and now and then a fierce flash broke forth; but, as yet, though through the trees we could see the clouds moving, the leaves were motionless, and not a drop of rain fell.

The missionary came to our little group, for we were all together, and observed:—

"Brother Godfrey, as I am to officiate at the funeral of Mr. Jones, and as you mean to attend, had we not better depart? I fear we shall have a storm."

We accordingly mounted our horses, and left the camp. When we were clear of the woods, and while we were ascending an eminence which commanded the prospect, the missionary asked Mr. Godfrey if they were subject to violent storms in that region? Being informed that we were not, he said that he had known a storm to force its way with such violence through a wood, as not to leave a tree standing in its path. "If you were subject to such storms here," he continued, "I should say, from my experience, that we should have one now. God grant that it come not over the camp."

He had scarcely spoken, when the rain began to fall in big drops, and the roar of the winds, afar off, could be distinctly heard, as if they were muttering their wrath, and gathering strength. He looked around, and said :—

"We must ride fast; there is not air enough stirring here to give an indication of the way the storm will sweep; but I believe it will be on this side of the run. We must on."

We accordingly put spurs to our horses, and rode rapidly toward the bridge. The dropping of the rain now ceased for awhile, but the heavens grew fearfully dark, and the air began to stir. Our horses threw back their ears, and seemed, like their riders, to observe the sky. At this moment, a bolt that seemed to rend the hills made our path lurid with light; while our horses trembled, like ourselves, at the awful peal which accompanied it. The rain now burst forth; and in an instant the blast was down upon us, sweeping the valley with resistless violence. We cast our eyes anxiously to the camp. We could see indistinctly the white tents through the trees, but nothing more. Yet the fury of the storm seemed to be there, for the air grew thick above it with leaves and the sundered branches of trees; and presently the horses, having broken from their fastenings, came dashing madly past us.

"We are in the hands of God, children!" said the missionary, calmly. "We must press for the bridge. The fury of the storm is not here, but *this* is dangerous."

We urged our steeds at the admonition, and an intervening hill soon hid the camp from our sight; but the frightened horses of the worshippers still came dashing on. A tree not fifty yards to our right, as we turned to the left, was prostrated with a terrible crash. We reached the stream in safety. The storm was not so furious there, but the mad waters came leaping down the ravine, and throwing their waves towards the bridge, as if anxious to sweep it away. Several horses from the camp stood by the bridge, evidently desirous to cross, but, apparently, kept back by an instinctive sense of danger.

"Will it not be hazardous to cross the bridge?" asked Mr. Godfrey.

"I think not," replied the missionary. "Let us pass one at a time. I see your horses are frightened—mine is not. I'll lead the way."

"No," said Adam, dismounting and giving to Harry the bridle of his horse, "let me lead yours over. You can walk; it will be safer."

But the missionary said there was no danger, and spurred his horse toward the bridge.

The well-trained animal drew back for a moment, and then passed on. The bridge was about ten yards long. We held back our horses, that now seemed to have no sense of danger, as their fellow had none. Those from the camp obeyed the same impulse, and, being unrestrained, sprang on the bridge after the missionary's. The frail structure shook from end to end.

"Father in heaven, be merciful!" ejaculated Jane, as the missionary, on discovering his peril, dismounted from his horse. His foot had scarcely touched the plank, when, with a tremendous crash, the bridge gave way, and rider and horse were precipitated into the foaming waves. That wild utterance which Cooper has so powerfully described in the "Last of the Mohicans," as proceeding from the horse when in distress, and which startled the brave Hawkeye and the intrepid Indians with a superstitious dread, now broke forth from the poor animals, and added, if possible, to the horrors of the scene.

"He's lost!" exclaimed Mr. Godfrey, in despair.

"Not if I can save him!" exclaimed Adam, throwing off his coat, and springing to the edge of the stream.

"My brother, he's a good man; God is with him! Die not as *you* are!" exclaimed Jane, in a tone of intense agony.

"My life is worthless, Jane," said Adam, with a calmness so strange, that it struck me, even at that awful moment.

Adam stood watching for the appearance of the

missionary. The bridge had caught edgewise between two rocks, on the other side of the stream. The horses from the camp, that were on the bridge, appeared first above the water, and were all borne down, except one that succeeded, by swimming, in gaining the bank near us, which was not more than two feet above the flood. On the other side, just below the spot where the bridge had rested, part of the rock which held it projected perpendicularly up several feet. It seemed that the missionary and his horse were both caught by the bridge. In a moment more, his horse, which was a noble animal, arose with his head up stream and high out of water, while his master was seen clinging to the bridle. On observing this, Adam hurried above us, plunged in, and, in spite of the angry element, by his great skill as a swimmer, succeeded in gaining precisely what he aimed at, the bridle of the horse. In an instant he raised the missionary from the waves. Both were evidently supported by the bridge, as was the horse. Quick as lightning Adam placed the upper end of the stirrup-strap in the missionary's grasp, and then holding with one hand the horse's head out of water, with the other he struck out for the shore. The animal seemed to know that a master spirit guided him, for he plunged bravely toward us. Wildly the waves broke over them, and the horse in vain attempted to breast their fury. The steed seemed stationary for a moment, and then yielded to the force of the element. Adam, however, still continued to keep his head in a proper position. When they got below the point where the concentrated rush of the stream from the obstruction of the bridge had nearly overwhelmed them, Adam made another effort, a desperate one, to gain the shore. Here we saw the missionary distinctly; his head arose above the back of his horse. I see the holy faith, then on his countenance, now; it is a picture on my brain, more distinct than that on the wall before me. As Jane said, "God was with him." In much less time than I have taken to tell it, master and horse, with their brave deliverer, stood safely upon the shore. Poor Jane swooned when she saw that her brother was safe.

The storm abated as rapidly as it arose. By a bridge some miles above, which had withstood the violence of the waves, we arrived safely at Mr. Godfrey's. As the missionary was preparing, though it was then nearly dark, to go to the house of mourning to perform the rites of sepulture, a messenger arrived to tell him that, in consequence of the storm having inundated the graveyard, the funeral would not take place until the next day, as another spot was to be selected for the repose of the dead.

Never shall I forget the holy evening which we spent after that awful storm. Uninjured in health, and with spirits gratefully and religiously calm and pure, the missionary joined the family circle. Jane looked the personification of pious gratitude, in its loveliest form—a religious woman. Harry gazed on her with reverence, while Mr. Godfrey, for the first time in many years, beheld with pleasure both his children. But the most remarkable feature of the group was Adam. That expression of desperate recklessness, which once possessed his countenance, had fled. I wondered, as I observed with what respectful earnestness he listened to the missionary, if it ever had been there. How kindly he answered his sister, and without a jest upon her piety! His very dog, that used to avoid him, because of the tricks he played him, went wagging his tail to his master, and laid his head upon his knee, the picture of faithfulness, as Adam placed his hand upon it.

But the prayer of that "old man eloquent" that night! I have heard the great ones of our land, in the pulpit, at the bar, and in the Senate, in the palmiest moments of ther oratorical power; but theirs could no more compare with the heart-touching pathos of this plain servant of God, than would the strut and stare of a fashionable tragedian compare with the simple majesty of Paul before Festus. He prayed for us all, for the father and for the children, and for their friend and for myself; and I have felt from that hour to this, however wayward my mood and imaginings, that in heaven's high chancery, I too had a claim and an advocate. Especially he prayed for Adam. "Let, O Lord!" he said, in tones that left no eye unmoistened, and no heart untouched, "the blessings of all the good I may hereafter be permitted to do, under thy providence, light upon his head, and be all the evil mine, as thou has vouchsafed to make him this day the instrument of thy mercy for the salvation of thy creature from the wrath to come! And when thy seventh and last angel, in the last war of the elements, shall pour forth the vials of thy wrath, and thy mighty voice shall proclaim unto all the nations of the earth, 'It is done!' forget not this little household! Shadow them under thy brooding and protecting wings! Let there be no wanderer from the flock, but let them all, a family in heaven, rejoice together in the light of thy everlasting love."

When the prayer was concluded, and we arose from our knees, Adam took a seat by his sister, and unable, iron-nerved as he was, to control the emotions that had been swelling in his heart for days, he laid his head upon her bosom, and "wept, and was forgiven."

After all, there is no love less selfish than a sister's.

> "My sister, my sweet sister! if a name
> Purer and holier were, it should be thine!"

So spake the wayward Childe to his sister; and when wife and daughter were deaf to his fame, and spoke not his name in their household, and Fanaticism refused his remains a resting-place among England's illustrious departed, where sleeps none worthier, his sister, his "sweet sister," gave them consecration, and built over them the monument which now guards them from the desecration of those who should have claimed to be nearer and dearer. And "she, proud Austria's mournful flower," where was her mournfulness, when they gave the hero of the world's history, and her lord, to the "vulture and the rock?" Cold, selfish, and sensual, she pursued the routine of courtly patrician observances, or hastened from them to common plebeian abandonment; while Pauline, not the less sensual, but the sister, was anxious to forsake, for that lonely rock, the voluptuousness of the soft clime she so loved, to whose glorious statuary her glowing form had given beauty, that she might share the exile, and solace the sorrow, and soothe the loneliness, of that forsaken husband, who was still to her the man of destiny; still to her a beloved brother; whose blood was her blood; who had given her renown and empire, and to whom, world-forsaken, she could give what is worth the world, a sister's unchanging love!

MY AUNT BETSY.

"WHAT GREAT EFFECTS ARISE FROM LITTLE THINGS."

It is wonderful how little the mother, father, and kindest relative of a child, understand his sensibilities and character, and how often they do violence to his feelings by a disregard of that public opinion which, of its kind, prevails among children as much as it does among men. The boy is as sensitive to ridicule as the man—more so; and he suffers just as much from being laughed at among his companions as the man does among his. How often a child has been compelled to wear a hat, cap, trowsers, or shoes of some ungainly cut, when they might just as well have been made after the fashion of his fellows; which has not only subjected him to ridicule, but given him a nickname, which made him a laughing-stock through life; and which was, perhaps, the first thing that led him to undervalue his own capacity and character, and to consort with those below him, who were the gradation to a still lower grade, when he should have directed his pride to the emulation of those who, as the world goes, are held above him.

A recollection of my Aunt Betsy draws from me these remarks. Each and every Sunday it was her custom to repair, with a precise housekeeper of a gentleman with whom we boarded, to Baltimore to church. We were spending the summer months in the country. She was a rigid Presbyterian, and was fond of doctrinal points; and to the ministry of the Rev. William Duncan, who then was of the old side, she delighted to devote herself. I know not whether that minister's more liberal opinions, which he teaches now, would be subscribed to by her, but I think not. The only place of worship in our country neighborhood was a Methodist meeting; the latitudinarian principles of that sect she could not sanction; for latitudinarians she was pleased to call them.

Our host, Mr. Stetson, was the owner of an old, shabby, shackling gig, which set low between the shafts, on wooden springs, with an old cloth top, and rattling wheels. To this vehicle, an old family horse, named Samson, halt, and nearly blind, was harnessed, and, thus conveyed, my Aunt Betsy and Miss Dalrymple rode to church. They might have ridden to Jericho if they had left me behind them; but, no, a stool was duly placed for me each Sabbath in the bottom of the gig, and on this, *nolens volens*, supported between the knees of my veteran aunt, to prevent my tumbling out, was I seated in front, with the bandbox beside me. My shoulders served to support the reins, which my aunt held far apart, one in each hand. Whenever Samson lagged in his gait, no whip was used, but the reins were flapped up and down on his back, and consequently on my shoulders.

Meanwhile, my respectable relation, with her spectacles on her nose, kept a sharp look-out for the stones and ruts; cautioning Miss Dalrymple to do likewise, and finding most unchristian fault with her whenever we received a jolt, if she did not receive notice.

"Miss Betsy, there's a stone," exclaimed Miss Dalrymple.

"Where, where!" exclaimed my aunt.

And before she received the intelligence as to which side it was, up went the wheel; my aunt screamed; but we righted again, though with a bounce that nearly caused the dissolution of the vehicle.

"Bless my soul! why could you not tell me on what side at once, Miss Dalrymple?" exclaimed my aunt, adjusting her spectacles.

"I couldn't think quick enough," was the reply.

"Think quick enough! Madam, you can see beyond your nose, can't you? Old as I am, I can;

but I can't see on both sides at once; do look sharp on your side, and I'll look sharp on mine. Willy, look ahead, for mercy's sake!"

The mortification I then experienced of being seen by my playmates in this condition, brings a blush to my cheek now.

My Aunt Betsy had a house in town, which she rented out during our summer sojourn in the country, but she reserved the privilege of putting the gig under the shed in the backyard, while we went to church; a narrow, steep alley (I forget the name of it) led to the back gate.

Arrived there, Miss Dalrymple would descend and open the gate, and my aunt would drive in; unless my aunt's tenant, who had an eye to the quarter day, and the indulgence he then sometimes required, bustled out, opened the gate, and let us in full dignity through. Then he would officiously conduct us into the house, leading me with one hand and carrying the bandbox in the other. For my aunt held also another privilege, by tacit consent, that of preparing the extras of her toilet in Mrs. Titlum's back parlor, the wife of Mr. Titlum, her tenant.

Then the bandbox was opened, her false hair and cap fixed primly on, and with care, though the church bells had ceased ringing. All ready at last, these worthies sallied out, stately as Juno's bird, between them leading your humble servant to the tabernacle.

This day of my eventful story my aunt had been more than gratified by Mr. Duncan's exposition. She came forth, leading me by the hand, as if she thought that she herself was entitled to some credit for the sermon, because it expressed her opinions so fully, and she had such firm faith in it. Miss Dalrymple, who, in some respects, was inclined to doubt certain of the divine's views on previous occasions, was glanced at triumphantly; she looked meek and mad accordingly. In this Christian frame of mind we reached Titlum's.

The quarter day was near, and while my aunt changed her cap and hair, Titlum got the gig in readiness. We were soon seated in it under the shed, Miss Dalrymple and my aunt, the bandbox and myself. Titlum led Samson through the gate, headed him right, and so we started fairly.

It was an alley just back of Calvert street (I forget, as I have said, the name of it, though I think it is "Grant street," giving the name of street to an alley, like many other streets and persons taking a higher style than they deserve); through this we emerged, taking our way along Market, now Baltimore street, with the intention of passing through Calvert street by Barnum's, into Monument Square.

That day, with masonic and military honors, one

of the soldiers of the fifth regiment, who fought bravely at North Point, was to be buried, and the military were parading in the square. My aunt had scarcely turned Samson into Market street, when the music burst upon her ear, and, ejaculating "Heaven preserve us!" she tried to turn Samson round, but Samson would not be turned round.

"I should not be surprised," exclaimed my aunt, "if this abominable violation of the Sabbath should cost us all our lives. To have trumpets sounding and see colors flying on the Lord's day, and we the innocent to suffer—my gracious!"

My aunt seemed like Othello in his agony, "*perplexed in the extreme.*"

"Boy, boy," she called out to a black boy on the pavement, "come and turn my horse's head round."

"What'll you give me, old 'oman?"

"Old woman! why don't he say lady? I'll give you a fippenny-bit."

My aunt was economical.

"I axes a quarter," replied he dictatorially.

"A quarter! bless me, this was not collection day, and I didn't bring any money. Miss Dalrymple, did you?"

Miss Dalrymple replied in the negative. My aunt said to the black fellow, after this short colloquy—

"Well, my good boy, you shall have a quarter of a dollar—when—"

"Shell out, old one," he repeated.

"I have not any change now, my boy. I'll pay you the next time we meet," replied my aunt.

"Do you see anything green here?" said the negro, shutting his right eye and pulling down the lower lid of the left one, until the whole of the white of it was exhibited. He stood a moment, as if to give my respectable relative a chance of full inspection, and then coolly walked off, saying, "There ain't nothing green about this child, old one."

"I protest," exclaimed my aunt, "if that boy belonged to me, he should have a severe whipping to-morrow morning early. I should almost be tempted to give it to him to-day, though it is Sunday."

But the boy didn't belong to my aunt, so he walked off haw-hawing, with contempt, like one who has detected an impostor in the act of defrauding him.

"Sir," said my aunt to a gentleman who was passing, "couldn't you turn my horse round, if you please?"

But no, the gentleman seemed to think with the negro, that my aunt was not respectable enough to receive that attention. If she had been a damsel fair, who had been left for a needful moment by her Jehu, the gentleman would have complied with most courteous alacrity, but an old woman, who had come out to take the responsibility of her own safe conveyance, let her take it; and the gentleman walked on. My aunt now applied her own energies to Samson. She succeeded in turning him nearly round, when she heard the noise of fife and drum, and, looking forth, discovered another company coming to join those already in the square. Her only chance now was to go straight out Market street, or to turn down Calvert street. Samson obeyed the rein quickly, which put him on his regular routine, but he made an obstinate stop at the corner of Calvert street, determined to turn into Monument Square. How my aunt flapped the reins, declaring that hereafter she would drive with a whip, and that Miss Dalrymple could carry it.

The company behind us had now got close on to Samson; and it was evident that the unusual proceedings of the day, on the part of my aunt, together with the noise and bustle, had done much to ruffle his temper. In depositing coal in the cellar of the corner house, as you turn down Calvert street, the proprietor had had a board laid over the curbstone on to the pavement, to prevent filling up the gutter, when it was discharged from the cart; against this Samson backed, as if desirous of witnessing the display, as the soldiers passed into Monument Square. Thinking himself perhaps still in the way, he backed a little, and finding his progress facilitated by the plank, he politely gave the soldiers the street, and betook himself to the sidewalk. His courtesy my aunt neither appreciated nor approved. Greatly alarmed, she waved her hand over the ragamuffin train, who surrounded the band, and called to the musicians in earnest expostulation :—

"Good people, do stop that noise! Don't you see what a condition we are in, and you are breaking the Sabbath?"

What soldier was ever known to regard, when on duty, the remonstrances of an old woman in a gig, with another of her sex and a child? No, though only on parade, they never *play* soldiers, and if all the old women and children in the world were to be killed by frightened horses, that would not abate their martial sounds.

The crowd of boys, when they beheld Samson, and the gig, and all the *et ceteras*, and saw my aunt's gesture of expostulation, though many of them could not hear what she said, burst into a yell of derision. One stout fellow, who was on the sidewalk, following the band close in the press, feeling valiant from the martial strains which rang in his ears, elevated a long lath, which he carried in his hand by way of soldiership, and smote Samson prodigiously. This Samson could not brook; the music had made him martial too, and it was evident that, like his great namesake among the Philistines, he was determined on revenge; for no sooner did the boy strike him, than he charged at once into the very band of music. The sound the soldier loves died upon their ears instantly—and well it might. The fifer started back in such haste from the advancing Samson, as to overturn the drummer, who fell flat with his drum-band around his neck, and, before he could recover himself, Samson's left leg was knee-deep through his drum-head; whereby he held the musician prostrate, as one antagonist would hold another by his neckcloth. The slide of the trombone seemed to have the power of engulfing the whole of it, for Samson's head struck the trombone, and it disappeared in the player's mouth. The man who played the serpent was nearly made a victim to it, as were our first parents—

> "In Adam's fall
> We sinned all."

He was a short, duck-legged individual, and wore the serpent, not exactly folded around him, but buckled on. It caught in the wheel, and held him there as the boa-constrictor twines part of its body around the tree, and part around its victim. The drum, however, saved the musician, though it nearly ruined us. As Samson raised his drum-incumbered foot to advance, he stumbled flat to earth, thereby ejecting my aunt upon the drummer, Miss Dalrymple into the embrace of the serpent, or rather the serpentine man, and myself and the violated bandbox and its contents into the street. The last thing that I remember, was the infernal yell of the ragamuffins, which rent the air at this catastrophe.

I do not know what my aunt would have done, if Mr. Titlum had not rushed to her assistance. He was fond of martial sounds, and, after helping us into the gig, he had scarcely entered his house, when the "stirring music of the drum" reached his ear. Desirous of witnessing the display, he passed out of his front door into Calvert street, and then to the corner. He was just in time to witness Samson's charge, and was the first to raise my aunt. On finding she was not hurt, with much delicacy he handed to her her cap, wig, and bonnet, which had escaped from her respectable person in the foul grasp of the drummer, who caught, in his terror, at he knew not what. Miss Dalrymple, unhurt, indignantly disengaged herself from the embrace of the serpent. I must do my aunt the justice to say, that I believe, before she ever thought of the predicament in which she stood, she looked around after me—a glance showed her that I was unhurt, for I was on my feet endeavoring to secure her false curls and cap from a black fellow who had seized them. I was, however, unsuccessful; for he made his escape in the *mêlée*.

All this while the soldiers were at a dead halt, stamping their feet with impatience, while those behind pressed front to learn the cause of the delay. The captain, in the confusion, had his coat skirts cut off by some dexterous pickpocket. As he was just behind the band, he was in the midst of the confusion, and a respect for the corps made him forgetful of all personal consequences; so it was easily done. But when it was done, he felt that although, in the tented field, 'mid battle and blood, if the foeman's bullet had deprived him of his skirts, he could have fought only the more valiantly; yet, considering the manner of the loss, and that the crowd had ceased to admire him, and were giving evidences of a contrary nature, and also considering the trombone man, the drummer, and he of the serpent, were disabled, therefore it was both proper and dignified that on the spot he should dismiss his company, which he forthwith did. He instantly retreated into a neighboring store, from the secluded backroom of which he sent for his citizen's dress, and with much meekness repaired to his own domicil.

It might, therefore, be admitted, that Samson won the day. In confirmation of this remark, it may be stated that, in consequence of the ridicule growing out of this contest, the captain resigned his command, under pretence of a press of business, and the company disbanded themselves, and many of them entered different volunteer corps.

But the matter did not stop here with Aunt Betsy. The drummer sued for the damage done to his drum, and also for an injury he had sustained by twisting his ankle under him as he fell, and spraining his wrist; asserting that, thereby, as a drummer, his occupation was ruined; for should his wrist get well, of which there was little prospect, his occupation was gone should any company to which he might be attached choose to take a long parade. He of the serpent sued my aunt for the damage done his serpent, and Miss Dalrymple for divers and sundry contusions and bruises, then and there received on various parts of his person; and the trombone man brought suit, not only for the utter annihilation of his instrument, but for the loss of three front teeth, which, he asserted, not only disabled him from playing with anything like his former proficiency, but which would, in all probability, shorten his life, from the fact that his digestion was delicate in the extreme, that his food had always required more mastication than he could bestow upon it, and now he would scarcely be able to masticate at all.

The captain magnanimously refused to bring suit against my aunt for the loss of his skirts, although a distinguished lawyer gave it as his decided opinion, that he was entitled to recover; because, although a pickpocket was the immediate cause of the loss aforesaid, yet the captain would not have sustained the loss, had it not been for the confusion occasioned by my aunt's want of control over the horse, and that, therefore, the captain was entitled to recover consequential damages.

These suits excited an interest at the time, which has not entirely died away yet. When the cause came up, my aunt's lawyers denied that there was any ground of action at all, but the judge, without hearing the other side, declared there was. He said, that if a man let loose a wild bull, which he knew to be wild, though he intended no mischief by it, yet he was liable for what damages the bull might do, because he ought to have informed himself of the nature of the beast before he threw him upon the community. The question would arise, the judge said, was my aunt capable of driving? If she was, did her near-sightedness prevent her? Could she with a child at her knees and a bandbox at her feet, drive safely through a crowd like that assembled on the occasion aforesaid? The judge, in conclusion, remarked, "that he did not mean to prejudge the case, but that it was clear to his mind, not only that there were grounds of action in the case, but also that the defendant must show, conclusively, that she was capable of driving; for, said he, this court never will sanction the doctrine that any old lady, however respectable, may be allowed, whether she can see or not, or whether she can drive or not, to start off on the Sabbath to church, with a feeble child between her knees, and a helpless woman beside her, and cause the great injury which it appears from the amount of damages claimed in this case has been done; men are not to be ruined in their professions, and their health irrecoverably impaired in this way, without a court of justice interfering and making the party guilty pay for it."

All legal readers are familiar with the case of "The Musicians *vs.* Betsy Hugersford," in the Maryland Reports. It twice got up to the Court of Appeals, and twice got back again, upon some informality. Then it was delayed for years, while a commission to take depositions was sent to New Orleans, and even to France and to England, to which countries several of the witnesses (we know that musicians are migratory) had emigrated.

The day before the case was to be finally tried upon its merits, the three musicians—the drummer, the trombone, and the serpent—went on a party of pleasure with many others, on board of a steamboat, to Fort McHenry. After the bottle had circulated briskly, it was proposed that each of the musicians should take the respective instrument upon which he had formerly played (for since that eventful day of parade they had asserted they were disabled), and try how much skill was left in them. In the hilarity of the moment, unsuspicious of consequences, they consented; and it was asserted by all, and particularly by the band of musicians on board, in their depositions, taken that night, that they never heard better playing.

The whole proceeding was a trick of a young lawyer, who had been taken by accident into the case. He was well acquainted with the three musicians, and had got them on the frolic for the purpose of showing by witnesses that they were as good players as ever, and, consequently, had sustained no injury.

Since the parade, the trombone had kept a tavern, the drummer an oyster-cellar, and the serpent a public garden; and in consequence of the great injury which the criminal negligence of my aunt had inflicted on them, they were each extensively patronized by a sympathizing public.

In the morning, when the suit was called in court, the plaintiffs' counsel, who had got wind of the depositions, and who considered that the witnesses were forthcoming, reluctantly dropped the suit, to prevent the accumulation of costs, which he felt his clients would have to pay. But a short time afterwards, when the band above mentioned, who were of the military, had been ordered to Florida, the suit was commenced again, their *ex parte* depositions amounting to nothing; and they themselves being without the jurisdiction of the court, and not likely ever to return to Baltimore again.

This case was pending when my aunt died, and the question is now agitating the lawyers, whether her heirs could be made parties to a new suit.

Notwithstanding all the trouble this business gave my poor aunt, I confess it was a great satisfaction to me, as it put an end to our gig rides thereafter.

MARY M'INTYRE HAS ARRIVED.

ON my way to St. Louis, safe and sound I arrived at Louisville on the steamer Madison, now years agone. The falls of the Ohio, at Louisville, were so low, that the captain resolved to go round by the canal, which was cut to obviate the necessity of unloading vessels to lighten them, so as to permit their passage over the falls. At ten o'clock A. M., we reached Louisville, and the captain told me, upon inquiry, as I wished to pay my respects to a friend or two of that hospitable city, that the boat would not leave until one o'clock, as he had to take on board a number of Scotch immigrants with their baggage, who had been brought thus far from Pittsburg on a boat that was returning. I therefore had ample time to make a morning call or two in passing, a pleasure of which I generally avail myself on our Western waters, whenever the boat on which I happen to be a wayfarer stops where I have acquaintances.

I resolved to pay my respects to "Amelia," the sweetest poetess of our land, in whose society I spent a most agreeable hour, which I would willingly have prolonged, but the admonition, that the boat started at one o'clock, arose to my memory.

I therefore repaired to the wharf half an hour before one, determined to be in time. Lo! as I approached the wharf, I beheld the Madison lumbering along in the canal, stopping every moment, as if to take breath, being, in fact, retarded by some obstacle or other, which she could not surmount without the aid of poles, and ropes, and a fresh start.

My only remedy was to ride round to Lockport, where the canal terminates by passing into the river, and wait an indefinite period for the arrival of the steamer, or get on board a row-boat, and have myself transported after her in the canal, and thus reach her, which I was assured could be effected in half an hour at farthest.

I accordingly feed two youths, who were paddling about in a boat, to convey me to the Madison. I was soon seated astern, and they pulled away for the steamer. We soon entered the canal, but owing to the waves the steamer threw in her confined track, and her lumbering movements from side to side, it was with difficulty and delay that we approached her.

The Scotch immigrants were what are called

on the Western waters, deck-passengers; of that class, almost all of whom are poor, but often very respectable, who, in the packet-ships, in crossing the Atlantic, take a steerage passage. Among the immigrants on the Madison, were many females, among whom there were some young and beautiful ones.

As I ripped out a strong Western oath (I am ashamed to write it, for I have not pronounced one for a long time) at the captain, for breaking his word with me, and leaving before the hour, one of the Scotch lasses said to me imploringly, for our boat had gotten immediately under the stern of the steamer, where she stood—

"Oh! sir, please don't swear so."

Struck with the tone and beauty of the Scotch maiden, my impulse of anger changed to one of admiration, and I instantly said to her—

"Well, I won't again; and you must be like Sterne's angel, when my uncle Toby swore; you must drop a tear upon the word in the high archives, and blot it out forever."

As I said this, I stretched out my hand to reach the railing of the steamer, but failed, as our boat gave a lurch at the moment. Again I made the effort, and should have failed again, had not the pretty Scotch girl leaned over the vessel's side and given me her hand. Thus assisted, in a moment more I was on the steamer's deck, beside my fair assistant. I thanked her with all the grace I could master, which she received with a blush, and said:

"But you forget, sir, that my uncle Toby's oath was to save life."

"But it was unavailing," I replied; "yet your fair hand, stretched out to me, may have saved mine; therefore, as I live and may err—

"Nymph, in thy orisons
Be all my sins remembered."

"Poor Ophelia," ejaculated the Scotch girl, sadly, "she went crazy for love."

"Ah," thought I, "here is intelligence as well as beauty taking a deck passage, and not the first time; for with poverty they have been companions before; and love, too, I suspect, is no stranger in this party."

Impressed with these reflections, I entered into conversation with my new-made acquaintance, and soon discovered that she was remarkably intelligent, as well as beautiful. It seemed to me that fair hair was never braided over a fairer brow. Her neck and shoulders were exquisitely turned, and added to the charm of features, which were decidedly patrician. There was a *näivete* in her manner, too, that had caught its tone from a position, I thought, evidently above her present one. She had also nothing of the Scotch in her accent, which was broad enough on the lips of her companions.

Though she was apparently poor, there was not only great neatness in her humble toilet, but a style that was above the " clay biggin." Several little trinkets upon her person—a ring, breastpin, and particularly a massive gold cross, attached to a handsome chain—attracted my attention, and indicated, not only from their value, but the manner in which they were worn, her superiority to her companions, as well as the fact, to my mind, that she was a Roman Catholic. Her companions were rigid Presbyterians, I soon learned; and my fair assistant into the boat, and reprover, did not attend, I observed, when an old Scotchman, in the afternoon, read the Bible to the group of immigrants gathered about him; but withdrew to the side of the boat, and looked over, pensively, into the water.

She interested me much. Being myself, at that time, the wearer of a large pair of whiskers, and an imperial to match, my humble travelling companions were rather shy of me; but soon observing that my fellow-passengers above stairs knew me well, and that I was not unpopular among them, the Scotch folks grew rapidly familiar and frank with me.

I learned, from a solemn and remarkably pious old Presbyterian, the history of the beautiful Scotch girl, whose name was Mary M'Intyre. He sighed heavily when he told it. Her father was an humble farmer of the better sort, and lived in Ayrshire. An old Roman Catholic nobleman, who dwelt in Edinburgh, had a daughter, who, on a visit which she made to Ayrshire, became acquainted with Mary, and treated her as an humble friend. When the young lady returned to Edinburgh, she took Mary with her, who was affianced to a young miller in the neighborhood, named M'Clung. In fulfilment of an old Scotch custom, which Burns and his Highland Mary practised, they at parting broke a piece of silver over a running brook, and on a Bible plighted their everlasting faith unto each other.

In the progress of events, Mary, to the horror of her lover's faith, became a Roman Catholic. Her lover wrote her what she thought a harsh and uncalled for letter on the subject. Her maiden pride, as well as her religious prejudices, were aroused, and she returned him his letter without a word of comment. Both were stung to the quick. The lover, though he went to Edinburgh, left for the United States without calling to see her, and wandered away up the Missouri River. Mary grew thin and absent-minded; and exhibited all the symptoms of a maiden sick for love. Three years passed; Mary's friend had died; and she had returned to her father's, the while wasting away; when, lo, a package came from the far Western wilds, from Mary's lover.

He implored her to forgive him for his conduct to her, in the humblest terms; and in the strongest terms he expressed the endurance of his passionate love. He stated that he had thought of nothing else but Mary since he left Scotland; that knowing every Sunday that she was worshipping in the Catholic Church, he went to one himself, that he might worship with her, and that he had become a Catholic, and sent her the antique cross she wore, in testimony of his love and of his faith. He furthermore told Mary that he was doing well in the New World; that if she said so, he would go for her, but that it would ruin his business (he was a true Scotchman); and he concluded by begging Mary to come to him. These immigrants were on the point of leaving Scotland; many of them were Mary's especial friends, and she determined to embark with them.

How I felt interested in that Scotch girl! In proud saloons since, in gay and wild Washington, I have many a time and oft felt all the impulses of my fitful and wayward nature aroused and concentrated to please some dark-eyed one from the sunny South, or some fair descendant of the Puritans, or may be, some dame of high degree from over the waters, cynosures of fashion in the capital; but remember I not women yet, who more struck my fancy than this bonnie lassie from the land of Burns. She could tell me so many things traditional in Ayrshire about Burns and his birthplace; and then she admired him so much, and could sing his songs so well. We had a long passage, and she kept herself aloof from the other passengers; I was all day and half the night by her side. She half made me a Catholic. I have since with uncertain steps and some short-comings, been trying to fix my conduct where my firm faith, and hope, and heart are fixed, in the simpler ways of Protestantism; and I know that Mary will think none the less of me when she sees this avowal; but then I was careless of everything but the enjoyment of the hour that was passing over me. It was just this time of the year (May), and the beautiful Ohio never was more beautiful. How many simple and frank questions she asked me! And as she did not know that I knew her secret, I could so plainly trace in all her thoughts the image of her lover the controlling one, as the bright moon above us was the controlling light. Several times, when she knew not that I observed her, I witnessed her devotions; and I thought, as I saw her clasp the crucifix, her lover's gift, and pray, that some earthly adoration mingled with her heavenly vows.

One day, as we sat chatting together with more than usual unreservedness, I observed—

"Well, you will soon marry some rich American."

"No," she instantly replied; "I prefer a

poor Scotchman." I must have felt a pang of jealousy of her lover at the time, for I remarked:

"Mary, you have asked me what I thought was the difference between a Scotch woman and an American; I will tell you: an American would make her lover come to her; a Scotch woman, as you know, would come to her lover."

Her brow and bosom crimsoned in an instant, and rising from my side, she looked at me and said:

"Sir, you have no right so to wound a lonely woman's heart," and bursting into tears, she walked away from me.

Whatever may have been my misunderstandings with men, and they have been few, I certainly never had one with a woman; and my uncourteous and uncalled for remark stung my own pride as a gentleman, as much as I had wounded Mary's womanly nature. I instantly followed her, and used every effort to reconcile her, but without effect. She walked away from me with a haughty inclination of the head, and entered her humble apartment.

I learned that one of her chief objections to her voyage, was this coming to her lover, instead of with him. Her refined education had taught her this refinement of womanly delicacy. I could not forgive myself for the wound I had inflicted on Mary's feelings, and I soon began to feel that I should not forgive her for her want of forgiveness.

At last we approached a point, not far below St. Louis, near by Jefferson Barracks, where the Scotch immigrants were to debark, and they were all bustle and preparation. I sat smoking a cigar on the guards, and watching them. Mary, in the certainty of meeting her lover, was, with a natural anxiety, practising all the arts of the toilet to make her scanty wardrobe do its best. I could see her arranging her hair and shawl, and consulting one of the Scotch girls as to their adjustment, whose opinion, but for her own anxiety, she would have disregarded. Doubtless, she often thought, years may have changed me much; and he, how he will be disappointed! She may have fancied that her very education, which gave her a different air and manner from what she had when he wooed her, might make an unfavorable impression upon him.

I never in my life thought I could easier read a woman's feelings.

At last we reached the point of the pilgrims' rest, and the boat rounded to; but, when they landed, Mary's lover was not there! She seemed stupefied; and the others were so busied with themselves and their own concerns, that they thought not of Mary or her lover.

She took a seat on her trunk on the shore amidst the baggage, which the immigrants were getting off, and looked the very picture of despair, as, with her hands clasped in her lap, she gazed now here, now there, as if she thought that from some point or other he must come. But he came not.

My provocation at Mary for her unforgiveness was gone. I arose from the guards of the boat, threw my cigar overboard, and went ashore. I had often been at this point on pleasure excursions from St. Louis, and I saw several persons that I knew. I went up to a young Frenchman, whose employment was carting wood to St. Louis, and after a profusion of compliments between us, for he was an old acquaintance, I asked him if he knew a Scotchman named M'Clung, a miller, in the neighborhood?

"Well, monsieur—ah, well."

"How far from here does he live?" I asked.

"Ah, about two mile."

"I will give you a five dollar gold piece, if you will mount a fleet horse and go to him, and tell him that the Scotch immigrants have arrived," and I showed the glittering coin.

"*Instanter*, monsieur," he replied, with a dancing eye.

"Stop!" I exclaimed; and taking one of my cards from my pocket, I wrote on it with pen and ink, which he got for me from the boat, the simple words, "Mary M'Intyre has arrived."

I saw my Frenchman in a few minutes more at

the top of his speed, on a Canadian pony, dashing like mad through the woods. As I walked towards the boat, I met Mary's eye; but she instantly averted it, as if she thought I was taking pleasure in her grief at not finding on the spot, to welcome her, the lover she had "come to." What strange creatures we are! I felt a proud thrill through my heart. No, my bonnie lassie, thought I, I'll have a braver revenge upon you than that; you *shall* forgive me.

Time flew on—the baggage was all landed; we were preparing to depart, when some one exclaimed—

"Look yonder! there's some chaps coming to the boat, or else they're racing it, for they've got all steam on."

We looked, and, sure enough, two horsemen were bounding towards us, as if with such intent, and one was my Frenchman, so I supposed, the other was M'Clung; and I soon knew it, for I could see his miller's clothes.

The whole boat was excitement, and the captain ordered delay for a moment till they should arrive, not knowing what their eager haste meant. I understood it; M'Clung was thinking of his Mary M'Intyre, and the Frenchman of his five dollar gold piece.

"They come on bravely," was the cry.

"Yes, and the miller is ahead!" exclaimed another.

I was glad to see love ahead of avarice ; but I suspect it was owing more to the steeds than their riders.

I looked at Mary. At the cry "the miller is ahead," she had risen from her listless posture, and was gazing intently at the horsemen.

In a moment, the miller's horse was bounding home without his rider, for he had not thought to fasten him as he threw himself from his back. He rushed towards Mary, and in an instant they were in each other's arms; such a wild embrace of joy I never witnessed. I thought their kindred hearts, like the "kindred drops" of the poet, would literally mingle into one.

"Ah, mon dieu!" exclaimed the Frenchman from the shore, for the captain had ordered our departure, mad at the delay, and we had left—"Ah, mon dieu! my five dollar, dat gold piece. I am a cheat." I stuck it in an apple, and threw it on the shore, and had the satisfaction of seeing the Frenchman bound towards it like the miller toward Mary, and grasp it, too; and I laughed heartily at the manner—so eager, and yet so gentle, holding it between his compressed legs—in which he made the golden pippin disgorge its truly golden treasure.

The last thing which attracted my attention on

the shore was the Frenchman, who stood beside Mary and the miller, with one hand restoring the gold piece to its lustre by rubbing it on his pantaloons, and in the other holding the pippin, from which he was taking large contributions, while he gesticulated with that member, when not applied to his mouth, towards the steamer, evidently trying to do a good many things at once, and among the rest to explain who sent him on his errand.

Ah, thought I, I have had my revenge. Years after this, I was again in St. Louis, in a very sickly summer. Partaking, may be, too freely of its hospitalities—for I never saw a more hospitable people than those of St. Louis—and not being used to the climate, I was seized with a bilious fever, in fact, it was yellow fever; I was in a boarding-house, and in a very confined room, and the physician said if I could not be taken to the country, I would die.

I became unconscious. I awoke one morning at last, with a dreamy impression of existence, but I had not the slightest conception of my location. I discovered that I was in the country; and as, in the progress of days, returning life grew keener, I found myself in a pleasant chamber, and a lady attending to me. She would not let me talk at first, but I at last learned that I had been there a week, delirious; and, farther, from a black servant, that her mistress had, without taking off her clothes, watched over me all the time. I was about questioning the black girl farther, when, from a moment's absence, her mistress returned; and after remarking how much better I was, asked if I did not know her? I looked at the beautiful lady before me, for she was indeed beautiful, though she looked wan, from her attendance upon me, I supposed, and replied—

"Indeed, my dear madam, I do not know you, though I shall never forget you."

She stepped to the mantle-piece, and took from it a small richly gilt frame, which looked as if it contained a miniature, and showing it to me, I beheld within it my card, given to the Frenchman: "Mary M'Intyre has arrived." Mr. M'Clung had greatly prospered in the world, and Mrs. M'Clung was what she would have been, in fact, in any situation, a lady in the land; and now an acknowledged and received lady. She seldom visited St. Louis, and when she did, she stopped at the house where I was so ill; and hearing my name mentioned, and learning who I was, she had me conveyed to her house in her own carriage, supporting my unconscious head all the way herself. Lucky for me was this last arrival.

I may speak again of this Scotch lassie, for we have met in other scenes, where, beaming the "bright particular star," fashion, and rank, and intellect did her homage.

THE UNSUMMONED WITNESS.

PART FIRST.

SOME years since, when I was in the practice of the law, one morning, just after I had entered my office—I was then an invalid on two crutches, and not a very early riser, so what clients I had, were often there before me—some few moments after I had ensconced myself in my chair with my crutches before me, like monitors of mortality, I heard a timid rap at my door. Notwithstanding I called out in a loud voice, "Come in," the visitor, though the rap was not repeated after I spoke, still hung back. With feelings of impatience and pain, I arose, adjusted my crutches under my arms, and muttering, not inaudibly, my discontent, I hobbled to the door and jerked it open.

The moment the visitor was presented to my vision, I felt angry with myself for what I had done; and the feeling was not relieved, when a meek and grief-subdued voice said—

"I am very sorry to disturb you, sir."

"No," said I politely, for it was a young and beautiful woman, or rather girl, of certainly not more than sixteen, who stood before me, "I am sorry that you should have waited so long. Come in; I am lame as you see, Miss, and could not sooner get to the door."

Adjusting her shawl, which was pinned closely up to her neck, as she passed the threshold, she entered, and at my request, but not until I had myself resumed my seat, took a chair. I observed it was a fine morning, to which she made no reply, for she was evidently abstracted, or rather embarrassed, not knowing how to open the purpose of her visit.

The few moments we sat in silence, I occupied in observing her. She had, I thought, arrayed herself in her best clothes, anxious by so doing to make a respectable appearance before her lawyer, and thereby convince him that if she could not at present compass his fee, he could have no doubt of it eventually; though it was also apparent to me that, in the flurry of mind attendant upon her visit and its consequence, she had not thought at all of adding to her personal attractions by so doing. That consideration, not often absent from a woman's mind, had by some absorbing event been banished from hers. She wore a black-silk gown, the better days of which had gone, perhaps, with the wearer's.

Her timid step had not prevented my seeing a remarkably delicate foot, encased in a morocco shoe much worn and patched, evidently by an unskilful hand—I thought her own. And though when she took a seat, she folded her arms closely up under her shawl, which was a small one, of red merino, and, as I have said, pinned closely to her neck, it did not prevent my observing that her hand, though small, was gloveless, and that a ring—I thought an ominous-looking ring—we catch fancies we know not why or wherefore—begirt one of her fingers. In fact, when she first placed her hands under the shawl, she turned the ring upon her finger, maybe unconsciously.

On her head she wore a calash bonnet; and as I again interrupted the silence by asking, "Is it the law you seek so early, Miss?" she drew her hand from beneath her shawl, and removing her bonnet partly from her face so as to answer me, she revealed as fair and as fascinating features as I ever remember to have seen. Her hair was parted carelessly back over a snowy forehead, beneath which, lustrous eyes, black as death and almost as melancholy, looked forth from the shadow of a weeping willow-like lash. A faint attempt to smile at my question discovered beautiful teeth, and I thought, as she said the simple "yes, sir," that there must be expression in every movement of her lip.

Observe, I was an invalid, full, at this very moment, of the selfishness of my own pains and aches, which, though not of the heart, and it would be difficult to convince a sick man that those of the body are not greater, were notwithstanding forgotten at once in my interest in my visitor.

"This is Mr. Trimble?" asked she, glancing at my crutches, as if by those appendages she had heard me described.

"That is my name," I replied.

"You have heard of Brown, who is now in—in jail, sir," she continued.

"Brown, the counterfeiter, who has been arrested for a theft," I asked.

"Yes, sir."

"I have repeatedly heard of him, though I have never seen him."

"He told me to say, sir, wouldn't you go to jail, and see him about his case?"

Brown's case, from what I had heard of it, was a desperate one. Not knowing in what relation the poor girl might stand to him, I shrank from saying so, though I feared it would be useless for me to appear for him: I therefore asked her—

"Are you his sister?"

"No, sir."

"His wife?"

"No, sir, we are cousins like, and I live with his mother."

"Ay, is your name Brown?"

"No, sir, my name is Mason—Sarah Mason."

"Where's Mrs. Brown, Miss Sarah?" I asked.

"She's very sick, sir; I hurried away just as she got to sleep, after morning; I have walked by here very often, and I thought, sir, you might have business out, and not be here to-day—do go and see him, sir."

"Why, Sarah, to speak plainly to you, I am satisfied I can be of no service to him; he is a notorious character, and there have been so many outrageous offences lately committed, that if the case is a strong one, there will be little hope for the prisoner; and Brown's case, I understand, is very strong. I am told, that after they had caught him in the woods, as they were bringing him to the city, he confessed it."

"My! my! did he, sir;" exclaimed Sarah, starting from her seat and resuming it as quickly.

"Yes, I think I overheard one of the constables say so. There are no grounds whatever in the case for me to defend him upon. I can do nothing for him, and should get nothing for it if I did."

I said this without meaning any hint to Sarah; but she took it as such, and replied—

"I have some little money, sir, only a few dollars now," and she turned herself aside so as with delicacy to take it from her bosom, "but I shall have some more soon; I had some owing to me for some fancy work, but, when I went for it yesterday, to come and see you, they told me the storekeeper had failed, and I've lost it."

As she spoke, she held the money in her hand, which she rested in her lap, in a manner that implied she wished to offer it to me, but feared the sum would be too small, and a blush—it was that of shame at her bitter poverty—reddened her forehead. I could not but be struck with her manner; and as I looked at her without speaking or attempting to take the money, she said, after a moment's pause—

"It's all I have now, sir; but, indeed, I shall have more soon."

"No, no, keep it, I do not want it," said I, smiling. Instantly the thought seemed to occur to her, that I would not accept the money from a doubt of its genuineness, as Brown might have given it to her, and she said—

"Indeed, sir, it is good money. Mr. Judah, who keeps the clothing-store, gave it to me last night. You may ask him, sir, if you don't believe it."

"Don't believe you! Surely I believe you. Brown must be a greater scoundrel than even the public take him for, if he could involve you in the consequences of his guilt."

"Sir, sir—indeed, he never gave me any bad money to pass. I was accused of it; but, indeed, I never passed a single cent that I thought was bad."

"Well, Sarah, keep the money; do not for your own sake, on any consideration, pass any bad money; go first and ask some one who knows whether any money you have is good, and keep that."

"But, sir, will you see him?" asked she imploringly.

"Yes, I will, and because you wish it; I cannot go this morning, I shall be engaged. This afternoon I have some business at the court-house, and I will, on leaving there, step over to the jail."

"Please, sir, to tell him," she said, hesitatingly, "that they won't let me come in to see him often. I was there yesterday, but they wouldn't let me in. On Sunday they said they would—not till Sunday. Please, sir, tell him that I will come then."

"I will, Sarah," I replied; "and if you will be at the jail at two o'clock this afternoon, I will contrive to have you see Brown."

She thanked me, repeated the words "at two o'clock," and again pressed the money on me, which I refused, when she withdrew, closing the door noiselessly after her.

She had not been gone more than half an hour,

when a gentleman entered, who was about purchasing some property, and who wished me, previously to closing the bargain, to examine the title. He wanted it done immediately, and in compliance with his request I forthwith repaired to the recorder's office, which stood beside the court-house.

I was then in the practice of the law in Cincinnati. My office was two doors from the corner of Main street, in Front, opposite the river, where I combined the double duties of editor of a daily paper and lawyer. From my office to the court-house was, as the common people say, a "measured mile;" and nothing but the certainty of the immediate payment of my fee, in the then condition of my arms and health *versus* pocket (the pocket carried the day, and it is only in such cases that empty pockets succeed), nothing but the consideration in the premises induced me to take up my crutches, and walk to the court-house. After I had examined the title, I determined, as it would save me a walk in the afternoon, to step over to the jail, which was only a square or so off, and see Brown. I did so, and at the gate of the jail found, seated on a stone by the wayside, Sarah Mason, who had instantly repaired thither from my office, resolved to wait my coming, not knowing, as she told me, but what I might be there before two.

I entered the jailer's room, in which he received constables, visitors, knaves, previous to locking them up, lawyers, &c., and handing a chair to Sarah, desired him to bring Brown out in the jail yard, that I might speak with him. While he was unlocking the grated door of the room in which Brown with many other criminals was confined, several of them, who were also clients of mine, called me by name, and made towards the door, with the wish each of speaking to me about his own case, perhaps for the fifteenth time. As soon as Brown heard my name, he called out—

"Stop! it's to see me Mr. Trimble has come; here, Jawbone Dick, fix that bit of a blanket round them rusty leg-irons, and let me shuffle out. Mr. Trimble came to see me." Controlled by his manner—for he was a master spirit among them, as I afterwards learned—they shrank back, while Jawbone Dick, a huge negro, fixed the leg-irons, and Brown came forth.

He had a muscular iron form of fine proportions, though of short stature. His face was intellectual, with a high but retreating forehead, and a quick, bold eye. His mouth was very large, displaying fully, when he laughed, his jaw-teeth; but it was not ill-shaped, and had the expression of great firmness, when in repose, with that of archness and insinuation, generally, when speaking. He gazed on me steadily for an instant, after he had passed the threshold of the door into the passage, as if he would understand my character before he spoke. He then saluted me respectfully, and led the way into the backyard of the jail, which is surrounded by a large wall, to prevent the escape of the prisoners, who, at stated periods, are suffered to be out there for the sake of their health, and while their rooms are undergoing the operations of brooms and water. Kicking, as well as his fetters would allow him, a keg that stood by the outer door into the middle of the yard, Brown observed—

"Squire, it will do you for a seat, for you and I don't like to talk too near to the wall; the proverb says, that 'stone walls have ears,' and those about us have heard so many rascally confessions from the knaves they have inclosed, that I don't like to intrust them with even an innocent man's story; 'twould be the first time they've heard such a one, and they'd misrepresent it into guilt."

The jailer laughed as he turned to leave us, and said—

"Brown, you ought to have thought of that when the chaps nabbed you, for you told them the story, and they not only have ears but tongues."

"Hang them, they gave me liquor," exclaimed Brown, as a fierce expression darkened his face. "I don't think a drunken man's confession should be taken, extorted or not."

As the jailer turned to lock up the yard, with the remark to me of, "Squire, you can rap when you have got through," I told him that it would save some trouble to him if he would let the girl in his room, who was a relation of Brown's, see him now. After a slight hesitancy he called her, observing it was not exactly according to rule.

"It's Sarah, I suppose," said Brown, taking a station by my side with folded arms, and giving a slight nod of recognition to the girl, as in obedience to the jailer's call she entered the yard. "You'd better stand there, Sarah," he said to her, "till Mr. Trimble gets through with me. It's no use for her to hear our talk; plague take all witnesses, anyhow."

Eyeing me again with a searching expression, Brown, as if he had at last made his mind up to the matter, said, "I believe I'll tell you all, Squire; I did the thing."

"Yes, Brown, I knew you did," I replied; "the misfortune is you told it to the officers."

"Yes, that's a fact. But may be you can lead the witnesses on the wrong scent if you know just how things are, could'nt you?" I nodded, and he continued. "I boasted when they got me, considerable; but the fact is, that I got the money. I was in the Exchange on the landing, where I saw a countryman seated, who looked to me as if he had money. I contrived to get into conversation with him, and asked him to drink with me; he did so, and I plied him pretty strong. The liquor warmed him at last, and he asked me to drink with him; I consented, and when he came to pay his bill he had no change, and had to dive into a cunning side-pocket, in the lining of his waistcoat, to get out a bill, though he turned his back round and was pretty cautious. I saw he had a good deal of money. I got him boozy, and when he left I dogged him. He was in to market, and had his wagon on the landing not far from the Exchange. He slept in it. He not only buttoned his vest tight up, but his overcoat tight over that, and laid down on the side where he hid away his rhino. Notwithstanding this," continued Brown, and he laughed at the remembrance of his own ingenuity, "I contrived to make him turn over in his sleep, and cut clean out through overcoat and all, got his pocket, with its contents, three hundred dollars. I had spent all my money at night with him. In the morning my nerves wanted bracing, and what must I do but spend some of his money for grog and breakfast. The countryman immediately went before a magistrate and described me as a person whom he suspected. The officers knew me from his description; and though I had left Cincinnati and got as far as Cleves, fifteen or eighteen miles, they followed so close on my track as to nab me that very day. I had been keeping up the steam pretty high along the road; they traced me in that way, and full of folly and the devil, for the sake of talking and keeping off the horrors, I made my brags, and told all. I suppose my case is desperate."

I told him that I thought it was.

"When I think of my old mother!" exclaimed he, passing his hand rapidly across his brow; he then beckoned Sarah to him, and I walked to the farther end of the yard so as not to be a listener. Their colloquy was interrupted by the jailer coming to the door. When I left him, Sarah followed me out; and, after requesting me to call and see him again, she took a direction different from mine, and I went to my office.

The grand-jury, of course, had no difficulty in finding a bill against Brown, and the day of his trial soon came. The countryman was the first witness on the stand. It was amusing, if not edifying, to observe the smirk of *professional* pride on the countenance of the prisoner when the countryman recounted how he carefully buttoned up his coat over his money and went to sleep on that side, and awoke on that side, the right one, and found his pocket cut out with as much ingenuity as a tailor could have done it. I tried to exclude the evidence of Brown's confession from the jury on the ground that it was extorted from him; but that fact not appearing to the court, they overruled my objection; and the facts of the case, with many exaggerations, were narrated to them by the officer who arrested the prisoner, as his free and voluntary confession. I had scarcely any grounds of defence at all. I tried to ridicule the idea of Brown's having made a confession, and presented the countryman in an attitude that made him the laughing-stock of the jury and audience ; but, though it was evident to them that the countryman was a fool, it was not less apparent, I feared, that Brown was a knave. I had some idea of an *alibi*, but that would have been carrying matters too far. I, however, proved his good character by several witnesses. Alas! the prosecuting attorney showed that he was an old offender, who had been more than once a guest of the State's between the walls of the penitentiary. The prosecuting attorney, in fact, in his opening address to the court and jury, attacked Brown in the sternest language he could use. He represented him as the violator of every sound tie; and as hurrying his mother's gray hairs to the grave. At this last charge the prisoner winced. I saw the lightning of his ire against the prosecutor flash through the tears of guilt and contrition. When I arose to address the jury in reply, Brown called me to him and said—

"Mr. Trimble, you know all about my case—you know I am guilty; but you must get me off if you can, for my old mother's sake. Plead for me as if you were pleading for the apostles—for the Saviour of mankind."

This was a strong expression to convey to me the idea that I must speak and act to the jury as if I held him in my own heart guiltless, was it not?

Poor Sarah was a tearful witness of his trial. She was spared, however, being present when the verdict was rendered. The jury retired about dark, with the agreement between myself and the prosecutor that they might bring in a sealed verdict. I told Sarah, for the sake of her feelings, before the court adjourned, that they would not meet the next morning before ten o'clock. They met at nine, and before she got there, their verdict of guilty was recorded against the prisoner.

As they were taking Brown to jail, he asked me to step over and see him, saying that he had a fee for me. I had been unable to get from him more than a promise to pay before his trial. I, of course, gave that up as fruitless, and appeared for him on Sarah's account, not on his own, or with any hope of acquitting him. I therefore was surprised at his remark, and followed him to the jail. He was placed in a cell by himself—the rule after conviction—and I went in with him at his request, and we were left alone.

"Squire," said he, with more emotion than I thought him capable of, "I don't care so much for myself; I could stand it; I am almost guilt hardened—but when I think of my mother—O God! —and Sarah, she has been as true to me as if I were an angel instead of a devil; but she wasn't in court to-day?"

"No," said I; "I told her that court would not sit until ten o'clock. I saw how deeply she was interested, and I saved her the shock of hearing your guilt pronounced in open court."

"Blast that prosecuting attorney," exclaimed Brown, gnashing his teeth, "why need he go out of the case to abuse me about my mother, before Sarah. I'd like to catch him in the middle of the Ohio, swimming, some dark night; if he didn't go to the bottom and stay there, it would be because I couldn't keep him down. But, Squire, about that fee—you trusted me, and as you are the first lawyer that ever did, I'll show you that I am for once worthy of confidence. Over the Licking River, a quarter of a mile up on the Covington side —you know, Squire, the Licking is the river right opposite to Cincinnati, in Kentucky—well, over that river, a quarter of a mile up, you will see, about fifteen feet from the bank, a large tree standing by itself, with a large hole on the east side of it. Run your hand up that hole, and you will take hold of a black bottle, corked tight. Break it open; in it you will find fifteen hundred dollars—five hundred of it is counterfeit—the rest is good. Squire, it is your fee. Your character and countenance is good enough to pass the whole of it."

I bowed to the compliment which Brown paid

my "character and countenance" at the expense of my morals, and said, "You are not hoaxing me, I hope."

"I am not in that mood, Squire," replied the convict, and asking me for my pencil, he drew on the wall a rough map of the locality of the river and tree, and repeated earnestly the assertion that he himself, in the hollow of the tree, had hid the bottle. I left him, rubbing the marks of his map from the wall, determined at the first opportunity to make a visit to the spot. The next day my professional duties called me on a visit to another prisoner in the jail, when Brown asked me, through the little loophole of his door, if I had got *that* yet.

"No, Brown," I replied, "I have not had time to go there."

"Then, Squire," he exclaimed, "you are in as bad a fix as I am, and the thing's out."

"How so?" I asked; I began to suspect that he thought I had been after the money, and that he was forming some excuse for my not finding what he knew was not there.

"You see me, Squire, without a coat; my hat's gone too. Job Fowler, the scoundrel—he knows about that bottle—he was taken out of the jail yesterday to be tried, just as they brought me in. I thought, though my respectable clothes hadn't done me any good, they might be of service to him, as his case wasn't strong, and every little helps out in such cases, as they help the other way when the thing's dark; so I lent them to him. He was found not guilty, and he walked off with my wardrobe. So the jury, hang them, aided and abetted him in committing a felony in the very act of acquitting him for one; and by this time he's got that money. Never mind, we shall be the State's guests together yet, in her palace at Columbus."

What Brown told me in regard to the bottle and Job Fowler, was indeed true.

Job was acquitted in Brown's clothes, and walked off in them, and wended instantly to the tree beside the Licking, where he found the bottle, which he rifled of its contents without the trouble of uncorking it. Mistaking the bad money for the good, he returned instantly to Cincinnati, and attempted to pass some of it. The man to whom he offered it happened to be in the court-house, a spectator of his trial. His suspicions were aroused. He had Mr. Job arrested, and on him was found the fifteen hundred dollars. A thousand dollars of it was good, but I got none of it; for the gentleman from whom Brown and Fowler together had stolen it was found.

The very day that Brown was convicted, and Job acquitted in the former's clothes, he was arrested for passing counterfeit money. A bill was found against him that morning. He was tried that afternoon and convicted, and the day after, he and

Brown, handcuffed together, were conveyed to the penitentiary.

PART SECOND.

THE interest which I took in Brown's mother and Sarah, induced me to visit them after he was sent to the penitentiary, to which he was sentenced for ten years.

His afflicted mother, overcome by accumulated sorrow for his many crimes and their consequences, rapidly sank into the grave. I happened to call at her humble dwelling the night she died. Sarah supported her by her needle, and a hard task it was; for the doctor's bill and the little luxuries which her relative needed, more than consumed her hard earnings.

The old woman called me to her bedside, and together with Sarah, made me promise that if I saw her son again, I would tell him that with her dying breath she prayed for him. The promise was made; and while she was in the act of praying, her voice grew inaudible; and, uttering with her last feeble breath an ejaculation for mercy, not for herself, but for her outcast child, her spirit passed to the judgment-seat; and if memory and affection hold sway in the disembodied soul, doubtless she will be a suppliant there for him, as she was here.

After the death of the old woman, I saw Sarah once or twice, and then suddenly lost all trace of her. More than a year had now elapsed since Brown's conviction, and in increasing ill health and the presence of other scenes and circumstances, as touching as those of the mother and cousin, I had forgotten them. I was advised by my physician to forsake all business, obtain a vehicle, and by easy stages, travelling whither fancy led, try to resuscitate my system. In fulfilment of this advice, I was proceeding on my way to Columbus, Ohio, with the double purpose of improving my health, and, by making acquaintances in the State where I had settled, facilitate and increase my practice, should I ever be permitted to resume my profession.

The sun was just setting in a summer's evening, as, within a half a mile of Columbus, I passed a finely formed female on the road, who was stepping along with a bundle on her arm. There was something of interest in the appearance of the girl which caused me to look back at her after I had passed. Instantly I drew up my horse. It was Sarah Mason. Her meeting with me seemed to give her great pleasure. I asked her if she would not ride, and thanking me, she entered my vehicle and took a seat by my side.

She had been very anxious to obtain a pardon for Brown before his mother's death. I had told her it would be fruitless, unless she could get the jury who condemned him, together with the judges, to sign the recommendation to the governor, and I did not believe they would do it. I, however, at her earnest solicitation, drew up the petition, and when I last asked her about her success, which was, in fact, the last time I saw her, she told me she had not got one of the jury to sign it, but that several had told her that they would do so, if she would obtain previously the signature of the presiding judge. By the law of Ohio a judgeship is not held for life, but for a term of years. The term of office of the presiding judge on Brown's trial had expired, and a new party prevailing in the Legislature, from that which had appointed him, he had failed to obtain the reappointment. He had removed to St. Louis for the purpose of practising law there; and thither Sarah had repaired with her unsigned petition. After repeated solicitations and prayerful entreaties, she at last prevailed on the ex-judge to sign it. She then returned to Cincinnati, and after considerable trouble succeeded in finding ten of the jury, some of whom followed the judge's example. The rest refused, stating, what was too true, that the ease with which criminals obtained pardon from gubernatorial clemency in this country, was one of the great causes of the frequency of crime; for it removed the certainty of punishment which should ever follow conviction; and which has more effect upon the mind than severity itself, when there is a hope of escaping it.

A new governor, in the rapid mutations of official life in the United States, had become dispenser of the pardoning power shortly after Brown's conviction, and it was his ear that Sarah personally sought, armed with the recommendation.

He was a good, easy man, where party influence was not brought to bear adversely on him, and after he had read the petition, Sarah's entreaty soon prevailed, and Brown was pardoned.

The very day he was pardoned he called on me at Russel's hotel, with his cousin; and after they had mutually returned me their thanks for the interest which I took in their behalf, he promised me, voluntarily, to pay me a fee with the first earnings he got, which he said solemnly should be from the fruits of honest industry.

He took my address and departed. I thought no more of it till, one day, most opportunely, I received through the post-office a two hundred dollar bill of the United States Bank, with a well-written letter from him, stating that he had reformed his course of life, and that it was through the influence of his cousin, whom he had married, that he had done so. He said that he had assumed another name in the place where he then dwelt, which he would have no objection to communicate to myself; but, as it was of no consequence to me, and might be to him, should my letter fall into the hands of another person, he had withheld it, together with the name of the place where himself and wife were located. The letter had been dropped in the Cincinnati post-office, and there was no clue whereby I could have traced him, had I entertained such a wish, which I did not.

Some time after this, I was a sojourner in the South, spellbound by the fascinations of a lady, with whom I became acquainted the previous summer in Philadelphia, where she was spending the sultry season. She lived with her parents, on a plantation near a certain city on the Mississippi, which, for peculiar reasons, I may not name. Her brother was practising law there, and he and I became close cronies. Frequently, I rode to the city with him; and, on one occasion, we were both surprised, as we entered it, by an unusual commotion among the inhabitants, who were concentrating in crowds to the spot, collected by some strange and boisterous attraction.

My friend rode into the *mêlée*, and presently returned to my side, with the crowd about him, from whom he was evidently protecting a man, who walked with his hand on the neck of my friend's horse. The man walked as if he felt that he was protected, but would die game if he were attacked.

"Sheriff," called out my friend to a tall person who was expostulating with the crowd, "it is your duty to protect Bassford; he has lived here with us some time, has a wife and family, a good name, and he must and shall have a fair trial."

"Colonel Cameron's empty pocketbook was found near Bassford's house," exclaimed one of the crowd, "and Bassford's dagger by the dead body."

"And Bassford and the Colonel were overheard quarrelling a few hours before he was killed," shouted another.

"Let Bassford answer, then, according to law," said my friend. "I will kill the first man who lays violent hands upon him."

"And I will justify and assist you," said the sheriff. "Mr. Leo, Mr. Gale, and you, sir," continued the officer, turning to me, "I summon you to assist me in lodging this man safely in jail, there to abide the laws of his country."

Awed by the resolution which the sheriff and his *posse* exhibited, the crowd slunk back, but with deep mutterings of wrath, while we gathered around Bassford, and hastened with him to the jail, which was not far off, in which we soon safely lodged him.

It occurred to me, when I first looked on Bassford, that I had seen him before, but I could not tell where. A minuter scrutiny, as I stood by his side in the jail, satisfied me that he was no other than my old client, Brown. Feeling that my recognition of him would not advance his interests, if I should be questioned about him, I maintained silence, and stood by a spectator. Brown stated to the sheriff that he wished my friend, whom I will call De Berry, to be his counsel, and requested that he might be placed alone with him, where he might have some private conversation with him. The sheriff said, "certainly;" and we all retired, De Berry asking me to wait for him without. I did so; and, in a few minutes, he came to me, and said that the prisoner wished to see me. "I presume, sheriff, you will have no objection?"

"Not the least," replied the sheriff. "Take Mr. Trimble in with you."

I accordingly entered; and, the moment the door was closed, Brown asked me if I remembered him.

"Perfectly," I replied.

"Mr. Trimble," he continued, "I saw you with Mr. De Berry, and knew that you recognized me. I supposed that you might tell him what you knew of me, to my prejudice. Here I have maintained a good character, and I therefore resolved to see you with him, and tell you the circumstances. I am as guiltless now as I was guilty then.

"Mr. De Berry says that the court, upon application, will admit you, if it is necessary, to defend me with him, and I wish you would do it. Let me tell you this affair. I know it looks black against me, but hear me first. After my cousin obtained my pardon in Ohio, I married her, swore an oath to lead a better life, and, before God, have done so. Sarah was and is everything to me. Not for the wealth of worlds would I involve myself in guilt which might fall upon her and her children. Knowing, Mr. Trimble, that in Ohio I could not obtain employment, or reinstate myself in character, I came here, with a changed name and nature, to commence, as it were, the world again. Since I have been here, my character, as Mr. De Berry will tell you, has been without reproach. But, old associations and companions dog us, though we fly from them. I have been located here on a little farm belonging to Mr. De Berry, which, with the aid of two negroes hired from him, I cultivate, raising vegetables and such things for the market. I had hoped the past was with the past, but last week there came along one of my old associates, who urged me to join with him and others in a certain depredation. I told him of my altered life, and positively refused. He insisted, and taunted me with hypocrisy, and so forth, till he nearly stung me to madness. I bore it all, until, on my telling him that my wife had reformed me, and that on her account I meant to be honest, he threw slurs on her of the blackest dye. I could bear it no longer, but leaped upon him, and would have slain him, had not some of his companions came up and rescued him. It was on the banks of the river, in a lonely spot that we met, and their coming up might have been accident or not. He vowed vengeance against me and mine, and left. Colonel Cameron, as you know, Mr. De Berry, bore the character of an overbearing and tyrannical man. We had some dealings together. He was in my debt, and wished to pay me in flour. I told him politely it was the money which I wanted. He swore that I should not have money or flour either. He raised his whip to strike me. I flew into a passion, dared him to lay the weight of his finger on me, and abused him, as a man in a passion and injured would do under the circumstances; perhaps I threatened him; I do not know exactly what I said in my anger. This was yesterday afternoon. It seems that the Colonel went to Mr. Pottea's afterwards, returned after night, was waylaid, and killed. How his pocketbook came by my house, I know not. As for the dagger, I had such a one. When I changed my name I thought, to make everything about me seem natural with it, that I would have Bassford engraved on it. I lost it some months ago, and have not seen it since, till to-day. Such, gentlemen, is the truth; but, great God! what is to become of myself and family, with such testimony against me? Two or three men in the crowd called out that they knew me before, that I had been in the Ohio penitentiary, that my name is Brown; and here is my quarrel with the Colonel, his murder on the heels of it, my dagger by his dead body, and his empty pocketbook by my house. Notwithstanding all this, gentlemen, I am innocent. Do you think that, if I had murdered him, I would not have hid my dagger? and would I have rifled his pocketbook and pitched it away by my own door-sill, where anybody might find it? No; my enemy must have contrived this to ruin me."

At this instant the door was opened by the sheriff, and Brown's wife admitted; she threw herself into his arms, exclaiming, "He is innocent, I know he is innocent!" while Brown, utterly overcome by his emotions, pressed her to his heart, and wept bitterly. I whispered to De Berry that we had better leave them, and accordingly withdrew.

That afternoon, Mrs. Brown called to see me. She asked me if I would aid her husband; and I promised that I would. She looked neat and tidy, said she had two children, and I saw that she was soon again to be a mother. She told me the same story that Brown had told me, and I could not but express the deepest regret for his and her situation.

The name of Brown's former accomplice, with

whom he had quarrelled, was Burnham. He was a desperate character, perfectly unfeeling and unprincipled, and possessed of great energy of spirit and frame. It is surprising that Brown should have overcome him. Brown's mastery originated, doubtless, in the fury of his insulted feelings.

De Berry became very much interested in Brown's case. The morning of his interference in his behalf, Brown had been taken upon the charge of murdering Colonel Cameron. While the sheriff, who was well-disposed towards him, was proceeding with him to the magistrate's, the crowd had gathered round them so thickly as to interrupt their progress, and Brown had been separated from the officer. The crowd, among whose leaders was Burnham, had made furious demonstrations against the prisoner; but his resolute manner had prevented their laying hands on him, when De Berry and myself rode up, and the sheriff, as we have related, took his charge to jail, to prevent an outrage, until the excitement had somewhat subsided.

The next morning De Berry insisted upon having a hearing before the magistrate, asserting that he meant to offer bail for Brown. As we proceeded to the magistrate's, we stopped at Brown's humble dwelling, and took his wife and children with us. The tidiness of his afflicted wife and children, and the evident order of his household and garden, made a most favorable impression upon us.

As we approached the magistrate's, we wondered that we saw nobody about the door of his office; but we learned, on arriving, that the officer of the law had determined to have the hearing in the court-house, in consequence of the anticipation of a great crowd, who would be anxious to hear. To the court we repaired. There was an immense concourse about the door, though the sheriff had not yet appeared with his charge. De Berry sent the wife and children to the jail, that they might come with him to the court-house, and by their presence and the sympathy that they would excite, prevent any outbreak from the mob. We took our station on the court-house steps, where, elevated above the crowd, we could observe their demeanor as the sheriff and Brown advanced. By our side stood a tall gaunt Kentuckian, clad in a hunting-shirt, and leaning on his rifle. He seemed to be an anxious observer of myself and friend. He soon gathered from our conversation the position in which we stood towards Brown, and remarked to us—

"Strangers, I suppose you are lawyers for Bassford; I am glad he has help, I fear he'll need it; but he once did me a service, and I want to see right 'twixt man and man."

Before De Berry could reply, we were attracted

by a stir among the crowd, and not far off, in the direction of the jail, we saw the sheriff advancing with the prisoner, who was accompanied by his wife and children. Approaching close behind them, were several horsemen, among whom we could not fail to observe Burnham, from the eagerness with which he pressed forward.

With not so much as the ordinary bustle and confusion incident upon such occasions, in fact, with less expressed emotion, the crowd gathered into the court-house, the squire occupying the seat of the judge, and the prisoner a chair within the bar, by the side of De Berry and myself, with his anxious wife to his right. The prosecuting attorney, who was a warm friend of the deceased colonel, seated himself opposite to us. Burnham pressed through the crowd within the bar, and stationed himself near the prosecutor, to whom I overheard him say—

"There are folks here who can prove that his real name is not Bassford but Brown, and that he was pardoned out of the Ohio Penitentiary; that man, by his lawyer, can prove it, so can I; but you had better call him, he knows—"

"Let me pass, let me pass!" exclaimed a female at this moment, pressing through the crowd with stern energy; "I'll tell the truth; Bassford is innocent!"

"She's crazy," exclaimed Burnham, looking

around with alarm, and making a threatening gesture, as if privately to her, to hush, forgetting that the eyes of all were upon him.

"Crazy!" retorted the woman, who was of slender person and fine features, though they were distorted by excess and passion, and who seemed to be possessed by some furious purpose, as if by a fiend. "They shall judge if I am crazy. Prove it, and then you may prove that Bassford is guilty. Gentlemen, John Burnham there, murdered Colonel Cameron! There is the money that Burnham took from the dead body; there are the letters, here is his watch! Bassford's dagger he got in a quarrel with him; he murdered the colonel with it, and left it by the dead body, and the pocketbook by Bassford's house, to throw the guilt on him!"

"How can you prove this, good woman?" inquired the magistrate, while the crowd, in breathless eagerness, were as hushed as death.

"Prove it! By myself, by these letters, by that watch, by that dagger, by everything—by what I am, by what I was! The time has been when I was as innocent as I am now vicious—as spotless as I am now abandoned; but for that man, that time were now. Hear me for a moment; the truth that is in me shall strike your hearts with justice and with terror; shall acquit the innocent, and appal the guilty. In better days I knew both these men; Bassford I loved, he loved me. My education had been good; that was all my parents left me, with a good name. He was thoughtless and wild then, but not criminal; he fell in with this man, Burnham, whom he brought to my father's house, and made his confidant. Burnham professed a partiality for me, which I rejected with scorn. He led Bassford into error, into crime. He coiled himself into his confidence, and made him believe that I had abandoned myself to him; at the same time he was torturing me with inventions of Bassford's faithlessness towards me. Each of us, Bassford and myself, grew reserved towards the other, without asking or making any explanation. Oh! the curse of this pride—this pride! Burnham widened the breach! He drove me nearly mad with jealousy, and Bassford with distrust. Bassford and I parted in anger. Burnham all the while pressed his passion on me. Bassford left that part of the country, Hagerstown, Maryland. I promised to marry Burnham; in a spell of sickness, which fell upon me in the absence of Bassford, he drugged me with opium, made me what I am, and abandoned me to my fate. After many wretched years of ignominy and shame, I fell in at Louisville, three weeks since, with Burnham; I came here with him. He saw Bassford—tried to draw him into his guilty plots—they quarrelled; and he—he never, never told me aught until he had done the deed; he murdered Colonel Cameron to ruin Bassford; and there, I repeat it," pointing to the watch, the money, and the letters of the deceased, "there are the evidences of his guilt."

"Sheriff," said the magistrate, "take Burnham into your custody."

"Kill him!" cried out an hundred voices from the crowd, while several attempted to seize him. Uttering a yell like a wild Indian at bay, Burnham eluded their grasp, and drawing at the same instant a bowie-knife from his breast, he darted forward and plunged it into the heart of the woman. The crowd shrank back in terror as the death-cry of the victim broke upon their ear; while the murderer brandished the bloody knife over his head, and, before any one could arrest him, sprang out of one of the windows of the court-room. It was a leap which none chose to follow; and all rushed instantaneously to the door. Before the crowd got out, Burnham had mounted his horse, and made for the woods. Several of the horsemen, who had come in the line, mounted and darted after, as if to take him.

"They want to save him," exclaimed several, who were also mounting other horses that stood by.

"Clear the road!" shouted the Kentuckian, who, rifle in hand, had sprang upon a mound, within a few feet of the court-house. The horsemen looked fearfully back, as if instinctively they understood the purpose of the hunter, and spurred their horses from the track of the flying man. The Kentuckian raised his rifle to his shoulder; instantly its sharp report was heard. All eyes were turned to the murderer, who was urging his steed to the utmost. He started, as if in renewed energy, then reeled to and fro like a drunken man, then fell upon the neck of his horse, at the mane of which he seemed to grasp blindly; in a moment more he tumbled to the earth like a dead weight. He was dragged, with his foot in the stirrup, nearly a mile before his horse was overtaken and stopped. The bullet of the sure-sighted Kentuckian had lodged in the murderer's brain. He had fallen dead from his saddle, and was so disfigured as scarcely to be recognized. The body was consigned to a prayerless, hurried, and undistinguished grave by the roadside.

Brown is still alive, where I left him, an entirely reformed and honest man. A stone slab, with some rude attempts at sculpture on it, at the foot of Brown's garden, designates the mortal resting-place of the woman, who, though fallen and degraded, was true to her first affection, and braved death to save him. His children, with holy gratitude, have kept the weeds from growing there, and ever, in their play, become silent when they approach it.

LIFE IN WASHINGTON;

SHOWING HOW

MR. THOMPSON, SECRETARY'S MESSENGER, SAVED HIS BACON ON A CERTAIN OCCASION.

"I find among office-holders, few deaths and no resignations."—*Thomas Jefferson to the Merchants of Boston.*

NONE but those who have had an opportunity of observing the characteristics of official life in Washington, can have any idea of it; and even they, unless they are fond of observing human character in its various developments, would not note the many scenes of farce, comedy, and tragedy, to which the pursuit of it gives rise.

Gliddon's mummy was pronounced by the lecturer to be a woman, an Egyptian priestess; but lo! after his many lectures and many unfoldings of the body, it turned out, so the doctors say (?), in spite of the learned lecturer's prophecy, to be a man after all. So, many an individual who considers himself ticketed for an office, by the recommendation of all his party, and about to be embalmed at least for four years in official ease, finds that some other individual has got into his place, either by mistake or design, and he is left, like the poor cripple at the pool of Bethesda, waiting for another movement of the political waters; but, alas, when it comes he is crowded out, and there is nobody to *put him in.* Patience, truly, does its "perfect work" in religion, but it seldom does in politics. It is the bustling, active, wide-awake fellow who generally gets in. And often, after all, the occupant sometimes continues to keep in from the press of the very multitude without. While the Secretary, for instance, who holds the subordinate place in his gift, is debating with himself to which of the many he shall give it, he discovers, maybe, the worth of the occupant who holds it, and concludes to retain him, at least for a while, until some urgent member of Congress, who has a casting vote upon some favorite scheme of the Secretary, presses the appointment of a personal and political friend for personal and political reasons. Glad to put the member under personal obligations to him, the Secretary makes the removal, no matter what may be the worth of the occupant. In Europe, it would be called a state necessity; here it is a party necessity, we should be told, and the maxim, "to the victors belong the spoils," though denied by one party, is practised by both; and necessity, the tyrant's plea, becomes a Whig or Democratic practice, as the case may be. But if the incumbent chance to be the relative or friend of the influential member, he is kept in just so long as that influential member keeps his influence.

I remember the case of a messenger in Washington, who had, to use his own expression, "an awful time of it, a monstrous awful time of it," to keep his place. He had been made a messenger in the early times of General Jackson, and he held on by the force of his politics through many successions of Secretaries, up to the time of General Harrison's election, when he began to fear his time had come.

I had gone on to the inauguration of Gen. Harrison, and this messenger knew that I was trying to save the heads of some Democratic friends of mine; so one day, when he was out of hope, and had been "keeping his spirits up by pouring spirits down," he gave me his confidence.

"I have an awful time of it, sir," said he; "awful! It's my duty to be at the Secretary's door and announce his visitors to him; in that way, you understand, I make the personal acquaintance of the Secretary, and he gits to like me, and I holds on. I have been in at the death of a great many messengers, clerks, and even Secretaries, too, but I feel bilious on the present occasion, though I havn't said a word about politics since Gen. Harrison has been elected. What kind of a man is the present Secretary, Mr. ——, is he an abolitionist or not?"

"No, he is not an abolitionist," I replied; "though, coming from a free State, he rather leans that way."

"He's not in favor of these regular nigger-traders, is he?"

"No, I should rather suppose he was not; no gentleman, no man of humanity is in favor of them."

In a thoughtful mood Thompson left me. A few evenings afterwards he came to my room, a sheet or two in the wind, and, after shaking me cordially by the hand, he took a seat, observing, in a very grateful manner—

"Mr. Horace, what you told me the other day about the Secretary's abolition notions helped me mightily. Sir, I've had my neck under the guillotine, hair cut close, hands tied down, and everything ready for the axe." And he wiped the perspiration from his forehead.

"Ah! well, I am glad you are alive and kicking officially yet," I rejoined.

"It was just touch and go; it happened this morning."

"Ah!"

"Yes. You know Robinson, the nigger-dealer,

who has the pen down town, Mr. ——? Well, I thought the fellow kind of looked smirking and consequential at me ever since the election. I sold him a nigger once; for, messenger as I am, I came from one of the first families in Virginia, one of the F. F. V.'s, and I was so long on here, waiting for office, that I had to sell my last nigger. I had, that's a fact. I brought the fellow on here to wait on me. I expected nothing short of a big clerkship, and talked of a foreign mission; and here I am, no more than a common messenger."

"The first shall be last, and the last shall be first," I said.

"Fact, sir; good in politics as well as religion. Well, I had to sell Robinson my last nigger; and he cheated me in the trade wofully. He cut South, and sold his gang, with Ben, before I got one cent of my money; and if I had not caught him in Baltimore, and put the screws to him, and put him in the pen there for debt, I never should have got the money. He had to pay, but he swore vengeance against me. He's down here, poor as I was when I sold that last nigger, the last button on Gabe's coat. He's been several times to see the Secretary; and as I stand at the door, as you know, I kind of bluffed him off, till at last he swore he'd inform on me if he didn't get in; and he came there yesterday, with a member of Congress, and I told them that the member had precedence, but

I couldn't let him in. The member wanted to take him in, but I told him it was the Secretary's express orders not to let anybody in without announcing him; but I said, 'Sir, you are privileged, being a member, a thing which I don't exactly agree to in a free country.' "

"You didn't tell him that?"

"Indeed, I didn't. I let him in, as smiling as a basket of chips. He hadn't been in two minutes when the Secretary's bell rings; in I pops, and he tells me to let in Robinson. So I shows him in. The fellow had a paper in his hand—an awful-looking paper. I took close note of it, I am used to papers.

"It seemed to have a line drawn down the centre of the paper, and names on each side. Signed as I live, I thought an application. I'll know you again, old-fellow, I said to myself (to the paper), if ever I should see you. Maybe I didn't listen at that door! Generally, I don't listen over particularly at anything that's a going on in the Secretary's room; because I know it's not etiquette; but who thinks of etiquette with his head under the guillotine, except some fool of a Frenchman.

"Maybe I didn't listen at that door! I heard the Secretary say to Robinson that his recommendations were very strong, and that he would think of it. Presently, out they came—the member and Robinson, and the scamp, the rascally nigger dealer, had no paper in his hand; I smelt a rat, I did somehow, and that's a fact. So when the Secretary left that afternoon, and I was dusting round, hang me if I didn't see that very paper stowed away back in his drawer: I knowed it the moment I set eyes on it, just as a revolutioner would have known a Britisher from his red coat. What do you think it was? Why, it set forth the petitioner, Robinson, as a Whig of the first water—had spent a great deal in the cause—had reduced himself to poverty—was fit for any situation that could be bestowed upon him—was most trustworthy—was most especially recommended to the Secretary's personal care — had a whole list of signatures, senators, members, blackguards — couldn't count 'em! That's not all. They made the biggest kind of charges against me, saying I drank—it's enough to make a man drink—and recommending him for my place.

"Well, thinks I, if I am a gone coon—I never was a coon—I'm a gone sucker."

"There's many a slip 'tween the cup and the lip," I said.

"Yes, sir, but what you told me about Secretary's abolition notions did the thing. Ever since I sold that last nigger, I've been a bit of an abolitionist myself. Says he to me next day—he's getting very polite to me lately, and always calls me Mister—says he, 'Mr. Thompson what kind of a man is Robinson, who came here yesterday from your State?' I pretended not to know what kind of a man he was. 'I mean what is his vocation—his business?' he said, playing with Robinson's recommendation, which he had just taken out of the drawer. 'Why, sir,' I replied, looking awful sorrowful, 'he's a nigger-dealer!' 'A nigger-dealer!' he cried. 'Yes, sir,' says I, 'he keeps the pen down yonder by the Capitol.' The Secretary started up, walked up and down the room two or three times, and just chucked Mr. Robinson's recommendation in the fire. I stood awhile till I saw the paper all ablaze, just as Robinson's soul will be all ablaze some of these days, and I left the Secretary signing papers."

LIFE IN WASHINGTON.

CONTINUED.

OTHER DIFFICULTIES WHICH MR. THOMPSON, SECRETARY'S MESSENGER, HAD IN RETAINING HIS PLACE.

"Hold on."—*Common phrase.*

THE "little month" of General Harrison's power, my acquaintance, Thompson, held on to his office without farther trouble. I knew the General very well when I first emigrated West, and before he had been announced as a candidate for the presidency. The easy familiarity and hospitality with which he had received me at the "Bend," gave me a frankness toward him which perchance I should not have felt, had I not known him before his elevation to the presidency.

"There's a divinity doth hedge a king,"

says the great portrayer of human nature; and

there's a divinity doth hedge power everywhere, in a republic as well as a monarchy — a president as well as a potentate of more patrician title and longer reign. And few kings have more real power, and certainly few exercise as much as the President of the United States.

Suspecting, from what Thompson told me of the "nigger-dealer's" attempt to get his office, that he held it by rather a ticklish tenure, I took the liberty of speaking to General Harrison about him; and General Harrison expressed a wish to the Secretary, as I afterward understood, that Thompson should be retained. The President's wish is, of course, law in such matters, as the following anecdote of General Jackson will show: A vacancy occurred, during his administration, in the bureau of one of the auditors, and General Jackson wrote a very strong letter of recommendation to the auditor in behalf of a young man from Tennessee, with whose fitness and character the General was well acquainted. With the letter in hand, the applicant called upon the auditor, who replied that he had the highest regard for the President's recommendation, but that Mr. Burns was so variously and strongly recommended that he should be compelled to fill the vacancy with his name. The applicant quietly took up his letter and withdrew; and with Western frankness and somewhat chagrin repaired to the White House, and returned the

General his letter. "What's the matter?" asked the old chief.

"He says he can't give it to me, General."

"Why not?" was the quick inquiry.

"He says he has the highest respect for your recommendation, but Mr. Burns is so strongly and variously recommended that he feels compelled to give it to him."

"Mr. Burns is his relative, sir. Compelled to give it to him!" And so saying, he pulled the bell sharply. "To have the highest respect for my recommendation is to follow it."

"Tell," he said to the messenger, "tell the auditor I wish to see him. Keep your seat, sir," to the Tennesseean.

In a few minutes, the auditor made his appearance.

The General, whose placidity apparently had returned to him, asked the startled official why he had not given the situation to the young gentleman whom he recommended.

"Why, Mr. President, Mr. Burns is so strongly recommended."

"I know Mr. Burns, sir; he is your relative, sir; and I also know this gentleman; and I should like to know whose recommendation is stronger than that of the President of the United States?"

The Tennesseean got the office; and it is needless to say the auditor came near losing his.

Thompson, in the snug enjoyment of his office, felt an increased respect for General Harrison, and began to think he would let politics alone when, lo! death, the king of kings and president of presidents, laid the chief in the place appointed for all the living. Here I could read a homily; but no matter. The query soon was, which way is "Capting Tyler" about to break, whom Mr. Botts is bound "to head or die?" Thompson smirked over the idea that "Capting Tyler" was said by the Whigs to have some of the original sin of Jacksonism about him; but he said nothing, as it was understood that Mr. Tyler would retain General Harrison's cabinet. Soon, however, rumor was rife that President Tyler and his Cabinet could not agree; and that there was going to be a break up. Yet the public knew nothing about it. Thompson had strong suspicions that all was not right, and while he was fearing what would be the state of things under a new Secretary of Mr. Tyler's appointment, fears of the incumbent, who had no longer the wishes of General Harrison to restrain him, came over him.

"Thunder on this office-holding," he said to me, one day; "our Secretary begins to call me Mister; it's no longer plain Thompson. I'm afraid he's agoing to butcher me. I might have been safe if the old General had lived, but hang it, this

Secretary can scent the least drop of Locofoco blood in a man, and he's bound to have him out."

I tried all I could to cheer Thompson, but his fears proved but too true; for one day he came to me and said —

"Well, the thing's up; my head's off, clean."

"'Taint possible!"

"Clean gone, sir."

"Well, but you are not absolutely removed?"

"No; but the Secretary gave me notice that he should want my place next Monday; and I think I'll go at once, and see what I can do for myself."

"What did he say to you?"

"Nothing. He was up and down; he just told me that he wanted my place."

"Well," said I, "hold on; Captain Tyler and his cabinet have had a muss. The Secretary told me himself that he quits to-morrow. Say nothing about it, but hold on."

"W-h-e-w!" ejaculated Thompson, "'There's many a slip 'tween the cup and the lip;' maybe I'm as good as old gold, yet."

And so it turned out; for the Secretary left with Mr. Tyler's retiring cabinet, and perhaps never once thought again of his humble messenger.

Like Mr. Webster, Thompson "breathed freer" for awhile; but he was all on nettles to learn who the new Secretaries would be. So were the public; many expressing the opinion that President Tyler could not get a cabinet. A friend told me, that upon such a remark being repeated to President Tyler, he replied: "That the situation and the salary would command the best talent in the land, to say nothing of what patriotism might do in the premises." Certainly, Mr. Tyler had a good cabinet.

"What kind of a gentleman is this new Secretary?" asked Mr. Thompson of me, one day.

"There you have me, Thompson. I don't know him."

"Is he a free liver? does he drink any?"

"I don't know. I understand he is a member of the church."

"Well," said Thompson; "between you and me, Mr. ——, I doubt if it will last him. I heard somebody say, the other day, that John McLean, the Judge of the Supreme Court, and a Methodist at that, was the only man who brought his religion to Washington, and I believe it."

"Yes," I replied, "it is certainly true of Judge McLean."

"And this new Secretary belongs to the church, hey? I wonder if he is a temperance man?"

"I don't know—I believe he is."

"W-h-e-w! there'll be all sorts of charges against me, now—all sorts. I bet you, sir, they'll have a dozen certificates as to my drinking."

Thompson, on the strength of the fear that these

certificates would be produced, took a regular spree; and on leaving the gallery of the House of Representatives, whither he had repaired to curry favor with the M. C's, he made a misstep, and fell—tumbled all the way down stairs, to the great damage of his nose, eyes, and character. He was laid up. He sent me a very humble message, would I would call and see him? and I did so. Poor fellow! he was terribly bruised, and but for the fact of his having been drunk when he fell, he would probably have killed himself. He made all kinds of inquiry of me as to what I had heard of, or about him, &c., &c., repeating them over and over again.

"Oh!" said I, "Captain Tyler is a Virginian; you must see him, and let him know that you are one of the F. F. V's, and he will save you."

"Well, sir," replied Thompson, raising himself upon his arm, in the bed, "it's astonishing what regard the first families in Virginia have for one another. Here I've been sick nine days—it was thought I would die—and every day there was a gentleman came to inquire after my health; he wouldn't leave his name, he only said he was a Virginian. I'll lay my life he knew my family; as soon as I get out I must hunt him up, and return my thanks."

When Thompson recovered, he learned that this

anxious inquirer after his daily health had understood he was about to die, and had obtained a promise from the Secretary that if he (Thompson) should "shuffle off this mortal coil," that he (the anxious inquirer aforesaid) should have his place!

THE DEVELOPMENT

OF

MIND AND CHARACTER.

As we turn over the pages of history, the events of by-gone days pass before the mind like a splendid panorama, glittering and gorgeous, making an impression of vastness and power; but which, from its very expansion, leaves but an indistinct recollection, in which the smaller objects are so overshadowed by the larger, that they escape the observation.

We mark the mighty stream that rolls by, and in the contemplation of its greatness, we think not of its source, or of its many tributaries.

To know men, we must study them. History tells us how they acted, and gives us the peculiarities of an age. Biography informs us why they acted; gives the motives and the means; and holds the mirror up so closely that we can scan every beauty and detect every blemish. In biography, we pass into a man's chamber with the familiarity of an acquaintance. History keeps us aloof for the pomp of the gala day.

We recur again and again to the memory of those departed friends, who have gone before us to the undiscovered country; while imagination pictures their very tone, and form, and manner, until they seem to stand in our very presence, and live over again the busy scene which has passed.

With a feeling akin to this, we delight to refer to those who have excited our admiration or our wonder. We read again and again of their rise, their progress, and their success; and we delight to dwell on every glowing scene in which they figured, until they seem to stand in our presence and to live. How thrilling is the recollection of the mighty dead! By it all the affections have been ennobled, piety endeared, charity enkindled. It has weakened every vice, and strengthened every virtue.

To study what may be called the philosophy of character, we must know all the circumstances that formed it. Not only the diversity of scenes through which the individual passed, but also the effect which they produced upon his character as he underwent their mutations. How much we are all influenced by the scenes around us — by friends, fortune, foes; by sickness and by health;

by every variety of being; by the past, by the present, and by our anticipations of the future. To the sanguine temperament, hope lends her thousand allurements; on the melancholy, doubt and dismay obtrude their thousand misgivings—glimmerings of hope that end in fears, and fears that end in despair.

Men of talents, more than other men, suffer under these varieties and mutations of feeling. Their acute sensibilities, their pride, their consciousness of talent, their ambition—all influence them at once, or by turns, and have made so many of them unhappy, even when all they hoped for was accomplished. How much keener were these influences when doubts and difficulties surrounded them; when, in their early struggles, they knew not what the morrow would bring forth; and when, judging from the past, it must bring forth anything but joy. To such, in their moments of despondency, when ambition beckoned them on, and stern and cold reality weighed them down, the prospect was almost as dark as Cato's in contemplating death:—

> "Through what new scenes and changes must I pass?
> The wide, the unbounded prospect lies before me;
> But shadows, clouds, and darkness rest upon it."

Providence, as if for the purpose of making each man's cup contain an equal portion of those ingredients which constitute happiness, gives to him, whose natural gifts are superior to another, ills of which the other never dreamed. She gives him the unquiet of ambition and sensitiveness, which those who have taken up their abode in the valley never feel. They reflect that Content, the wise man's personification of all earthly good, sits smiling at their door; and what, without it, are sway, and empire, and glory? And yet there are few who do not feel the thirst of emulation, the panting to reach the goal, when they reflect upon those who have reached it. They forget how many have fallen in the race; how many have been pushed aside by the strong and the determined, who, in their turn, have shrunk from those of higher powers. How much circumstances have done, circumstances which seemed but a feather, wind-wafted any and everywhere! How often the best laid schemes, the profoundest plots, the most cunning contrivances, have passed away like the bubble in the stream, or turned to the ruin of those who were exulting in their handiwork! How often the best talents, adorned with every virtue, have fallen before inferior talents, disgraced with every vice. Yet, nevertheless, the development of the talents and character of those who have struggled through difficulties and danger to eminence and power, is interesting and instructing; no matter whether the individual used good or bad means to attain his ends. And if interest attaches to him who struggles ardently in a bad cause, how much more does he excite who struggles nobly in a good one? Our Washington, no doubt, in contemplating the actions of Cæsar and Cromwell, felt that if they dared so much for mere selfishness, he could dare more for patriotism; that if they pledged life and fortune for their success, he would pledge "life, fortune, and sacred honor," for the success of his country. Besides, to show to aspiring ambition the rock on which so many split, victims to unhallowed passions, is as salutary as the Spartan's practice, when he exhibited his intoxicated slave to his sons, that they might shun the beastly vice to which the menial was a victim. And again, to show, on the other hand, the undaunted perseverance with which so many great men have struggled in a good cause, is to lead by the hand the unsteady and the wavering until their foothold is sure. A great author used to observe that, whenever he sat down to write, he always placed the Iliad on the table open before him. "For," said he, "I like to light my taper at the sun." And, certainly, the actions of an illustrious individual may be said to be a great moral luminary, from which all who choose may borrow light. That which elevates us above the brute, which does us service, is moral energy; which, like the fabled gift of the alchemist, extracted gold—golden rules, I mean—from everything around us.

It determines us, in the pursuit of that which we seek, with the spirit which may become a man.

The man of natural capacity, who relies upon his sagacity and disregards books, often, it is true, takes a just view of men and things; but he is very apt to think that events, which have happened before his eyes, are the most wonderful that ever did happen, because he is not familiar with those of other times; and he will exaggerate an occurrence of comparatively little moment for a very natural reason, it is the most remarkable he has heard of or witnessed. On the other hand, the mere bookworm is worse than he who disregards books; because he is perpetually endeavoring to mould the occurrences of the day with some fancied theory of the past, and in looking at events, to use Dryden's expression, "through the spectacle of books," he is, consequently, more apt to use his memory and imagination in tracing the resemblances of the past with the present, than his judgment in marking their differences and acting accordingly. The light of the past dazzles him; he has gazed on it too much; and when he turns to the present, if he cannot fashion some theory of compatibilities and agreements, he is bewildered in perplexities; and, if he does fashion a theory, it is one to which Utopia is a commonplace.

Some men would have to new-mould their minds before they would be qualified for the active and stirring scenes of life. They undertake everything with preconceived notions on the subject; and, through all changes of circumstances and of opinion, they go on by a kind of predestination in the path of error. Others, again, legitimate descendants from the family of Wrongheads, have, as they think, a natural chart to discover truth, as honest Jack Falstaff knew the true prince by instinct; and by instinct they blunder on all their lives. Such persons, in an intellectual point, belong to the hospital of incurables.

There is an anecdote, happily illustrative of those who see things just as they wish to see them. An old clergyman, and the lady of his love, who, though rather an old lady, was still an admirer of the romance of the tender passion, were once looking through a telescope at the moon.

"My gracious!" exclaimed the lady; "those two figures, who incline towards each other, are evidently two lovers who have met after a long absence." "Two lovers!" exclaimed the astonished clergyman. "My dear, you are certainly crazy; they are plainly and palpably the steeples of a church."

To watch the development of talent is one of the most pleasing studies in which the mind can possibly engage; for the whole being is displayed before us, from the feverish impulses of the boy to the fixed resolutions of the man. For every passion acts upon the intellect, and the intellect acts upon every passion. Ambition, perhaps, has had more martyrs even than religion, and the torch of science has lighted the funeral pyre of many a victim.

To keep the mind in continued action requires the strongest motive. Lord Mansfield loved laughingly to observe to his friends, "that particularly favorable circumstances, fortune, friends, talents, often made a great lawyer; but," said he, "the best thing in the world to make a great lawyer is great poverty." There is much truth in this remark; and it would seem that it applied with equal force to talents in whatever field of literature or science their possessor sought to become distinguished. So prone are many men of mind to indulgence and ease, that, if there is not something always goading them on, they are very likely to stop by the way, like the traveller in the shady spot, until night overtakes them, when they are apt to lose their path, and spend the time they should be pursuing their journey in seeking to find it.

Ambition has been called the last infirmity of noble minds; yet how often is it the first impulse to their nobility! A generous emulation acts on the mind like the fairy in the legend of romance, who guided her votary, amid innumerable difficulties and dangers, till she led him to happiness. To awaken the pupil's ambition should be the first object of the tutor; for, until that be awakened, he will teach in vain. This is the reason why so many eminent men have passed through school with so few honors, and won so many from the world. They have been "the glory of the college and its shame;" and not until their energies were aroused, and their ambition called forth, by the stirring strife of the world, did they exhibit those faculties which have made memorable an age or a country. Had not these men genius at school? Certainly. It was only dormant, like the strength of the sleeping lion. And many boys have been thought dunces at school, because their teachers had not penetration and sagacity enough to discover the latent spark of intellect within them.

Swift's college mates and teachers thought him a dunce at the very time that he was writing his "Tale of a Tub," the rough draft of which he then showed to his friend and room-mate. The Tale was not published until many years afterwards. He got his degrees at college by the "special favor" of the faculty, as it stands recorded in the archives. It appears he would not read the old works on logic, but preferred laughing over Rabelais and Cervantes. His teachers did not understand his character. They should have studied it; and then they could easily have controlled him, and have prevented the lamentation on his part, in after-days, that he had thrown away seven years of his life. Let those students of talent who may have acted as Swift did, remember what Dr. Johnson said of him, namely, "that though he had thrown away seven years of his life in idleness, he was determined not to throw away the rest in despair." Doubtless some young man, who ran away with all the honors of the college as easily as all the honors of the world afterwards ran away from him, used to quote Swift as a proverb of stupidity; and it was this after-resolution of Swift that gave him the world's honors, and perhaps contentment with the college honors, and a want of continued industry that caused his competitors to lose them.

One of Byron's teachers pointed to him one day, saying: "That lame brat will never be fit for anything but to create broils." Poor Byron, it is true, had great talents for creating broils; but Dr. Drury, another of his teachers, discovered that he had talents of a far higher kind, and successfully sought to awaken his emulation. It is pleasing to know that, though Byron was always satirizing his other teachers, and setting their authority at defiance, for Dr. Drury he entertained the highest respect, and has so expressed himself in language that will not die.

When Scylla was about proscribing Cæsar, some one asked him what he had to fear from that loose-girdled boy! "In that loose-girdled boy," said he, "I see many promises." Cromwell's associates thought him a foolish fanatic; and it was his relation, Hampden, who discovered his capacity, predicting that he would be the greatest man in the kingdom, should a revolution occur.

Patrick Henry gave so little promise of mind, that, when he went to be examined touching his qualifications to practice, one of the gentlemen who were appointed to examine him, absolutely refused the duty, he was so struck with the unpromising appearance of the applicant. Yet, but a short time afterwards, Henry made his great speech in the Parsons cause. His talents were so little known, even to his father, that the old gentleman, who was one of the Judges, burst into tears on the bench; while the people raised their champion on their shoulders, and bore him in triumph through the streets. How much sooner would have been the development of Henry's mind if his emulation had been earlier aroused, and a fit opportunity had been given him for display. And when he was driving the plough, or officiating as the barkeeper of a common tavern, or roaming wild through the woods in pursuit of deer, if he had met with some kind friend, who would have taken him by the hand, assisted him in his studies, excited his ambition, talked to him of the immortal names of history, and cheered him on to emulation, we should now look up to him, not only as our Demosthenes, but his own glowing pages would have been the best monument of his renown.

Dr. Barrow's father said, that if it pleased the Lord to take any of his children, he hoped it would be Isaac, as he was fit for nothing but to fight and set two dogs fighting. Nevertheless, when this Isaac grew to manhood, and his emulation was awakened, he was thought in mathematics to be inferior only to Newton, and was the greatest divine of his age.

It has been the misfortune of a great many young men of talent, over whom the dark cloud lowered in their younger years, to be placed among those who did not understand their characters or their merits, and who would rather crush than assist them. And, too, there is a passion in this world called envy—

> "That fiend that haunts the great and good,
> Not Cato shunned nor Hercules subdued"—

that ill-omened bird that, like the raven o'er the haunted house, is always croaking evil—that will tower at the highest names and burrow for the lowest—that twin sister of jealousy, which has so many buts and ifs to throw, like stumbling-blocks, in the way of rising talent. At that time, too, when the cheering voice of a friend falls upon the ear like a blessing; when darkness and doubt are before the aspirant, and behind him all the ills of life—

> "Despair, and fell disease, and ghastly poverty,"

like bloodhounds from the slip—then it is that envy goes forth, like the assassin at night, with the felonious intent hot at heart, against the youthful and aspiring genius. How easily, like the cameleon, she can change her color, and fawn the parasite of the successful! I remember once hearing a sycophantic hanger-on at the skirts of the bar, who was neither here nor there, one thing or the other, but between the two, like Mahomet's coffin, compliment the late Mr. Wirt on an effort which that gentleman had then just made, and which was certainly not one of his best. "Sir," said Wirt, in a deep tone, which came from the bottom of his heart, "when a youth in Virginia, in a little debating society, to an audience of six, and one tallow candle, about fourteen to the pound, I have made a better speech than that, when there was no one to discover the merit of it, and none to say, 'God speed you.'"

Doctor Parr, the celebrated teacher, who used to boast that he had flogged all the bishops in the kingdom, and who, whenever it was said that such and such a person had talents, would exclaim, "Yes, sir, yes, sir, there's no doubt of it; I have flogged him often, and I never throw a flogging away." This reverend gentleman was remarkable for discovering the hidden talents of his pupils. He was the first who discovered Sheridan's. He says: "I saw it in his eye, and in the vivacity of his manner, though, as a boy, Sheridan was quite careless of literary fame." Afterwards, when Richard felt ambitious of such honours, he was thrown, as Dr. Parr says, "upon the town," without resources, and left to his own wild impulses. This, no doubt, was the cause of many of Sheridan's errors and wanderings, which checkered the whole of his splendid but wayward career. A teacher wanting the observation of Dr. Parr, might have concluded that because Sheridan would not study, and no inducements could make him apply himself, he wanted capacity. This was the case with Dr. Wythe, his first teacher, who did not distinguish between the want of capacity and the want of industry. It appears, from the exploits of the apple-loft and the partiality which Sheridan's school-mates entertained for him, that he was more ambitious of being the first at play than the first at study. Sheridan had not then verified the proverb, of "Good at work, good at play;" but it often happens that he who wins the game among boys, afterwards wins the game among men, when there is a far deeper stake, and when, too, there is not half so much mirth among the losers, and, alas, not half so much happy-heartedness with the winner.

A great man is almost always a great boy; that is, in proportion as the man is superior to the men around him, the boy was superior to the boys around him in everything in which he sought to be superior. I do think that an observer of character will discover this, if he at all applies himself to trace the history of the mind.

Locke tells us, and it is generally admitted among metaphysicians that he tells us truly—that we have no innate ideas—that sensation and reflection originate them in the mind, which, until they make their impress, is like a blank sheet of paper. Now, if it is sensation and reflection which write ideas upon the mind, of course the intellect depends greatly upon circumstances to develop it, and give it that bias of thought which seems like instinct to determine its possessor to a particular pursuit: for instance, to poetry, oratory, mathematics, or mechanics. The poet, the orator, the mathematician, or the mechanic, will often tell you that he felt a great inclination to devote himself to his particular vocation; and he will tell you, too, whence he received it; but you will immediately reflect that many have been placed in his situation without feeling the least propensity towards that pursuit. Observing an apple fall from a tree, led Newton to his sublime speculations and discoveries; but how many have observed an apple fall, in whose minds the inquiry never arose, Why did it fall? and how many have asked themselves why it fell, without pursuing the subject farther than the inquiry; and how few, if they had pursued the inquiry, would have arrived at the correct conclusion.

The biography of many eminent men teaches us that, in their early contemplations, they felt many impulses to different pursuits at different times, which arose from an unaccountable train of reflections suggesting themselves to their minds; or, what is oftener the case, the impulse originated on reading the life or studying the work of some eminent man.

The first wish of Julius Cæsar was to be an orator; and, according to Sallust and others, his qualifications for oratory were of the highest order. He might have been the first orator of Rome; he preferred being the first warrior. Lord Mansfield's first wish was to excel in poetry. Pope says of him —

> "Oh! what an Ovid was in Murray lost."

So was it with Burke, Sheridan, and Canning. Dr. Franklin says, that if his father had not dissuaded him from poetry, he feared he should have been but a bad verse-maker. Dr. Johnson set off from Litchfield to London with an unfinished tragedy in his pocket—all that he had in the world. Blackstone, the celebrated author of the "Commentaries," was passionately fond of poetry; and his "Farewell to the Muse," which he wrote on commencing law, shows that he had a talent for it. Byron's first passion was for oratory. Dugald Stewart, the celebrated author of a work on the mind, contemplated writing an epic poem, but abandoned the idea to devote himself to metaphysics.

Sir Humphrey Davy, on leaving poetry for philosophy, thus expressed himself:—

"Once to the sweetest dreams resigned,
The fairy fancy pleased my mind,
And shone upon my youth;
But now, to awful reason given,
I leave her dear ideal heaven,
To hear the voice of truth."

The first mental impulse of Chief-Justice Marshall was to poetry. As Americans, we may congratulate ourselves that, when the muses lost a favorite, the law gained a votary, whose sagacity, judgment, impartiality and patriotism have never been surpassed. He held the scales of Justice with an impartial hand, amidst all the conflicting claims of the sovereign States, and amidst all the agitations of party violence; and he has made sure, and safe, and firm, all the great landmarks of constitutional law. There was not a spot upon his ermine. Peace to his ashes, and eternity to his memory!

It would seem as if fortune had thrown impediments in the way of many eminent men, merely to test them, as the Spartan boy was compelled to undergo the severest trials of skill previous to being admitted to the companionship of men.

The governments of Greece and Rome were happily suited to foster emulation and energy in their youths, and to fit them for the highest exertions and the most desperate enterprises. The prizes awarded to the successful at their various trials of physical and intellectual strength, at their shows, in their schools, and on all public occasions, promoted and encouraged the ambition of the parties, and made it the constant study of their lives to excel. Intellectual power, of whatever kind, or to whatever purpose devoted, was almost deified by the ancients; and every person, from the highest patrician to the lowest plebeian, might be said, from the smallness of the ancient republics, to come under the influence of its possessor. Therefore it was that every art was practised to obtain popularity; for, in a city with the government and manners of Athens or Rome, popularity was power, place, emolument — everything to which ambition could aspire. Mind will govern wherever it has a fair opportunity of displaying itself. We observe the truth of this remark in every diversity of civilized and savage life. It is more the intellect of the Indian than the prowess of his arm that makes him leader. What an influence, for instance, Tecumseh, who has been called the

"Napoleon of the West," possessed over the various tribes of his people!

Demosthenes addressing the "stormy wave of the multitude," Napoleon upon the field of battle, Washington in so many situations of his eventful life, exhibited the highest powers of human energy. It is in such situations that the force of the mind is tried; and a great one, then, like the oak, gathers strength from the very fury of the storm.

Certainly this energy, and self-control, and power of controlling others, arise in a great measure from education and the force of circumstances; but much of it must also arise from what we cannot account for, if we do not attribute it to an idiosyncrasy of the mental constitution.

How many of those who wished to march against Philip, quailed if Demosthenes was not by? It was the mind of Napoleon which won the great battles of his armies; and our fathers might long have continued the subjects of England, had they not been guided by the wisdom and virtue of Washington.

Trace the characters of these men in their habits, their feelings, their impulses, and their associations, and will you not find that the boy was the miniature of the man?

The remark is as old as Cicero, and its truth has made it a proverb, that if a man has excellence of one kind the world will deny that he has excellence of another. Burke's enemies used to say: "Burke has no judgment, he has too much imagination." Chatham, it was said, declaimed so well that it was evident he could not reason. Sheridan was pronounced too witty to be wise. If you have an intellectual gift which your neighbor has not, he thinks it almost a matter of impossibility that you should have it. And he will immediately tell some such tale of you as the envious Cassius told Brutus of Cæsar:—

"I can endure the winter's cold
As well as he."

Demosthenes had more sublimity of thought than any orator of his time. Who had the best judgment? Demosthenes. Cicero had more wit and imagination than any orator of Rome. Had he not as profound judgment? Chatham had more imagination and greater powers of declamation than any statesman of his age. Had any of them greater sagacity, knowledge, or penetration? Who had greater powers of declamation than Canning? Brougham has; and has he not more judgment than fell to the lot of the departed premier? Charles James Fox pronounced Napoleon's bulletins and letters models of style and sublimity. Did Napoleon want judgment? Mirabeau, who controlled the deliberations of the National Assembly of France in the stormiest time of her Revolution, was as remarkable for the gorgeous splendor of his imagination as he was for the far-reaching profundity of his views.

The opinion that talents are like a piece of cabinet-work, fit only for a particular purpose for which they were made, seems to be more prevalent among moderns than it was among the ancients. This may arise, in a great degree, from the accumulation of knowledge and the necessity there now is to know more, to be called eminent. The invention of letters has wrought like a fairy gift, and spread knowledge abroad to all. But the facilities which this divine invention gives in the acquirement of knowledge, have, by the accumulation of it, made it necessary that the aspirant should devote himself with the greater closeness to the particular science in which he seeks success, as the mistress is said to require the greater devotion from her lover in proportion to the allurements around him which might lead him astray. Now it would take all the time of the closest student to keep up with the increase of knowledge in many branches of study. This was not so among the ancients. The philosophers, from their academies, delivered their precepts to their disciples, which passed among them as the undisputed truth. We observe, that individuals among the ancients excelled in many different pursuits, which, among the moderns, are held to be incompatibilities. Themistocles, for instance, was the greatest statesman of his time, one of the best orators; and he commanded at the sea-fight of Salamis, which saved the liberties of Greece. Cato, the censor, was at once a statesman, a warrior, an orator, and an author. "Plutarch's Lives" are full of the truth of this remark. Napoleon and Chatham placed this work under their pillows every night, and read it in the morning previous to entering on the duties of the day, as the ancient priest repaired to the inner sanctuary that he might catch inspiration from the presence of the divine itself.

I can no more believe that every poet placed in Byron's situation would have written as he did, than I can believe that every man so situated would go into voluntary exile. I merely say that every man, to be great, must have natural capacity, genius, or whatever metaphysicians please to call it; and there must be sufficient motive acting upon his mind to awaken its powers; and that the motive and circumstances that arouse them will always give them a peculiar bias, which might seem to the individual himself a very instinct determining him to his particular pursuit.

Some minds need a much stronger incitement than others to call forth their energies. A man with Dr. Johnson's indolence and habits of procrastination, requires a much stronger motive to make him exert his talents than a man with Newton's industry. One who, like Sheridan, had a thousand temptations to allure him away from intellectual toil, should have the very strongest motive to keep him to it. The ball, the rout, the dinner-party, the club, in each of which he cut such a conspicuous figure, all led him away from those studies which he should have pursued. Perhaps nothing but stern necessity would have made him a student. While Dr. Franklin would sit up half the night, not by compulsion, but as a pleasure, when there was almost a necessity that he should retire to rest to enable him to undergo the labors of the coming day—Dr. Johnson, to use his own expression, "had to provide for the day that was passing over him" by his intellectual toil, and he shrank from it as if he considered it all labor.

Then, if these remarks be correct, a man must not only have genius, but he must be placed in circumstances favorable to its development; and it requires different circumstances to call forth the intellect of different individuals.

The mind, its purposes and impulses, previous to receiving its bias, is in the state of a mass of water that has been diked in, and which, when it forces its way, rolls an irresistible flood, bearing on the bosom of its onward wave every leaf and stem so naturally, that, in contemplating it, either of us would say—"Nature, surely, formed that channel. See how beautifully the willow bends over it, how gracefully it winds around the hill, expanding with such ample volume, as it stretches through the plain! Surely, it must have rolled there when time was young. No, not so; if it had found vent in another place, that willow would not have grown there; there would have been no flower at the foot of the hill, and that fertile plain would now be a barren waste, herbless, fruitless, treeless." Thus it is with the mind. Corregio, no doubt, felt many stirrings of ambition very different from an artist's, previous to becoming a painter; but when he saw the painting which struck him more than anything he had ever seen before, the whole tide of his feelings burst forth, and, starting back, he exclaimed with enthusiasm—"And I also am a painter," devoted himself to the art, and became one of the greatest painters that ever lived. When a man has talents and firmly applies himself, he must be great.

Montesquieu, the author of the "Spirit of Laws," was twenty years completing the celebrated work which has given his name to immortality. He remarked on its completion, that he had read and re-read the works of the great luminaries of science; "and," said he, quoting Corregio, "I also am a painter."

Milton, too, said in his youth, feeling the flame from the divine altar burning within him, that he meant to write something which the world would not willingly let die. And who, in his imagination, has not contemplated the wan, attenuated, blind old man apostrophizing that celestial light which shone but upon his mind?

> "Hail, holy light! offspring of heaven, first-born
> Of th' Eternal, coeternal beam;
> May I express thee unblamed? since God is light,
> And never but in unapproached light
> Dwelt from eternity."

And Bacon, too, that great luminary of science, in sickness, in poverty, and in disgrace, bequeathing his name to posterity, after some time should have passed away!

It is this deep, heartfelt enthusiasm, and far-reaching aspiration, and high hope, that make the great man. As soon as his mind has received its bias, and he has determined his particular pursuit, with a devotion that falters not—with a toil that never tires—with a singleness of love that nothing woos him from winning, he pursues his purposes; and is it to be wondered that he gains his point?

Leander crossed the Hellespont, to meet the lady of his love, though the billows heaved high, and the tempest broke over him; and thus must the poet, the statesman, the orator, and the philosopher, bear on to his purpose—

> "He must keep one constant flame
> Through life unchilled, unmoved,
> And love in wintry age the same
> As first in youth he loved."

What, then, do these facts impress upon one? Why, that no matter what others may think of your intellectual powers, press on, and you may strike the mine; for who knows but what you possess it. Feel as Sheridan felt when Woodfall told him, after hearing his first speech in Parliament, that he would never make an orator. "It is in me, however," said Sheridan, "and it shall come out." It was in him, and it did come out. He lived to make, on the impeachment of Warren Hastings, for effect, the greatest effort that was ever heard in the British Parliament, and which has only been equalled by Burke's eulogy upon it; an effort of which Burke, Fox, and Pitt, became rivals in eulogy; which caused Pitt to move an adjournment of the House, declaring that he himself "was under the enchanter's wand;" an effort which made the culprit Hastings confess that, for awhile, he believed himself guilty; which brought from brothers and sisters, and the remotest connection letters that boasted of their relationship to him; an effort which drew from his lovely and devoted wife tears and words of heartfelt, womanly, and holy pride, in which his very servant participated; for we learn that he was "long celebrated" for the manner in which he imitated his master's closing words. It was an effort that made every Irishman proud of his country, and every Englishman prouder of his language. A man of genius should feel as did Burns, who concluded, that because he could plough as well as another youth who wrote verses, that he could write verses as well. If you fail once, do as Jacob Faithful advises: "Try it again, and you may have better luck next time."

But remember that these trials be in the cause of virtue, and that your talents be devoted not only to your own advancement but to the public good. One of the most touching productions of the modern muse, is the lines entitled "My Birthday," from the pen of Ireland's favorite bard, in which he laments the birthdays that will not return and give the power of amendment; and speaks—

"——— of talents made,
Hap'ly for high and pure designs,
But oft, like Israel's incense, laid
Upon unholy earthly shrines."

A still more memorable lamentation over errors that could not be corrected, is narrated by Dumont in his "Recollections of Mirabeau." At the commencement of the French Revolution, Mirabeau went to Paris, ruined in fortune and reputation. His wild passions were as reckless as the swollen mountain stream, the proclivity of which to the valley is not more certain than were his impulses towards excess. He set up the sign of "Mirabeau, tailor," and was elected to the States General. Such was the low ebb of his moral character that hisses, curses, and execrations followed him as he entered the National Convention. By the power of his talents he forced his way; and when the Jacobins rose up against him, he exclaimed in his loudest voice, shaking his "boar's head" at them, "Silence, those thirty voices!" and they were silent at his bidding. But, alas, in the midst of his power, he felt how much greater it would have been had his moral character stood as high as his talents. Dumont states his belief that Mirabeau would have gone "seven times through the heated furnace" to have purified his name, for he was conscious that if his personal reputation had been good he would have had the control of all France. Mirabeau's friend has seen him burst into a passion of tears when reflecting upon this subject, and heard him, in a voice almost inarticulate with grief, exclaim: "I am cruelly expiating the errors of my youth." At the age of forty-two he died of his excesses; and all Paris, forgetting his errors in the splendor of his talents and services, went weeping to his funeral. But for these excesses, he might have lived with a virtuous as well as a brilliant renown, and have saved France from the horrors of her fearful revolution. What a lesson! What a moral!

Alas! we have too many instances to prove that talents, though they may win for their possessor public admiration, fail to secure him public confidence if he wander from the paths of rectitude. On the other hand, behold the respect and reverence which gathered in blessings around the brows of Chatham, Henry, Marshall, and Washington. Emulate their example; and, though you may not all be great, the saying is as trite as it is true, that you can all be good.

A CHAPTER OF ACCIDENTS:

THE AUTHORESS OF "CONSTANCY."

AFTER spending three or four days in that hospitable city, Louisville, most delightfully, I embarked on board the steamboat Mary—I use a fictitious name, and, like the lord of poets, "I have a passion for the name of Mary"—to return to Cincinnati. All was bustle on board; the captain was hurrying to and fro among the hands, uttering strange oaths, and vowing that he must be off before the other boats.

Ah! a race on the carpet—or, to speak without metaphor, on the river—thought I; and as one on crutches, unless he has certain powers possessed by the devil on two sticks, which, for his soul's sake, he had better not have, unless he has the gift of Asmodeus, if any accident happens, is just in as bad a predicament as the liveliest imagination, expatiating on our western waters, could possibly fancy. "I cannot swim," thought I; "it will be a tempting of misfortune; I'll quit the boat." I passed out of the cabin to carry this resolution into effect, and beheld the firemen pitching the huge logs into the furnace, as though they were so many Lilliputian splinters. The heat from the apparatus passed over my face like the breath of the sirocco. At this instant, the steam gave a hiss full of fumy fury; it seemed to me the premonitory symptom of a bursted boiler, just as the hiss of a snake is the *avant-courier* of a bite. I could not pass that boiler; it was impossible. While I stood eying it, irresolute, I heard the paddles splash in the water, and the boat moved under me; we were on our way. I now hurried into the cabin, determined to get the sternmost berth, Number one, the farthest off from the boiler, and ensconce myself in it until supper, and then I could just pop out and take the nearest seat at the table.

When I opened the book to set my name down to Number one, lo! every berth was taken but Number ten, the nearest of all to the boiler.

"There must be some mistake about this," said I, aloud; "I believe I took Number one."

"No mistake at all, sir," exclaimed a thin, dyspeptic old man, starting up from a chair which stood jam against the door that led to the stern of the boat; "no mistake at all, sir; I came three hours ago and took that berth. I have no idea of being near that boiler. Did you see that account in the paper this morning of the bursting of the boiler of the Return? Horrible! horrible!!"

Here the conversation among the passengers turned upon such accidents, and we talked ourselves into a perfect fever. Every jar of the boat—and somehow the boats on the western waters have a knack at jarring—seemed to be the last effort of the boiler to contain the boiling waters within. I tried to philosophize. I began to think about Napoleon, and to reason myself into a belief in destiny. I always was something of a predestinarian. "But confound it!" thought I, just as I was settling down into a fatalism as doubtless as a Mussulman's, "if I had quitted this boat, or even got berth Number one, it would certainly influence my destiny should that boiler burst."

I determined to try once more to get the berth, and I addressed the old codger again; but in vain. He vowed he would leave the boat, be put ashore, before he would give up Number one. He, I discovered, had never been out of sight of his own chimney before, and had often sat in its snug corner, and read of steamboat accidents. He had a decided taste for such things. A connection near Wheeling had left him a piece of property, of which he was going to take possession, and I verily believe the price of it could not have induced him to change berths with me.

Habit is everything. By the time I had dispatched more cups of coffee than I choose to tell of, and more eggs and bacon than might, under other circumstances, have been compatible with the health of a dyspeptic, for such I was, and seated myself on the stern of the vessel, with a fragrant cigar, watching the setting sun as it threw a gorgeous hue on the glittering waters—by this time, by a process of ratiocination with which, I fear, the sensual had more to do than the intellectual man, I had partly reconciled myself to the dangers that encompassed me.

I discovered that the other boats were out of sight, and I began to reflect that every situation has its pleasures as well as perils. And then arose, vividly to my mind, the fact that when, not a very long time previous, I was approaching Dayton, through the woods, in a carryall, all alone by myself, as an Irishman would say, with a greater desire for a straight course than the trees would allow me to practise—I like a straight-forward course, and if there has been an obliquity since in my scribbling or conduct, it is attributable to this circumstance—the fore-wheel of my vehicle—I was in a full trot—quarrelled with a tree that stood in its way, got the worst of it, and broke short off. The consequence was, I was pitched out into the road with much less ceremony than a carter unloads his cart. My better half, my crutch, kept its seat, and bounced up, I thought, with a spirit of rejoicing and deviltry, delighted, no doubt, to get rid of a burden that I had compelled it to carry for years—a burden which, unlike Æsop's, grew heavier on the journey. Crutch and I have never been friends since. In taking a long walk, after this event, it bruised my arm so terribly, that I have been an invalid for five months. This infused into my arm a spirit of nullification. It ran up the single star at once, and vowed it would not bear the weight of the whole body—that it was not made for that purpose, and wouldn't and couldn't. I have several times threatened this unruly member with dismemberment, but it knows very well it is bruised too near the shoulder for *that*, and is, like South Carolina, too close a part and parcel of my body to entertain many fears on that score. In fact, I played politician with it, and brought in a compromise bill. I have agreed not to use the crutch until my arm gets well, and to endeavor to contrive some other means of walking. For amusement, and to get rid of ennui, in the meantime, I scribble.

But where was I in my story? Ah! away went the horse with the broken carryall, my crutch driving, while I lay in the road, happily unhurt; but, like King Darius, "deserted in my utmost need." In an instant I recovered myself, and cried out "Wo! wo!" in the most commanding tone I could assume. The horse stopped, but you may depend I had a hop of it to reach him.

Some one of old boasted to one of the philosophers—which one was it? I forget—that he could stand longer on one leg than any man in the country. "That you may," replied the philosopher, "but a goose can beat you." Now, the fact is, I can beat the best goose of the whole of them; and this is something to brag of, when we remember that these sublime birds saved the now "lone mother of dead empires," then in her high and palmy state, by cackling. A good many cackle nowadays in vain, to save our State; but, gentle reader, they are not geese. And, my fellow-citizens, if you think I have any qualities for saving the State—which our statesmen want, though even geese had them of old, but they were *Roman* geese, and the last of the Romans, both of geese and men, rests in peace—if you think I have any qualities for saving the State, be it known to you that I have adopted the motto of various elevated, disinterested patriots of our country, viz.: "Neither to seek nor to decline office." I have a right to jest with my misfortunes: it is the best way to bear them.

I had to lead my old horse up to the broken carryall to mount him. He feared to look on what he had done, like Macbeth; and the ghost of

Banquo never startled the thane more than did that ghost of a vehicle my steed. How he curvetted, twisted, turned, kicked up! At last I mounted him, and shared, with my crutch and the harness, the honor of a ride into Dayton.

In this way I entered that town for the first time, and drew up at Browning's in a style of grotesque dignity, I ween, that has seldom been surpassed.

I chewed the cud of this incident for some time, and then thought of another. The winter before last I was returning from Columbus, in the mail-stage. We had passengers, a reverend gentleman, who, with myself, occupied the front seat. He was one of the biggest parsons you ever saw. Opposite to the reverend gentleman sat a Daniel Lambert of a Pennsylvanian—one of your corn-fed fellows. He believed emphatically that Major Jack Downing was as true-and-true a man as ever wrote a letter, and his political bias led him to remark that he "didn't think the major any great shakes, after all." Alongside of the Pennsylvanian, face to face with your humble servant, was a young man with demure features, saving and excepting a twinkling eye. He was a Southerner, he said, travelling for his health. On the back seat sat an old and a young lady, with an elderly respectable looking man between them. The young lady was like a dream of poetry; her features were finely formed, and her eyes were the most expressive and intelligent I ever beheld. She was not only "beautiful exceedingly," but she had exceedingly cultivated and graceful manners—that chief charm in woman, after all. She mechanically—from the impulse of good feeling—stretched out her hand to take my crutch, as I ascended the stage; and, remembering Dr. Franklin's tale of the deformed and handsome leg—I often have cause to remember it, and I pronounce it a test—I felt an instinctive admiration for the fair lady.

We were soon dashing along, not on the best roads in the world. I like to observe character; I'd shut Shakspeare any day, and turn a deaf ear to Booth any night, though representing his best character, to hold converse with an original in the lobby. I sat in silence, and listened to the talk of my travelling companions for a mile or two, when I made up my mind as to their dispositions. My mind was made up from the first, as to the fair lady. In coming to a fine prospect, I caught her eye glancing over it, and I commenced, gently, to expatiate upon it. I made a hit; I thought I would. We broke out at once into a chattering conversation, in which our imaginations sported and played on the beauties of the poets and of Dame Nature. I tried to find out who she was, but you must remember I had to deport myself with great delicacy and tact—she was an accomplished, young, and most beautiful woman, and I was merely a stage-coach acquaintance, without not only the pleasure of an introduction, but ignorant of her name. These parsons beat us young men out-and-out, for when we stopped to dine, the reverend gentleman took a seat by the fair lady, in the corner, on the left hand side of the fireplace; and they carried on a conversation in a low voice for some time. I began to form a bad opinion of the whole tribe of black coats, and to think them no better than the "*gentleman in black*, with the black waistcoat, inexpressibles, and silk stockings, black coat, black bag, black-edged papers tied with tape, black smelling-bottle, and snuff box, and black guard," whose adventures have lately been published. "Well," thought I, "if I were an old limb of the law instead of a young one, I might play old Bagsby with him; but I am not, and"—I was interrupted agreeably in these reflections by the reverend gentleman, or the "gentleman in black," leaving the fair lady, and walking to the other side of the room to the fireplace, for there was a fireplace in both ends of the room, and commencing a conversation with the elderly gentleman and and lady seated there. I was left *tête-à-tête* with the fair lady, and divers and sundry things were said by both of us not necessary to record. How fast the time flew! I felt a cold chill as the driver entered the room. We arose; he said he was sorry to have kept us waiting so long, but he was having the wheels of the stage greased; the former driver had neglected it, and his horses couldn't stand it. "So long!" I sat down--you know my feelings---and I hoped and hope my fair companion did not regret a great deal this delay.

Long ere this, of course, I had discovered the lady was as intelligent as she was beautiful; and I offered her a newspaper I had put in my pocket at Columbus, that I might read for the third time a beautiful tale which it contained. The editor of the paper praised the story very highly, and I commended his taste and the public's.

"What is the name of the tale?" asked the lady.

"'Constancy," said I; "I fear it is but a day-dream—but the story is beautifully told—and I hope the author, if ever he has a love affair, may realize it."

She blushed, and asked me to read it. I pride myself somewhat upon my reading—I had a motive, you see, for offering the newspaper—and, in a voice just loud enough for her to hear, I complied.

We were soon seated in the stage, again, rattling away. The Pennsylvanian had eaten to sleepiness; he nodded and nodded fore and aft. The young man beside him, with a face as grave as the parson's, would every now and then slyly tip up his hat, so as sometimes to cant it nearly off; at which the unsuspecting sleeper would rouse up, replace his beaver, cast his eyes to the top of the stage, as if he wondered if a bounce of the vehicle could have pitched him so high, and then nod again.

We changed horses at the Yellow Springs. I did my best to beat the preacher, but these preachers are hard men to deal with; they stand on a place Archimedes wanted, for while I was musing upon some fairy thought the fair lady had uttered, the reverend gentleman, or the "gentleman in black," took advantage of the pause, and proposed that we should sing a hymn! I have no voice in the world—I mean for singing—and, with a jaundiced mind, I thought at once the reverend gentleman wished to show off. I asked him rather abruptly if he was married. He smiled peculiarly —I didn't like his smile—moved his head—I couldn't tell whether it was a shake or a nod—and gave out the hymn.

Just as you pass the Yellow Springs, on your way to Cincinnati, is a branch, which, at this particular time to which I allude, was very muddy. We descended into it in full drive—the ladies and the parson in full voice—and sweetly sounded the fair lady's. I was just watching her upturned eye, that had the soul of the hymn in it, when the forewheel on my side entered a mud-hole up to the hub, and over went the stage! Were there bones broken? you ask. Bones broken! I would have compromised the case and used a dozen crutches.

We had a verification of Dean Swift's proverb—it gave consolation to him to whom the dean addressed it, but none to me—

> "The more dirt,
> The less hurt."

The big parson fell right on me! Do you wonder that I felt myself sinking into the mud? I seized time as I was rapidly disappearing, as I thought, altogether, to ask the fair lady if she was hurt. She was not, she assured me, and, in a plaintive voice, inquired if I was. There is consolation, thought I, in that tone, if I should sink to the centre of the earth; and when I reflected how muddy I was, I contracted myself into as small a compass as possible, determined to disappear. Here the Virginian called out in a long angry voice, which satisfied us that he was not killed, though he felt himself in danger—

"Halloo, Pennsylvany, are you never going to get off of me?"

The sleeper was not yet fairly awake.

"Don't swear, don't swear," said the preacher persuasively, and, making a stepping-stone of my frail body, he got through the window. The Pennsylvanian used the body of his neighbor for the same purpose—engulfed him—and followed after the parson. The fair lady was unhurt, and, not to be too particular, we all got safely out. And—and, no matter—it's no use for a man to make himself too ridiculous—I shall not commit a suicide on my own dignity—I forgot my situation but for a moment, and that was in observing the parson by the roadside on his knees, with his clasped hands uplifted, and his hat reverently cast aside. I forgot my situation but for a moment, and in that one moment my opinion of the parson was entirely changed.

The stage was uninjured; in ten minutes we were on our way. I—I—I can jest with some of my misfortunes—with my crutch—but there are some misfortunes a man can't jest with.

In about half an hour the stage stopped at a neat farmhouse, and the fair lady with her companions left us, but not before I seized an opportunity of uttering — notwithstanding my discomfiture — in my very best manner, one or two compliments that had more heart in them than many I have uttered to many a fair acquaintance of many years' standing.

When we were on our way, again, I learned from the parson—he had caught it all between the two fireplaces where we stopped to dine; it gave me serious notions of reading divinity—that the fair lady was travelling under the protection of the old lady and gentleman, who were distantly connected with her. She was on her way home from Mr. Archer's Seminary,* in Baltimore; she had stopped at a relative's. Her parents lived at —— (a great distance, thought I). She was the authoress, he told me, of "Constancy."

Not long after this event, I received a newspaper, the direction—my address in full—written in a fair delicate hand—a hand meant for a "crow-quill and gilt-edged paper," containing a beautiful story by the authoress of "Constancy." I didn't think it possible for my name to look so well as it did in that direction.

Whenever I travel, and often when I don't travel, and am an invalid as now, that fair lady is the queen of my imagination; but, a cloud always passes over my face (I've looked into the glass and seen it), and another over my heart (I feel it now), whenever I think of the branch of the Yellow

* Mr. Archer's Seminary, in Baltimore, is deserving of especial notice. It has been ten years in successful operation. Mr. Archer is of one of the old families of Maryland; is a graduate of West Point, and is in every way qualified to be at the head of such an institution—a refined and intellectual gentleman. His pupils are most of them from the South, of the wealthiest and most respectable families; and there is not only the greatest attention paid to mental and moral cultivation in this thriving institution, but there is also a degree of refinement and womanly dignity in the deportment of its inmates, which is a subject of general remark.

Springs. Yet, in spite of the upturning, even on board of the boat, in the fear of a boiler's bursting, when her image crossed my mind, gone were the dangers around me. The smoke ascended from my cigar, not in a puff like the steam from the boiler, but soothingly, lingeringly, placidly; it curled above my head like a dream of love. I fixed my eye on the rapidly varying landscape, and renewed a vow—that if—bah! your "if" is a complete weathercock of a word, a perfect parasite to your hopes and to your fears; used by all, faithful to none, a sycophant, but I must use it—if I ever —no matter—if it turns up as I hope—I'll make a pilgrimage to the shrine of that fair lady, though I go to the uttermost parts of the earth.

THE LATE CHARLES HAMMOND,

OF CINCINNATI.

The death of Mr. Hammond has smitten a large circle of personal and political friends throughout the Union with grief; though it was an event which we have been daily expecting for months—for occasionally we would hear that there was hope, which made us forget that Death sometimes delays the blow, to make his aim the surer. When the news reached us that he was better, we would flatter ourselves that it was a prognostic of recovery, when we should have reflected that it was but a gleam of sunshine through the closing clouds—but the quietude of increasing debility, which had not energy to be restless.

For many months he was confined entirely to his room, and for many weeks past entirely to his bed, in which he could not change his position without assistance. With heroic fortitude he bore his sufferings, with resignation he bowed to the high behest, and breathed his last as quietly as an infant sinks to rest.

Truly, we may say in the oft quoted language of Scripture, not often more justly applied: "A great man has fallen this day in Israel." Mr. Hammond's talents were of the highest order. As a lawyer, he was sagacious and profound; he not only applied to the case before him the energies of a great mind, but he traced it up to the first principles, and illustrated it by the light of various knowledge. While the subtlety of his discrimination partook somewhat of scholastic refinement, he was remarkable for generalizing his subject, and viewing it philosophically. Though he never figured in the cabinet or on the bench, and held, but for a short time, many years ago, a seat in the Ohio State Legislature, yet his editorial disquisitions prove him to have been a statesman who took his views from the fathers of the constitution, and who could expound it as though he sat at its adoption. As a constitutional lawyer, he was thorough and practical. He handled the great questions, as they arose, with the ease of a county court lawyer filing a declaration on a promissory note. In such questions he delighted. His celebrated argument, many years ago, on the constitutionality of the Bank of the United States, was pronounced by Judge Marshall the ablest effort on the subject he had ever heard. The graces of the orator were denied to Mr. Hammond, but "he spoke right on," and with a force, directness, and mental power, which commanded the closest attention. He was very fond of the study of theology; and when he first went to Cincinnati, he held an anonymous controversy with a certain clergyman, in which he gained so decided an advantage, that the clerical gentleman was at some pains to learn who his antagonist was; and when he did so, he called on Mr. Hammond and begged him to drop the controversy, and spare him. When the controversy occurred in Cincinnati between Bishop Purcell and Mr. Campbell, Mr. Hammond was a constant attendant; and all who heard him converse on the subject, who did not know how various was his information, were astonished at his display of Biblical learning. He kept himself acquainted with the current literature of the day. Such authors as he held vicious he would not read, farther than to catch their opinions; and if he spoke of them in his paper, it was with stern denunciation. Of the imaginative writers of the day, Walter Scott was his favorite; and he was very fond of James's works. In almost the last conversation the writer of this held with him, he spoke of the latter's "Gentleman of the Old School" in terms of praise. Bulwer and Byron he would not read. In the authors of Queen Ann's time, he was deeply versed; Dryden, Pope, Swift, and Addison were as familiar to him as his law books. He was, too, a general reader of history, and no partial garbling of the historian could bias his accurate judgment of the actor and the event. In our own history, next to Washington, the man whose memory he loved the most was Chief-Justice Marshall. He used to say that the argument of the Chief-Justice, in the case of Jonathan Robbins, on the floor of Congress, was, take it all in all, the most argumentative and conclusive speech on record. Philip Doddridge, who died some years since, in Congress, was the friend whose memory he cherished the warmest. He thought him one of the finest minds the country has produced; and it was a mental luxury to hear him repeat passages from his deceased friend's speeches, and narrate anecdotes of his intellectual triumphs.

But Mr. Hammond was not more distinguished for the qualities of his head than for those of his heart. While he was inflexibly upright in his judgment of men, he had an apologizing indulgence for the frailties of humanity, which yielded assistance even where he condemned; and which loved to recount the traits of better deeds, even in the condemnation. His charity was not confined to words; it was, in fact, practised more than preached. When the cholera was at its height in Cincinnati, the writer of this dwelt in Front Street below Elm, and one of the inmates of the family being prostrated by the scourge, he was sitting at his door about twelve o'clock one night, anxiously looking out for the doctor. At this time Mr. Hammond came up from the lower part of the street, and asked after the sick person. After answering, as the writer had seen him pass by before, and never knew him to do so except during the cholera, he inquired what brought him down there in what was called the most infected part of the city. "Why," said he, "there is an old man down here whose father I knew; he was a great Indian fighter; I have got a person to nurse him, and I step round occasionally to see that he does his duty." A hundred anecdotes like this could be told of him.

The late venerable Matthew Carey observed to the writer, and he was certainly a judge of men, that he considered Mr. Hammond not only one of the ablest, but one of the most philanthropic men he had ever known.

Mr. Hammond's integrity was stainless. He would not have compromised the independence of his character for any earthly consideration. His editorial career proves this. If ever to a man the phrase of the poet could be applied—

> "He would not flatter Neptune for his trident,
> Or Jove for his power to thunder,"

it was to Mr. Hammond. Of servility and time-serving, he had a hatred that amounted to abhorrence. When it became necessary, in his opinion, to comment upon the public conduct of any man, or any set of men, Mr. Hammond never asked himself what injury he or they could do him; his inquiry was, what injury has been done to others, and why was it done? To the last he felt a deep interest, not only in our general, but in State and city politics, and so expressed himself.

In politics, he was what is called a Federalist of the old school, what demagogues are fond of calling an aristocrat; but there was no aristocracy in Mr. Hammond, saving that of personal independence. He loved to live plainly. His wants were few. He seemed only to value money as far as it enabled him to assist others. The glare of fashion he despised. He, who was called by certain politicians the aristocrat, was seen on the most familiar terms with his humblest neighbors, with whom he delighted to converse, while he was too apt to cut short a colloquy with those who held themselves entitled to his consideration. Wealthy pretension, without merit, he frowned down if it but glanced dictation, or passed it by with cold indifference. For meanness he had a loathing; while the generous action or the noble sentiment brought the tear to his manly eye. Often, when attempting to narrate an affecting incident, his feelings would choke his utterance, and he would change the subject.

For religion he had a profound respect, and always so expressed himself.

Mr. Hammond had his frailties; but it is not for the writer of this notice to dwell upon them. It was said of the Roman Cato, that he "sometimes warmed his patriotism with wine," and that was the "head and front" of Mr. Hammond's offending, and no more.

Almost the first hand which greeted the writer when he landed, a stranger in Cincinnati, was that which is now cold in death; from that hour until the last it always was extended to him in kindness. He feels as if one of the great sources of his pride, gratification, and instruction, was dried up, and is ready to exclaim with Fisher Ames over the bier of Alexander Hamilton: "Penetrated with the fond recollections of the man, my heart grows liquid while I write, and I could pour it out like water."

A few days before his death he requested to be buried without any pomp, and that a plain slab, bearing his name and the date of his birth and death, should be placed over him.

His monument is in the memory of the philanthropic, the intelligent, and the good, and in those hearts round his hearth, who have garnered up so many affectionate memorials of him, and who cherish his virtues and practise them.

CHANGES IN OUR CITIES.

SUMMERFIELD PREACHING TO THE CHILDREN, ETC.

On one who has sojourned occasionally in the different cities of our Union, at different times, their various and changeful physiognomies (so to speak) must have made an impression. Cincinnati, for instance, changes much more than Baltimore. On returning to Cincinnati, after a five years' absence, one is more struck with the changes and improvements than he is in Baltimore after fifteen years' absence. Yet Baltimore has improved as rapidly as any city on the Atlantic border, with, perhaps, the exception of New York. "Well, how does Cincinnati look to you?" asked a friend of ours, on a return there, after a five years' absence in Washington. "Up to Seventh street," we replied, "like an old friend with a new coat on; beyond that like a perfect stranger." And so it is.

Almost all that portion of Cincinnati called "Texas" has grown up in that time; crowded streets, where I saw nothing when I left it but cow-paths over the common. Walk even down Main street, and almost all the signs that the business houses knew a few years ago are broken down and broken up, like the firms they proclaimed. So with the private residences, as many a northern or southern sojourner who has been entertained there finds out.

In Baltimore, particularly in the heart of the city, one finds things pretty much as he left them. We pass down Calvert street, for instance, and there is Balderston's wire establishment, which has been there to us time out of mind; and there is the Mechanical engine-house in the old place, and a large flagstone in the pavement tells us it was founded in 1763. What was Cincinnati then? We have talked with Simon Kenton, "the last of the pioneers," who was taken prisoner by the Indians in the wilderness where Cincinnati now stands. In New Orleans and St. Louis, how fast all traces of the French population are fading away! Boston and Philadelphia hold a good deal of their old look, we mean of fifteen years ago, for that is old in our calendar; while Charleston has not changed much since our childhood, and we are now of a "certain age." In Baltimore, the population has a oneness, an identity of appearance, different from that of Cincinnati. Beyond the court-house, in the Queen City, you hear more of the German language, particularly on Sunday, than of your own, from the passers by in the streets. Their very clothes you see were made in the old country, and scores of them have just arrived. Their friends, who are walking beside them, and pointing out different objects with great volubility, as you can see and hear, have been here only a little while before them, as some portion of their habiliments, which are Americanized, show. In fact, the German population have that part of Cincinnati almost entirely to themselves. In Louisville, you see comparatively few foreigners. It has the look of Baltimore. Louisville, in population and character, resembles Baltimore. In Baltimore, however, there are fewer dandies—I mean, fashionable young men; young men who seem to have nothing to do but to dress themselves foppishly, and idle about—than in any other of our large cities. This impression has frequently occurred to us; and while the Baltimore women are remarkable for their beauty, the men certainly are not remarkable for their personal appearance.

We believe that there is more social equality in Baltimore than in any other large city in the Union. The mechanic here stands higher, and he is more conscious of the fact. Many of the highest public offices here are filled by mechanics. As a class, here, they are very intelligent, and very independent in their bearing; none more so. One is struck, too, with the prevalence of Methodism in Baltimore. Methodism thrives better in the South than in the North. Its warm and trusting faith, so full of sunshine and hope, suits this meridian, and is compatible with the comparative equality which prevails here.

You do not see so many negroes in the streets as formerly, and there are not so many of them slaves. We have not looked at the census to test this fact; but to the eye it certainly appears so. If Baltimore has not her public squares, like Philadelphia, filled with trees, she has her Monument Squares and her City Springs, in all of which Cincinnati is so wofully deficient. The only thing like a public square in Cincinnati is in Eighth street, if we remember rightly; and there half the time, in fine weather, the inhabitants round about are kicking up a dust in the way of cleaning their carpets. The dwellings in Cincinnati are extremely neat, and you see at once that white labor has had the care of them.

Recurring to Methodism. We go sometimes to the Light street Methodist Church, whither we were frequently led, in our boyhood, by our good old maiden aunt, and where, too, now we are met by the spirit of improvement, at least in the better arrangement of the church, if not in the spirit of the worshippers. The old "bird-nest pulpit" is removed, and a more modern and roomy one substituted. And, by-the-by, it has often occurred to us that those "bird-nest pulpits," as somebody calls them, of the olden time, must have been great foes to the display of eloquence. Perched away off from the worshippers, the preacher must have felt himself with them, but not of them; his *nearness* to his congregation must have been lessened in them. We do not wonder that Whitefield preferred preaching in the open air, with the "heavens for a sounding-board," as he said. With all his powers, he must have felt himself cramped in one of those pulpits, with the sounding-board, looking like an extinguisher, raised over his head. "Mother, why don't they let that poor man out?" said a little child to his mother, who had taken him for the first time to a church in which there was one of those "bird-nest pulpits," where the urchin thought the preacher was caged, and, by his eager gesticulations, in the situation of Sterne's starling.

Light street meeting-house used to be filled on occasion of worship, and we shall never forget our good aunt taking us there when a child, to hear Mr. Summerfield preach to the children. That saintly apostolic pale face is before us now, after the lapse of many years.

The body of the church was crowded with children, of which crowd we formed one. We noticed, even then, that not a girl played with her neighbor's ribbon, or her own; and that the boys entirely forgot their mischief, and were won from their general listless indifference in church, while all gazed into the face of the preacher with deep earnestness. One of his remarks we shall never forget. It was something in this wise: "Little children," he said, "if you were away from home, and your parents—your father or mother—should write to you, how eagerly you would open that wished-for letter, would you not? And how eagerly you would read every line of it, and how you would treasure their admonitions, their good advice, in your memory! You would resolve to do what they wished you to do—just what they desired. That you would resolve should be your steady aim, and again and again you would unfold that letter in some quiet room, or when you were apart from your playmates, and read and reread it to yourselves, that you might know it all by heart, and do just as they bid you. You would remember how that dear parent loved you, how much trouble and anxiety he had felt when you were ill, and how affectionately he had watched over you! Yes, you would think of all this, I know you would, for you look like good children—and you are here in church to-day, and this is another proof that you are good children. Yes, you would think so much of that dear letter. Well, little children, your Father who is in heaven, your Heavenly Father, has sent you a letter also, and here it is in the shape of this book which I hold in my hand, and of which you have all heard—I mean the Bible." And so speaking, he dwelt upon the history of the Bible and the character of our Redeemer to the children. What we remember most distinctly, though, is that passage, and such a manner! Notwithstanding the improvements in Light street Church, which my taste could not but admire, we own we longed for the old appearance of things, that we might call up the more vividly the spirit of that eloquence, now gone, which so interested and charmed our boyhood. We have just been reading Summerfield's Sermons and Sketches of Sermons, and in so doing we have been trying to recall his manner and tones as he stood in that old pulpit, and account for the effect which he produced in their delivery, for they are certainly not remarkable sermons in matter, and we can in a measure realize their effect. But it requires one, in doing so, to keep constantly in the "mind's eye" the living, breathing utterer of them, to their very interjections.

Baltimore is called the Monumental City. It might also be called the City of Societies. For scarcely a day passes that some one of these numerous bodies do not turn out, often, alas, to bury their dead. But in a country like ours, such societies (for they are almost all of them of a benevolent character) do incalculable good in the examples which they set of temperance and philanthropy. And as man is a social being, these associations bring men together without the need of their resorting to the bar-room, or the theatre, to gratify a questionable sociability and love of excitement. There is one kind of association, however, though, may-be, the most useful of all in our cities, which is, nevertheless, the source of a great many outrages. We allude to the different fire companies. Proverbially, Philadelphia is the city of brotherly love (on paper), and of firemen's most unbrotherly riots in fact. They arise in the first place from emulation among the firemen, but they end, like emulation in many other places, too often in strife, bloodshed, and murder.

How often do we hear that a fire company was outrageously assaulted, in returning peaceably from a fire where they did good service, when it is shrewdly suspected that the assaulters were members of another company, or worse, that the alarm was raised that they might meet, and fight. These matters are a disgrace to a civilized community, and there seems no likelihood of an end being put to such proceedings. It strikes us that it would be well if none but appointed and paid firemen, selected by the authorities, were allowed to act as firemen; or it would be well to make all firemen give bonds for their peaceable behavior at fires, if such a thing were practicable. Even Washington City was once (we do not know how it is now-a-days) subject to such disturbances. We remember, more than once, to have made our escape in at Fuller's (now Willard's) window, to get out of the range of brickbats, which one fire company was hurling at another. Give us any law but mob law, say we, and almost any kind of riots rather than those which spring up between such a useful class of citizens as that of which our different fire companies are composed. To see firemen destroying each other's engines, and taking each other's lives, while a fire is raging, is about as bad as Nero's fiddling while Rome was burning.

SHOBAL VAIL CLEVENGER,*

THE SCULPTOR.

The Queen City of the West may indeed be proud of her arts, and her artists. Powers, Beard, Frankenstein, Powell, Clevenger, will give her a reputation, we believe, which will be honored wherever the arts are cultivated. Many of their productions already grace the halls of her citizens, where the travelling stranger, in partaking of their hospitality, often gazes in wonder on their works, which he pronounces to exhibit a genius kindred to that which guided the pencil and the chisel of the masters of the olden time.

Situated so beautifully by the "beautiful river," Cincinnati, as if conscious of her advantages, already displays an architectural elegance, which is

* This sketch was written some time ago, when Clevenger was living, and was just about to depart for Europe. Poor fellow! while returning, he died at sea.

not surpassed by any city in the Union. She now numbers fifty thousand inhabitants; yet there are many who well remember when the glancing river rolled on unshadowed by anything that denoted civilization. In patronizing her artists, her citizens will not only reward merit, but cultivate their taste, and thus, adding the graces of ornament to the beauties of situation, will crown the queen with an enduring magnificence.

Clevenger is a "born Buckeye." Middletown, a small village in the interior of Ohio, is the place of his birth. He was born in 1812. His father is by trade a weaver, and Shobal is the third child of a family of ten. His parents are still living to rejoice in the rising reputation of their son. A year after the birth of Shobal, his parents moved to Ridgeville, and afterwards to Indian Creek. At the age of fifteen, Shobal left his parents, and went with his brother to Centerville, to learn, under his direction, the art of stonecutting, in which employment his brother was engaged on the canal. It was indeed fortunate for the future sculptor, that he thus early learned the use of the chisel, and it accounts for the accuracy and tact with which he handles it.

On the canal, the future artist, at his humble occupation, caught the ague and fever, and was compelled to return home. As soon as he recovered, he went to Louisville, from which, after being engaged for a short time, he came to Cincinnati, and stipulated to remain with Mr. Guiou, a stonecutter, for the purpose of learning the trade. While he was with Mr. Guiou, an order, among others, came to the establishment for a tombstone, which was to have a seraph's head chiselled upon it. Mr. Guiou undertook the task himself, and formed the figure, which Clevenger criticised. His master said, satirically, "You shall do the next." This remark galled Clevenger, and he determined to try. The next day was Sunday, and instead of enjoying its recreation, he repaired to the shop and busied himself all day in producing a seraph's head. On Monday, when his fellow-workmen saw it, they pronounced it better than Mr. Guiou's. This, as may be supposed, gave great pleasure to the youthful aspirant, and inflamed his ambition. He used to visit the graveyard on the moonlight nights, and take casts from the tombstones, particularly from those sculptured by an English artist, which are thought to be very good. Mr. Guiou now gave Clevenger all the ornamental jobs to do, which sometimes provoked the ill-humor of his fellows, as was to be expected, but the amiability of the artist and his acknowledged skill soon reconciled them to the justice of the preference.

Soon after Clevenger's time expired with Mr. Guiou, he married Miss Elizabeth Wright, of Cincinnati, and repaired to Xenia, an inland town of

Ohio, where he commenced business. Meeting with poor encouragement there, he returned to Cincinnati and worked as a journeyman for his former master, but shortly after entered into partnership with Mr. Basset, and they established themselves in a little shop on the corner of Seventh and Race streets.

It was this shop that Mr. E. S. Thomas, the editor of the "Evening Post," chanced to enter one day, attracted, as he glanced in, by the figure of a cherub, which Clevenger was carving. Mr. Thomas, who has a fondness for such things, and who has had an opportunity of seeing the best statuary of Europe, was instantly impressed with the genius of Clevenger, and warmly told him that he had great talents in the art. The next day Mr. Thomas noticed Clevenger in his paper, and expressed firmly his conviction that his genius was of the first order, and that, if encouraged, he would be eminent.

Powers, the sculptor, who is now in Florence, pursuing his art, and who will shed fame on the Queen City, was then in Washington, where he had modelled the heads of some of our leading statesmen, with an accuracy and talent that were winning universal commendation. Clevenger, still at his stonecutting, understood that Powers was about to return to Cincinnati, and bring with him his clay model of Chief-Justice Marshall, from which he meant to take a bust in stone. On hearing this, the youthful aspirant said, to use his own expression, that he "would cut the first bust from stone in Cincinnati, if he couldn't cut the best!" He accordingly forthwith procured the material—the rough block of stone—and asked Mr. Thomas to sit to him. Mr. Thomas did so, and from the rude block, without moulding any model previously in clay, with the living form before him, and with chisel in hand, in his little shop, the young artist went fearlessly to work; and, without having seen anything of sculpture but the memorials of the dead in a western graveyard, casts from which he had taken by moonlight, unaided, by the inspirations solely of genius, he struck out a likeness that wants but the Promethean heat to make it in all respects the counterpart of the veteran editor.

This bust was executed about three years ago. The press of the city spoke in just terms of praise of the performer. Patronage followed. Many of the wealthiest citizens had their busts taken, and the accuracy of each successive one seemed to strike more and more. The artist's shop—now dignified with the name of studio—attracted the attention of all classes of the citizens. There the visitor might behold him eagerly at work, apparently unconscious of the attention he attracted; his fine clear eye lighting with a flash upon the model, and then upon the stone, from which, with consummate skill, he would strike the incumbrance which seemed to obscure from other eyes (not his own), the form which he saw existing in the marble.

Clevenger is now in Boston, where he has moulded a bust of Mr. Webster, said universally to be the best likeness ever taken of the great lawyer. Among his best efforts are said to be his busts of Messrs. Biddle, Clay, Van Buren, and Poindexter. The visitor stands in his studio, and gazes at the models, even of those he has not seen, with the conviction that they must be likenesses—there is ever something so lifelike about them.

This spring Clevenger goes to Italy, for the purpose of studying the masterpieces of his art, 'mid the scenes where they were fashioned. We can sympathize with the deep devotion with which he will gaze on the glories of his craft, and call up the memories of the mighty masters of old upon the very spot where they bent, chisel in hand, over the marble, and almost realized, without the aid of the gods, the fable of Pygmalion. While he is over the waters, in that classic land, we shall send glad greetings to our bold Buckeye, and bid him not despair. Let him assist to make his land classic too—what man has done, man may do.

POWELL, THE ARTIST.

PICTURES IN THE ROTUNDA IN WASHINGTON—STATUARY IN WASHINGTON.

SOME fifteen or more years ago, a stranger in Cincinnati, if he had turned from Main street into Fourth street, south, might have observed, three or four doors from the corner of Main, a bonnet, and some little articles of millinery in the window, and passed on—nothing conveying to him the impression that anybody belonging to the race of artists harbored there. Yet, had he opened that humble door, he would have discovered a delicate boy-artist at his easel, laboring away so intensely as at first not to be aware of his entrance.

When made aware of it, the visitor would have been struck with the manly countenance of that diminutive youth, and his pleasant tone and his engaging manners. If he were an observer of countenances, the well-developed forehead of one so young, and his clear and animated blue eye, would have attracted his notice. Perhaps he would have found the artist engaged in finishing the likeness of Mr. Longworth, a wealthy gentleman of Cincinnati, who has encouraged several young artists in their first attempts—artists who have since become distinguished.

The name of this youth—boy-artist we might call him—is William Henry Powell, who is now abroad, putting the finishing touches on his picture of "The Discovery of the Mississippi by De Soto, in 1542." In this house, his mother and sister carried on a little millinery establishment, up stairs. The window designated their locality, while that of the youthful artist needed no indication, as there were none except his personal friends and admirers who sought for it, as he had not yet become an artist by profession, and was, in fact, a boy.

Soon, however, his pictures were talked about, and the press noticed him; and in the progress of events, and in the development of his genius and resources, he was enabled to go to the East, and subsequently to Europe.

When the choice came to be made as to who should paint the picture for the last unoccupied panel in the rotunda, he was selected, through the influence of the western members of Congress.

This picture is spoken of in the highest terms—

and these high terms come to us with such indorsements as to satisfy us that they are not the mere eulogy of friends. Mr. Bryan, of Philadelphia, a connoisseur in such matters, who has a large collection of pictures, speaks of it with high praise, and so has Count D'Orsay. De Soto is the chief figure, and there are many others prominent on the canvas—we fear too many, from what is said of the picture. The Indian figures on the canvas contrast strikingly, in their wild costume, with the steel-clad warriors of De Soto; and the priests, planting a cross as the sign of possession, furnish another contrast. There is a figure of a horse in the picture, which is said to be excellent.

We rejoice in the success of Mr. Powell. To say the truth, the pictures in the Rotunda are not remarkable for excellence. That of "The Pilgrims," by Wier, is the best. "The Baptism of Pocahontas" has very little merit. And that of the "Signers of the Declaration of Independence," from the various exhibitions of legs in it, was justly called by John Randolph the "shin-piece."

But everything must have a beginning, and we like this encouragement of our American artists; and we have no doubt that Mr. Powell's picture will do him great credit, and reflect honor upon the Great West, which has already given Powers to the world of Art.

The best piece of statuary in Washington is the full-length bronze statue of Mr. Jefferson, in front of the White House. There stands the illustrious author of the Declaration of Independence, with the Declaration in his hand, attired in the style of dress worn when he presented it to the American Congress. We feel at once the individuality of the representation when we look upon it, and we recognize Thomas Jefferson. Pass from the White House to the Capitol, and look at Greenough's statue of Washington, disguised, as far as the form is covered, in that outlandish drapery, and we venture to say that unless one was told that it represented Washington, it would be a long time before the guess was made, unless by chance. The face of the statue has the Washington look, but the drapery, style of the figure, &c., take the mind away from the Father of his country. We saw in the Patent Office the very clothes that General Washington wore, and we look at the statue and at once feel how unlike him it looks. Fancy General Washington sitting to a Daguerreotypist and arraying himself in a Roman toga for the occasion. A statue should be as much as possible a Daguerreotype of the man.

"Paint me as I am—warts and all," said Cromwell to the artist, "or I will not pay you for the picture." The bluff and bold Protector showed what was the artist's duty in this remark. If the artist is painting a Venus, he takes ideal beauty; but when he is painting a man, he should give us humanity. In this consists the power of Thom's celebrated Tam O'Shanter group. Human character is there, in the listener's pausing in the act of rising to listen to the story, and in the turned-in toes of Souter Johnny.

Lamartine says that Robespierre always presented himself to his countrymen in the same color and style of dress, and always had his pictures taken and busts modelled in the same fashion. "The man of the People" did not wish the identity of his appearance changed in the eyes of the people. There he was, the "incorruptible" and the unchanged. Like Cromwell, the Frenchman showed not only his taste, but his knowledge of human nature. Furthermore, "the little corporal" would strike a French soldier much more in his cocked hat and coat buttoned across the breast than in his coronation robes. The charlatanism in Napoleon's nature (and he had a great deal of it) never struck us more than when looking at the picture which represents his coronation.

Much praise is due to Mr. Mills, who is at present engaged on the equestrian statue of General Jackson, for the great pains he has taken to represent his subject just as he appeared in nature. In this model the erect, energetic self-will of General Jackson is apparent, and there is no doubt that the artist, following the suggestions of his own genius, will make for himself a reputation as enduring as the metal from which he is to mould his lifelike model.

DEATH OF MR. WEBSTER.

AN ORIGINAL LETTER FROM HIM.

THE last of the triumvirate (composed of Calhoun, Clay, and Webster), the great expounder of the constitution, is no more. Though his death has just occurred, the telegraphic wires have transmitted the sorrowful fact to every intelligent mind in the Union.

How impressibly the lesson strikes us! Calhoun —what a deep pulsation there was in the public heart over his ashes! And then, again, how profound and universal the sorrowing for Mr. Clay! And now, the last of the immortal three has departed; and while all parties lament his death, the conviction of what the country has suffered lately in the loss of her greatest citizens, crowds upon every mind.

Lord Morpeth has said, that in one respect at least the republican experiment has failed, and that is in the fact that our greatest men do not reach our highest office—the Presidential chair. Be this as it may, it does seem truly singular that neither of them reached it; though they were all for a long time eager aspirants for its honors. This is a subject for moral as well as for political reflection, and may well exercise the judgments and the consciences of the thoughtful men of all creeds, as well as of all parties.

In intellect Mr. Webster was superior to either of his illustrious rivals. He had more expansion of mind and information, perhaps, than Mr. Calhoun, and much greater power of argumentation than Mr. Clay; but he had not Mr. Calhoun's or Mr. Clay's quick intuitive readiness, nor would he as boldly rush into responsibility, but when he did take his position, what he said of himself was true, he "took no step backwards." He could not see at a glance results like Mr. Clay, nor would he defend an abstraction like Mr. Calhoun on his own resources and responsibility. He was emphatically the "great expounder." To expound and explain a great political truth was his great power. And in this respect, particularly in the exposition of constitutional law, he was without a rival. Wirt, Clay, Calhoun, Pinkney, of Maryland, even Marshall was not his equal; for to the powers of the greatest of these—Pinkney and Marshall, the first celebrated for his intellectual resources on a constitutional question, and the latter for his judgment—he added a transparent clearness of style superior to either of them—an earnest, and at the same time poetic diction, at times reminding one of the Bible.

In a bad cause, he was not calculated to be successful. Many a county court lawyer would have won from him the ordinary run of cases. Truth looked him so brightly and boldly in the face, that she put him out of countenance when he turned from her side. But by her side, in law or on a constitutional question, all opposition paled before him; as, for instance, when, on the question of Nullification, he met Mr. Hayne in the United States Senate, and not only buried that question on the spot, but delivered, in our opinion, the greatest speech, intellectually, recorded in the English language.

The profound statesmanship exhibited by Mr. Webster in the Ashburton treaty, has elicited the praise of the statesmen of the Old as well as of the New World.

As we contemplate the mighty dead, now gone to another judgment than that of their fellow-men, we marvel that they should have troubled so much themselves and others with aspirations which are mere dust and ashes, and no more. We wonder that they did not look more at the one thing needful. But this wonder strikes us at so many death-beds!

as well over the humblest, as over those for whom the tolling bell, the muffled drum, and the funeral display, proclaim a nation's honor.

It is a gratification to know that Mr. Webster's last hours were cheered by the presence of his family and friends; and that he died calmly, after an earnest prayer to Him through whose intercession only the proudest as well as the humblest can be saved.

But we would introduce, we trust not ungracefully, an original letter upon an interesting subject, from Mr. Webster. The letter speaks for itself, and was handed to us to publish if we wished. It was written in answer to an invitation from Mr. F. D. Anderson and others to attend a celebration of the Temperance cause, in Harford County, Maryland. The motto on the seal is—"*Vera pro gratis.*" The letter is here first published.

MARSHFIELD, *October* 8, 1851.

GENTLEMEN: It is a matter of deep regret to me, that I did not receive your kind letter of the 9th of August till a very late day. I was in the mountains of New Hampshire, taking a breath of my native air, and it was the last of August before I returned. I know not whether, if I had received your communication sooner, it would have been in my power to attend the meeting to which I was invited, but I should have been able to have given a more timely answer.

There can be no question that the Temperance movement, in the United States, has done infinite good. The moral influence of the Temperance associations has been everywhere felt, and always with beneficial results. In some cases, it is true, the Temperance measures have been carried to excess, where they have invoked legislative penalties, and sought to enforce the virtue of Temperance by the power of the Law. To a certain extent, this, no doubt, is justifiable and useful; but it is the moral principle of Temperance, it is the conscientious duty which it teaches, to abstain from intoxicating draughts, such as are hurtful both to mind and body, which are the great agents for the reformation of manners in this respect.

Your order is quite right in connecting benevolence and charity with Temperance. They may well go hand-in-hand. He whose faculties are never debauched or stupefied, whose mind is always active and alert, and who practises self-denial, is naturally drawn to consider the deserving objects which are about him, that may be poor, or sick, or diseased.

LOVE, PURITY, and FIDELITY, are considered Christian virtues; and I hope that those "banners" which bear these words for their motto may rise higher and higher, and float more and more widely through this and all other countries.

You have invited me, gentlemen, if I could attend the meeting, to address the members of your order on the great subject of Union. I should have done so with pleasure, although I do not propose to continue the practice of addressing great multitudes of men; yet I could not have refused to have expressed my opinions on the great topics of the day, in the State of Maryland. Out of the abundance of the heart the mouth speaketh.

I pray you to be assured, gentlemen, that I value highly the opinion you have expressed for my public character and conduct; and I indulge the hope that I may ere long meet some of you in the city where my public duties are discharged; and most of all, I fervently trust that you and I, and your children and my children will remain fellow-citizens of one great united Republic, so long as society shall exist among us. While I live, every effort in my power, whether made in public or in private life, will be devoted to the promotion of that great end.

I am, gentlemen, very respectfully, your obliged friend and fellow-citizen,

DANIEL WEBSTER.

www.ingramcontent.com/pod-product-compliance
Lightning Source LLC
LaVergne TN
LVHW021251110826
845151LV00002BA/384

* 9 7 8 1 4 2 5 5 3 9 2 0 7 *